Praise for *Walking the Twilight Path*

"In this profoundly deep necromantic-shamanic tome, death is neither glamorized nor idealized, but looked at in a realistic, intelligent, and spiritual light."
—Raven Digitalis, author of *Shadow Magick Compendium*

"A sane, practical and inspiring look at Death, covering everything from epitaphs to the afterlife to returning from the Beyond. Michelle Belanger writes from personal and magickal experience, engendering psychological and spiritual progress via the confrontation of personal extinction, and subsequent resurrection."
—Kala Trobe, author of *Invoke the Gods*

About the Author

Michelle Belanger is an author, lecturer, and occult researcher who has appeared on a number of television and radio shows in the United States and abroad. Although she is best known for her expertise on vampires, Michelle studies a wide range of topics, including energy work, paranormal phenomenon, shamanism, folklore, and the Gothic subculture. She is the founder of House Kheperu, a magickal society based in part upon the concept of death and rebirth. Together with the other members of House Kheperu, she teaches a unique style of energy work and ritual at private workshops as well as national conventions.

In addition to her esoteric studies, Michelle is also a talented vocalist and song-writer. She has performed with several musical groups, including the dark metal band URN and the Gothic duo of Nox Arcana. In the 1990s, she was the editor of *Shadowdance*, a maga-zine dedicated to dark and fringe culture that has since been reborn as a free podcast on the web.

To Write to the Author

If you wish to contact the author or would like more information about this book, please write to the author in care of Llewellyn World-wide and we will forward your request. Both the author and publisher appreciate hearing from you and learning of your enjoyment of this book and how it has helped you. Llewellyn Worldwide cannot guaran-tee that every letter written to the author can be answered, but all will be forwarded. Please write to:

Michelle Belanger
℅ Llewellyn Worldwide
2143 Wooddale Drive, Dept. 978-0-7387-1323-6
Woodbury, Minnesota 55125-2989, U.S.A.

Please enclose a self-addressed stamped envelope for reply,
or $1.00 to cover costs. If outside U.S.A., enclose
international postal reply coupon.

Many of Llewellyn's authors have websites with additional information and resources. For more information, please visit our website at
http://www.llewellyn.com

WALKING THE TWILIGHT PATH

A GOTHIC BOOK OF THE DEAD

MICHELLE BELANGER

Llewellyn Publications
Woodbury, Minnesota

First Edition
First Printing, 2008

Book design by Steffani Sawyer
Cover art © 2008 Tom Maday/LuckyPix/PunchStock
Cover design by Gavin Dayton Duffy
Editing by Nicole Edman
Interior photos © 2008 by Patricia Gonzalez
Interior illustrations © 2008 Dover Publications. Illustrations on pages 31, 43, 81, 83, 86, 97, 123 from *Devils, Demons, and Witchcraft* by Ernst and Johanna Lehner, and illustrations on pages 107, 110, 128, 189 from *Egyptian Designs* by Carol Belanger Grafton.

Llewellyn is a registered trademark of Llewellyn Worldwide, Ltd.

Library of Congress Cataloging-in-Publication Data
Belanger, Michelle A.
  Walking the twilight path : a Gothic book of the dead / Michelle
Belanger. – 1st ed.
    p. cm.
  Includes bibliographical references and index.
  ISBN 978-0-7387-1323-6
  1. Death–Miscellanea. 2. Occultism. I. Title.
  BF1442.D43B45 2008
  130--dc22

                              2008022627

Llewellyn Publications
A Division of Llewellyn Worldwide, Ltd.
2143 Wooddale Drive, Dept. 978-0-7387-1323-6
Woodbury, Minnesota 55125-2989, U.S.A.
www.llewellyn.com

Printed in the United States of America

Acknowledgements

A number of people have helped provide insight as I journeyed through the process of creating this book. I would like to extend my thanks to Wraith, for his insights on modern mortuary techniques, Kantrip for long discussions on selfhood and rebirth, Patricia Gonzalez for her amazing photographic work, Christopher Penczak for unflagging friendship and support, Leilah Wendell for providing an early outlet for my articles and experiments, and my mother who, in her process of dying, taught me much about life. I would also like to thank Elysia, Jennifer, Brett, and Nicole at Llewellyn for all their hard work and support. Without them, this book would still be nothing more than a file sitting on my hard drive.

CONTENT/

Introduction: A Prelude to Death   *XI*

PART ONE: 1
APPROACHING THE THRESHOLD

1: An Initial Approach   3
   Journal Exercise: The Allure of Death   *14*
   Icon Meditation: Beautiful Death   *18*

2: Bringing Death Into Your Life   21
   Journal Exercise: An Altar for the Dead   *34*

3: Erecting the Threshold   39
   Journal Exercise: Getting Into Ritual   *47*

4: Walking the Spaces Between   49

5: Protecting Yourself   57
   Icon Meditation: Death as a Journey   *72*

PART TWO: 75
THE WAY OF ALL FLESH

6: Accepting Impermanence   77
Journal Exercise: *This Life, Now*   87
Icon Meditation: *Death as Tragedy*   90

7: Facing Your Fears   93
Journal Exercise: *The Weight of the Years*   98
Journal Exercise: *You Are Not That*   103

8: The Weight of Eternity   105
Journal Exercise: *The Everliving Dead*   115
Icon Meditation: *Death as a Threshold*   116

9: Disposing of Bodies   119
Journal Exercise: *Planning Your Own Funeral*   129

10: Return to the Elements   131
Journal Exercise: *Elemental Affiliations*   146

11: Giving Up the Ghost   149
Journal Exercise: *The Art of Crossing Over*   159
Icon Meditation: *Death as Transcendence*   162

PART THREE: 165
THE BRIDGE BETWEEN WORLDS

12: A Fine and Private Place   167
Journal Exercise: *Cemetery Thoughts*   180
Icon Meditation: *Death as Struggle*   182

13: A Necromantic Medicine Bag   185
Journal Exercise: *The Power Inside*   193
Icon Meditation: *The Personification of Death*   194

14: Life Among the Dead   197
   *Journal Exercise: Companions on
   the Otherside*   208

15: Preparing the Way   211
   Icon Meditation: Death as Initiation   220

16: The Gates of Life and Death   223
   Journal Exercise: Starting a New Life   248

17: Walking the Twilight Path   251

**Appendix I: Twilight Path Incense
and Oils   259**

**Appendix II: Leyden Papyrus
Recipes   273**

**Appendix III: Offerings for
the Dead   277**

**Appendix IV: Some Deities
Associated with Death   283**

Bibliography   295

Index   301

INTRODUCTION

A PRELUDE TO DEATH

This book is about death. What's more, it's a how-to manual for immersing yourself in the energies of death. Considering that most of us have a deeply held fear of dying, at this point, you're probably wondering, "Why on earth would someone want to immerse themselves in death energy?" Consider that, in the tarot deck, the Death card does not necessarily mean that the person in the reading is going to die. Instead, the Death card represents change. The energies of death are in fact the energies of change, which pulls us out of stagnation and encourages us to grow. However, both death and change are still frightening, intimidating processes so, to understand the purpose and importance of this book, it's necessary to first understand how death came to me.

Introduction

On a cold and snowy afternoon in January 1973, I was born. Six months later, I died. Obviously, I got better, but the condition that caused my heart to go into cardiac arrest as an infant could only be repaired with major surgery. For the first four years of my life, I literally danced with death, undergoing numerous heart-related procedures that were profoundly pioneering and risky for their time. By the age of five, I had at least two feet of scars on my small body and I had endured no fewer than two near-death experiences. Coming face to face with my own mortality at such an early age left me forever changed.

Because all of this happened when I was so young, it took me a while to fully comprehend the nature of that change. From as far back as I can remember, I have been able to perceive and interact with spirits. The capacity came so naturally to me that half the time I didn't even realize that I was speaking to the dead. Only as I got older did I begin to wonder if it was all in my head. As an example, when I was very little, my mother had a friend who would often take me aside and play fun games. I only saw her when my mother was visiting with other friends at her college, and so her appearances never seemed strange to me. Years later, when I inquired about this beloved friend from my early childhood, my mother informed me that I had accurately described the person for whom I was named. The problem with this, however, was that this friend of my mother's had succumbed to ovarian cancer while I was still in the womb!

An avid fan of Sylvia Browne, my mother attributed the intensity of my psychic gifts to my early brushes with death. Since psychic gifts run in that side of my family, I can't say with certainty that dying and coming back made me psychic. But there is strong evidence that near-death experiences can change people in this way. Some of the classic hallmarks of a near-death experience involve the changes people undergo subsequent to their return to the living. They tend to look at life differently, doing things that they had never dared to before and regarding each moment as something precious. They no longer experience a fear of death, but regard it as a natural and even positive process. And many report heightened levels of psychic sensitivity.

How is this possible?

Death and rebirth lie at the heart of many ancient mystery religions. In shamanism, death and rebirth form the basis of the shaman's initiation, and this early trip to the realm of spirits is directly responsible for the shaman's ability to heal disease. Time and again, in cultures around the world, death is seen as something that can be profoundly transformational. In the teachings of Tibetan Buddhism, there are techniques for practicing dying that are thought to bring about liberation from the limitations of this worldly existence. Clearly, the touch of the Grim Reaper is not as horrific as many people make it out to be.

Seizing Death's Legacy

I believe that, because my life hung so completely in the balance when I was a child, a part of the Otherside still clings to me. I think this process is at work in any near-death experience. A person may depart the world of the living for only a few moments, but even a brief sojourn will leave them changed. Those who die and then return are forever touched by the world of spirits. In the language of shamanism, they become "twice born." They no longer properly belong to either the world of the living or the world of the dead, but walk with a foot in each.

It's all well and good to say that someone who has experienced a death and rebirth is a walker-between, but what is the point of it, really? A near-death experience typically occurs spontaneously. The circumstances are almost always traumatic. Why would someone actively seek out this process and submit themselves to it?

Once I realized that my perspective of the world was changed because of my early encounters with death, I asked myself those questions. I look back at the terror and trauma of my early surgeries and would not willingly repeat them, but I know for a fact that I would not be the person I am today without those experiences. Death has left me a complicated and profound legacy. There is, of course, the deeper connection that I experience with the world of spirits. This is significant in itself, but it is not the only gift given to me by death. The first and most valuable thing that I brought back with me from the Otherside was an absolute certainty that death is not the end. Death is certainly one end, but it is a doorway that leads out of one place and into another. And along with that certainty comes a freedom from fear.

How much of one person's life is wasted in uncertainty? How completely do we surrender ourselves to fear on a daily basis? The fear of death is one of the main anxieties that underscores every human endeavor. Our fear of death extends to a general fear of change. We don't like to see things pass from our lives. According to the Tibetan Buddhists, every change in our life is a little death, and humans certainly act as if this were the case.

Imagine what your life would be like if you could be more flexible in the face of change. Imagine not only a freedom from fear, but a freedom from anxiety as well. Why do we get ourselves so worked up over morning traffic? Why do we lie awake at night worrying about whether a certain person really likes us? How many of the little things that plague us day to day ultimately come down to our fear that something important to us is going to be taken away? Death teaches us that eventually, everything in this world is going to be taken away. It's not a punishment—it's simply the nature of things. The knowledge that comes from this lesson is what the Buddhists would call "non-attachment." It's not apathy, as some might interpret it. Instead, non-attachment is a deeper appreciation for all of the things that you have, without any of the emotional baggage that comes from worrying about when or if you won't have them anymore.

Touching death gives a person a more profound appreciation for life. Less encumbered by fear, a person who has endured a near-death experience is also better equipped to enjoy life. This is true for anyone who has experienced a profound reminder of their own mortality. In facing death, such people understand the brevity of life. Everyone is going to die, but most people struggle to hide from this fact. And somehow, in that struggle, most people forget how to live.

My mother was a perfect example of this. A talented artist and musician, for thirty-nine years my mother worried more about the things that had been taken away in her life than she worried about living with the gifts she had. If she wasn't fretting over the past, she was worried about the future. Her fears of what people might think or do if she lived the life she wanted kept her from doing exactly that.

When my mother was thirty-nine, she was diagnosed with breast cancer. On her fortieth birthday (because reality has a grim sense of humor), she had a radical mastectomy. Only after her bout with cancer did she drum up the courage to submit her sculptures to galleries and to lend her voice to community theater events. In dying, she learned how to live. Cancer ultimately claimed her in 2004, but by then, she'd done pretty much everything she'd set out to do, and she'd gained the courage to do it regardless of what others might think.

This example brings me to another gift brought back from the Otherside. My brush with death has left me better able to understand and accept the mortality of those around me. My mother struggled on and off with cancer for nearly thirteen years. When she finally died, my step-father was devastated, even though there was nothing shocking or unexpected in her dying. By that point in her illness, my mother had been dying for several of those thirteen years. It seemed as though every six months, they gave her only six months to live.

I viewed her death as a blessed relief, just as my mother did when the time finally came. The hard work of actually dying was over, and now she could move on to another life, or, perhaps, rest a little in between. Although he's a devout Christian, my stepfather's grief came from the fear that he would never see her again. I didn't have to rely on promises or faith. My own personal experiences had taught me beyond any doubt that death is only an end for our physical bodies. Furthermore, it is a natural and necessary process, and, especially at the end of a long illness, it can be a very good thing.

Living the Good Death

I was on the phone with my mother the night that she died. My mother could barely talk by the time that she called, so we did not waste words on tearful goodbyes. Instead, I did my best to make good on a promise I'd made to my mother. I talked her through the process of dying, drawing upon material I had learned from the *Bardo Thodol*, also known as the "Tibetan Book of the Dead."

If I have one regret about my mother's passing, it's the fact that I could not fly from Ohio to Texas quickly enough in order to do this at her bedside. Early on in her illness, my mother had asked me to help her make the transition out of life. I have been working on the book you now hold in your hands since 1996, when I decided to develop a system that would harness the transformational power of a near-death experience. In addition to my own experiences, the work was strongly influenced by my studies of the Tibetan *Bardo*. In their system, when someone is dying, a person sits at their bedside and reads from the Tibetan Book of the Dead. This book is essentially an instruction manual for the process of dying, and it explains each stage of physical death so the dying person can better understand what is happening and therefore suffer less from uncertainty and fear. The book also describes what the Tibetan Buddhists believe occurs immediately after death, and the passages are supposed to be read even after the person has physically died, in order to help their newly released spirit navigate the Otherside.

Still more or less Christian, Mom didn't want me reading directly from the Tibetan Book of the Dead, but she did want me to be at her side, giving her a pep talk and doing energy work to help make things easier when the time came.

Mom hung on for years after they said that she would die, but, when the process of dying actually began, it happened very quickly. To this extent, it was unexpected. One day, she was at home and it was business as usual. She was in pain, and she definitely wasn't going to get up and dance a jig any time soon, but she had been hanging on so long in this state that it had become her version of normal. And then, without much warning, she was slipping away. Her breast cancer, which had been chemo'ed and radiated into remission for a few years subsequent to the mastectomy, had come back in her bones in 1999, and at this point, her marrow was no longer producing enough red blood cells to keep her body oxygenated. Essentially, she suffo-cated to death.

That part was pretty obvious while I was on the phone with her. Every breath was labored, and those lungs, which had powered her operatic soprano through many triumphant high C's, barely had the strength to make her voice audible on my end. So I told her not to talk, and I did all the talking. I told her everything that I remem-bered from my own near-death experiences, and I told her, above everything, not to surrender to fear. I stayed on the phone as long as I could. Then I headed off to work, because life rarely stops for death, as the poet Emily Dickinson so eloquently observed. I was absolutely unsurprised when a relative called me at the front desk to tell me that she had passed not long after our phone conversation.

The Book of the Dead

All of my life, I have been touched by death, and I consider this a good thing. My relationship with these concepts started with the near-death experiences, but my ability to perceive and interact with spirits meant that I continued to work closely with the dead from childhood on, even though I often vacillated between belief and doubt when it came to spirit communication. Somehow, before the age of twelve, I had stumbled onto the concept of shamanism. I remember watch-ing a show where a young white man was put through a ritual death and rebirth by a Native American shaman as part of his initiation. Even though the young man was wholly modern and from a different culture, he had been called to be a shaman, and the old man finally convinced him to submit to the rite. I have no idea what movie or show I was watching (though I suspect it owed something to the pop-ularity of Carlos Castaneda at the time), but it left quite an impres-sion on me. I read anything on the topic that I could get my hands on, and I was trying my own hand at vision-questing and death and rebirth rites by the time I was in my early teens. All of these studies went hand in hand with some other experiences I was having at the time, which demonstrated a significant and somewhat disturbing tie between my physical health and my ability to do energy work. That issue, however, is another book entirely.

I grew up in a small town in northeast Ohio, and I found myself naturally drawn to the local cemeteries. This was in the early eighties, and most people had no idea about Gothic anything, least of all me. I had no idea how quintessentially Goth I was being by dressing all in black and meditating on graves in local cemeteries. I wore black as a sign of vocation. Raised Catholic by a well-meaning great aunt, in my world, black was the color worn by all priests. Even in my teens, I felt dedicated to a calling, and black was my way of committing to this calling in a visible way. Cemeteries were places where I could gain perspective. They were always quiet, and such a sense of peace radiated from the stones. Every headstone told its own story, and to lie in the grass above the corpse slumbering beneath was a potent method for remembering the lessons of mortality: life is brief, and every moment is precious.

In many ways, this book had its start among the stones of Maple Hill Cemetery in Hinckley, Ohio. When I first asked myself the question, "How can someone gain the benefits of near-death experience without having to literally die?" I thought back to those early meditations. Many of them are reproduced in this book exactly as I practiced them, because those meditations seemed to be the first steps that I took toward consciously and actively harnessing my affinity for deathwork. Some of this early work also led to articles that were published in the 1990s in the *Azrael Project Newsletter*, a publication run by artist and author Leilah Wendell, whose underground classic, *Our Name is Melancholy*, is concerned with deathwork and the personification of the Angel of Death. Leilah's other works, like *The Necromantic Ritual Book*, helped enlarge upon some of my own ideas of how to reach across the Veil and work with spirits of the dead.

My studies on death and rebirth, and particularly on shamanism, led me eventually to develop a death and rebirth ritual that coupled guided meditation with intense energy work. In the mid-nineties, I was performing this rite on individuals to help force an awakening experience. In a Buddhist sense, a person awakens when they realize the illusory nature of the world. I borrowed the term "awakening" from the Buddhists because the process I was witnessing in people definitely involved a sense of waking up and suddenly seeing the world with different eyes. And yet, there seemed to be more to it than just a change of perspective. Awakening opened hidden doors in the psyche, typically unleashing latent psychic abilities and, for some people, vivid past-life memories. It was hard not to see the connection between this process and the psychic side effects of a near-death experience, so it only seemed logical to try to trigger an awakening through the use of a death and rebirth rite.

The individual rituals I performed between 1994 and 1999 were invariably intense—sometimes too intense for people who had to get up the next morning and go to college classes or a daily-grind job. I learned that most people cannot simply be thrown head-first into such an experience without being at least a little overwhelmed. I refined the technique over the years, adding more preparation and aftercare, and reading everything I could on similar rituals practiced around the world.

For the past several years, I've been performing a modified version of my ritual death and rebirth called the "Rite of Seven Gates." Usually, I do this for small groups, but I've also run it at several large conventions. The largest group to undergo this rite involved no fewer than seventy-five people at ConVocation in Troy, Michigan. The solitary rite in Chapter 16, which is the culmination of all the work in this book, is based directly upon the Rite of Seven Gates. This self-initiation ritual has benefited greatly from the input provided by all of the people who have participated in the group versions of the rite over the years. It re-creates a shamanic death and rebirth, allowing the Ritualist to reach across to the spirit world, and then to return to the world of the living, enriched and changed.

The Threshold of the Unknown

So what is the work laid out in this book? *Walking the Twilight Path* is a complete ritual system that seeks to reproduce the beneficial effects of near-death experience. You start from the position of life (because

I can only assume that those reading this are among the living), and you seek balance by immersing yourself equally in death. The ultimate goal is a threshold state, where you have equal experience with both death and life, and you can freely interact with one side or the other at will. This is accomplished by bringing into your life the energies of death, which are simultaneously the energies of change and transformation.

First, you will confront your own mortality and you will work to gain acceptance of death as well as a sense of non-attachment to your physical body. Anxiety over our physical bodies, especially in terms of damage, scars, and pain, is one of the biggest sources of fear when it comes to death, so we will address this directly. Once you have made your peace with death, you will begin to open a door to the Otherside, inviting spirits into your ritual space so that you may learn from these partners from across the Veil. You will seek out one partner in particular, and this spirit will become a helper who reaches across from the realm of the dead just as you will be reaching across from the realm of the living. The point of this is to meet in the middle and facilitate a threshold state—that ideal state of the shaman who walks with a foot in both worlds. Ultimately, you will undergo a self-initiation strongly influenced by both shamanic and Tibetan rites of death and rebirth. This self-initiation will cement your identity as a Walker-Between, allowing you to harness the benefits of near-death experience in a safe and controlled environment. You will then integrate your experience of both life and death, embrace change and personal transformation, and became a mediator between the realms of the living and the dead.

This is ambitious work, and it is not for the faint of heart. The path laid out in this book is not something you should casually undertake, and if you are going to succeed in this path, it will take a great deal of dedication and hard work. But the benefits are worth all of that. The goal of this process is as multilayered as the repercussions of a near-death experience itself. First of all, in making peace with mortality, you will overcome fears and anxieties related to death and dying. This can help you gain a remarkable level of courage for living your life. Once you realize that the worst is already inevitable—that today or tomorrow or sixty years from now, you *will* die—then anything else that can go wrong in your life seems relatively inconsequential. All things are fleeting—even sorrow, even pain. Replete with the knowledge of death, you will find that you have the strength to survive anything, because, in surviving, you still have your life. Something can always be built from there.

This courage will also lead you to another main goal of pursing this path: learning to truly live. Once you face the truth that your life is finite, you will find that even the little pleasures in life become more precious. Instead of wasting all of your energy in the pursuit of some item or state that is supposed to buy you happiness, you will learn to look around your life and find the things that make you happy now. Working toward the betterment of your future is a noble goal, but your achievements will ring hollow if you fail to appreciate the good things in your present that can help carry you toward that goal.

Strength, perspective, courage, and a deeper appreciation for life. These are the main things that you are seeking if you choose to walk the Twilight Path. In addition to these qualities, you will also come closely into contact with the world of spirits, and you will learn how to reach out and communicate with those beings who exist beyond the Veil. This is a powerful aspect of the Twilight Path, and it can grow into a sacred responsibility. As someone who can navigate the shadowy threshold between this world and the next, you will be able to identify and resolve hauntings, and you can help reassure the living that the dead are not lost to them forever. This role as a mediator between the world of flesh and the world of spirits is the very definition of a shaman, and it can extend even to the ability to help the living make an easier transition into death once the time comes.

Gothic Mystique

Walking the Twilight Path is subtitled "A Gothic Book of the Dead." This is not meant to make the work seem trite or trendy. Simply put, there is almost no way in this modern age to produce a work that presents a positive approach to the mysteries of death without that work sounding Gothic. Certainly, if I am the one writing that book, Gothic elements cannot fail to appear. The modern Gothic movement owes a lot to the poets and philosophers of the Romantic era, and I often read the melancholy and insightful words of Lord Byron or Percy Bysshe Shelley as a prelude to my cemetery meditations. When I was a teen, I had no conscious awareness of what was Goth, but as I've gotten older, I cannot deny that I fit the profile. I have a passion for the twilight world, and I harbor a great love for those dark and elegant aesthetics that sometimes make "normal" people look askance and back away. I see a peaceful beauty in death, and a profound elegance in the fact that life is brief and must be savored.

All of this combines to make me quintessentially Goth, and as a result, there is a Gothic flavor to some of the rituals and many of the meditations. However, *Walking the Twilight Path* is not intended to be the Dark Book of Darketty Darkness. "Twilight Path" implies a balance between darkness and light. Death is a natural and indivisible part of life, and to fully appreciate one, you must also learn to appreciate the other. This not only holds true for people so immersed in life that they deny death at every turn—you will also fail to benefit from this book if you immerse yourself so completely in the energies of death that you forget how to live. Death gives us perspective on all things fleeting in our lives, and if you pursue this path correctly, at the same time that you delve into the mysteries of death, you will also take time to enjoy the mysteries of life.

Seekers of Twilight

How do you know if this path is right for you? Arguably, if you have found your way to this book, it probably has something to teach you. Consider the circumstances under which you were drawn to picking up this text. How much of that was fate and how much mere coincidence? Everyone living must eventually face death, and so every single person alive can benefit from learning more about that process. Perhaps the Universe is telling you that now is a good time to learn.

Some of you have already started upon the Twilight Path, and this book is simply the most logical step for the next portion of your journey. There is a restlessness in you, a need for greater balance in your life. Perhaps you find yourself seeking out the shadows, partly because the darkness is in such danger of being completely eclipsed by the light. Too many people equate death and darkness with evil, and so they shun these things. And yet, instinctively, you see life and death not as forces working in opposition to one another, but instead, forces that are necessary complements to one another. You know this profoundly, because you feel the dark places in you coexisting with the light, and rather than shrink from this dichotomy, you have studied it and come to realize that your power comes from the two forces working in tandem.

Others of you may have had this path suddenly thrust before you. Perhaps someone close to you has died, or you have experienced a close call yourself. Either way, you find yourself more curious about death and its meaning than you were before. A part of you wants assurance that death is not the end. Another part of you wants to touch it, taste it, come to know it intimately so that your fear will melt away. Still others of you have had an encounter with something from the Otherside. Maybe this was a ghost. Maybe you don't really know what it was you experienced. But the encounter has left you curious, and you have come here seeking answers. You want to understand how to reach out and make contact with that other side, and you've realized that such knowledge can be obtained by learning more about the threshold that separates life from death.

Whatever your story, something in your life has whispered to you about the existence of a door, and you want to see what waits on the other side. This book offers the key to the threshold, and a path that will teach you balance so that you may explore the mysteries of both life and death from a safe and firm foundation. The goal of this path is not to wallow in death, but to discover a threshold state, so you can achieve a more profound experience of both sides of your existence, as well as a deeper appreciation for the power of change. The wisdom you will attain on this path can be used in service to the living, to help give them perspective; in service to the spirits of the dead, to help communicate with them on the Otherside; and finally, you can use what you gain here in service to the dying, to help guide them to a peaceful and fearless transition.

The benefits of following this path are compelling, but even if you feel called to the twilight, you should ensure that you are prepared for the journey. The work laid out in this book is emotionally demanding. If you seek to walk the Twilight Path, you must be in a healthy and balanced emotional state. Otherwise, your work is likely to fail, and you may very well endanger yourself and possibly others around you. There are signs that make it clear whether or not now is the right time for you to begin this work. Look over the statements outlined below. If any of these statements are true for you, now is not the right time to pursue this path.

- You think obsessively about harming or killing yourself.
- You think obsessively about harming or killing others.
- You find yourself crying, screaming, or needing to hit things uncontrollably on a regular basis.
- You regularly cut yourself to relieve emotional pain.
- You are taking intoxicants (drugs, alcohol) on a daily or near-daily basis.
- You are experiencing mood swings that noticeably affect your interactions with others.
- You hear voices that tell you to harm yourself or others.
- You hear voices that berate you or threaten to hurt you.
- You have regular black-outs in your memory where you cannot remember where you were or what you were doing.
- You are so uncomfortable around other people that you start cutting classes, calling in to work, or canceling appointments just to avoid contact.
- You engage in any behavior *expressly because* you know it will endanger your health and well-being.

Please keep in mind that this list is only to be used to determine whether or not you are in a state of mind healthy enough to embark on this path. It is not intended to professionally diagnose mental ill-ness, even though many of the statements above can be symptoms of mental illness. If you suspect that you are suffering from a mental illness, you should consult a qualified mental health professional as soon as possible. As far as hearing voices is concerned, understand that this may be a sign of mental illness, but it may also be a sign of legitimate spirit contact. If those voices are violent or threatening, however, even if they are legitimate spirits, they are still trouble. If you really have a spirit that is telling you to kill yourself, and the voice is not just all in your head, then you have attracted something very negative. Before you open yourself any further to the spirit world, you will have to resolve this negative attachment.

Final Notes on the Text

This book is essentially a workbook for those who wish to follow the Twilight Path. It contains lessons, exercises, and rituals that will help the diligent student to embrace change by exploring the mysteries of both life and death. As you delve into this book, you will learn how to open your life to the positive influence of death energy, in the form of personal transformation. I don't recommend that you jump around in this book or start at one of the final chapters and move backward. There is a set progression in which these lessons should be taken, and I strongly recommend that you take them in their proper order so you can get the most out of this book. Without the proper preparation, *Walking the Twilight Path* can lead you into some psycho-logically dangerous territory. Fears and anxieties about death are very real and very human, and it is impossible to adequately progress on the Twilight Path without first having come to terms with those anx-ieties and fears. Many of the early exercises are designed to prepare you—spiritually as well as psychologically—for deathwork, and these should not be skipped over lightly.

Throughout this book, you will encounter special sections known as "Icon Meditations." These two-page interludes feature an image paired with a brief contemplative meditation. The images are all pho-tographs of cemetery art—monuments which I have personally found both evocative and compelling. The images are all drawn from Wood-lawn Cemetery, an amazing, historic cemetery in the Bronx. The photographer, Patricia Gonzalez, who has a special eye for capturing the solemn, contemplative mood of these memorials, has graciously provided her work for this book. The icon meditations are like a virtual tour through your own private cemetery, and they will help you reflect upon key concepts and ideas raised throughout the text.

The best way to approach these meditations is to first study the photograph without reading the accompanying text. Project yourself into the image until it feels as if you are standing in the cemetery. Contemplate the monument, and allow your mind to drift along whatever currents of thought the image inspires. You may even want to have your journal handy so you can record ideas and reflections as they come to you. Once you have allowed yourself to engage in five or ten minutes of free association with the image, read the meditation itself. Approach the icon through the lens of the meditation, allowing yourself to perceive things that perhaps you had overlooked. Immerse yourself in the experience, and continue to focus on the feeling that you are observing the monument in the virtual cemetery.

Like many exercises that occur throughout this book, these meditations can be performed again and again, and as you progress along the Twilight Path, you are likely to discover new layers of reflection and meaning when you take the time to re-explore certain icons. You can expand the application of the icons by using them as a kind of gateway to a certain mood or state of consciousness, using the image as a mental touchstone to bring you more completely in touch with the theme that it represents.

You will also encounter journal questions at the end of nearly every chapter. Your journal will be an invaluable tool as you progress along this path. In many ways, it will become your own personal "Book of the Dead." Your Book of the Dead should include your insights and experiments concerning your work with this path. You should keep a log of each exercise, recording your observations and experiences. Analyze your experience with the exercises, measuring your level of success, and try to develop strategies for improving that success. Although the Twilight Path is a mystical journey, it helps to take a scientific approach to your experience. Experiment, record, and analyze your progress at every step. The notes you take will help measure your progress and point the way to further development.

In addition to the journal questions that appear at the end of each chapter, you will sometimes also encounter an additional exercise entitled "Back to Life." These exercises take the main lesson of the chapter and turn it around, applying it not to deathwork but to the art of living. These exercises are intended to remind you that this is a balanced path, and the wisdom you gain throughout this book is meant to be applied to both life and death. Record your experience with these exercises in your journal as well, to provide a necessary counterpoint to all of the work you'll be doing with death.

The entire process outlined in this book culminates in a self-initiation ritual, but that alone should tell you that your work with the Twilight Path is not finished once you reach the end of this text. This book is merely an introduction, and the door it allows you to open is a portal you should return to again and again. By learning how to approach that threshold, you are taking up the sacred duty of the shaman, walking a path that winds between the worlds of both the living and the dead.

In many ways, your journey along this path is a healing journey. Our culture has become fragmented. Too many of us live only in the light, denying the existence of death and darkness. As a result, we resist change to the point of crippling ourselves. Our fear consumes us. And yet, death is nothing more than the ultimate change, and, as we will discover in this book, death energy lies at the heart of every little change we encounter in our lives. To deny the positive aspects of death is to deny the healing power of personal transformation. As you integrate the mysteries of death into your daily life, you will come to fully understand the power and liberation represented by the threshold state, and you will be able to share that revelation with others. The final chapter in this book will offer some ideas of how to apply this wisdom so that, in healing your own attitudes toward death and dying, you can help to heal the rest of the world.

Mors Janua Vitae
"Death is the Gate of Life"

PART ONE

Approaching the Threshold

"It is easy to go down into Hell;
night and day, the gates of
dark Death stand wide;
but to climb back again,
to retrace one's steps
to the upper air—there's the rub, the task."
—*Virgil, Aeneid*

1.

AN INITIAL APPROACH

If death is the greatest unknown faced by humanity, how can we possibly begin to approach it? For some of us, there is a temptation to confront death head-on, but the only way to do this is to experience it. This supposes a project as reckless as it is dangerous. In 1990, a film debuted called *Flatliners*. In this film, a group of medical students sought to solve the mystery of death by flatlining—artificially inducing the cessation of brain activity. They each took turns crossing the boundary into death and bringing one another back—with disastrous results. Artificially inducing brain death in order to conquer one's fears is best left to fictional characters. There are better ways to connect with death and come to understand the impact it has upon us.

3

Death is not simply a one-time event that looms at the end of our lives. According to the Tibetan Buddhists, death is a part of everyday living. Every time we abandon a habit or undergo some significant change, we experience a little death. For every single transition we experience in our lives, one way of being dies and we achieve rebirth into something new. If we look at things from this perspective, once we get to the death of our physical bodies, we have essentially been practicing the art of dying all along. If a person was wise enough in life to learn the lesson of letting go, then the process of physical death becomes no more frightening than the act of changing one's clothes. This is the Death that we encounter in the tarot deck—death as the imperative to change.

And yet, even this aspect of death may seem intimidating at first. Especially in our Western culture, we are taught to cling to things, amassing quantities of objects and material wealth, and hoarding these in order to feel accomplished in our lives. Letting go does not

Tomb of baby Caleb, aged 15 months, located in Woodlawn Cemetery, in the Bronx, New York.

come easily to a culture that so fears the process of growing old that it considers it acceptable to paralyze muscles with deadly poison in order to present a less wrinkled brow. In a world of face-lifts and Botox treatments, where do we find the courage to gracefully accept the imperative of change?

The Art of Letting Go

As we undertake the journey of coming to understand death, it is best, at first, to start small. From there, we can work our way up to greater acts of personal transformation. If the Tibetan Buddhists are right, and we experience a little death with every significant change, it follows that our first step would be to initiate such a change in our lives. We experience a type of death whenever we let go of an old habit or self-image. When we change from one career to the next, there is that moment of transition when we launch ourselves into the unknown. Every time we cut away the old to make way for the new, we are making that transition. Especially when there is an element of sacrifice and an element of the unknown, the change we make can be viewed as a type of death.

Sacrifice is an important part of coming to understand death. Many people view death as terrible without ever stopping to wonder why. But at the root of the fear of death lies the fear of the unknown. This is coupled with an unwillingness to let go of something we love. The real tragedy of death is founded upon loss. For the person dying, it is the loss of a life that has grown familiar. When death is upon us, we do not cling to our bodies because we enjoy the suffering and the pain; we cling because we don't want to lose the flesh that has become such a comfortable set of clothes. Family members and friends mourn less for the dead person and more for themselves, because they will never hear that voice or see that smiling face again.

If we are going to come to terms with death, we must first come to terms with the idea of sacrifice. Sacrifice is nothing more than learning to let go, especially when we are reluctant to lose whatever it is we're giving up. In some magickal circles, sacrifice has developed a very negative connotation, largely because it can be associated with the bloody practices of the Aztecs or even the ancient Hebrews. In the past, sacrifice often involved the slaughter of an animal, but sacrifice goes wrong when you are offering up something that isn't yours to give. The life of another is not a proper sacrifice. It teaches nothing of the lesson of letting go. A sacrifice is only meaningful if it is something that you would rather keep.

There is a meaningful story about Alexander the Great. As a youth, he was expected to make a sacrifice to the gods to secure for himself a prosperous and bright future. When the priest handed him a container of incense so he could take some for the offering, instead of grabbing a pinch or even a handful, Alexander dumped the entire container upon the flames. Incense was a sacrifice in Alexander's culture because of its expense, and the priests were horrified at the young prince's extravagance. Yet from Alexander's point of view, it could not be a sufficient offering if it did not hurt. This is our first lesson along the Twilight Path.

In many mystical traditions, when individuals finally commit to their chosen path, that commitment is marked with some obvious, physical change. Sometimes this is as simple as adopting a new style of clothes. In some cultures, such a commitment is marked with an extensive, full-body tattoo. Still others mark this transition by shaving the initiate's head. Cutting off the hair is symbolic of cutting away the past, and the initiate is given a clean start, unburdened by any old images of the self.

The following ritual is intended to serve as a commitment ceremony to mark your dedication to the Twilight Path. The ritual centers around the concept of sacrifice, focusing on an intentional physical change as the point of transition. Your speaking parts in this rite, as well as in all of the other rituals that appear in this book, are designated by the term "Ritualist." I use "Ritualist," rather than "Priest" or "Priestess," to emphasize that these are not necessarily religious rites. Although you can certainly integrate the Twilight Path into your particular religious system, this path is not necessarily a religion itself. Deathwork is something anyone can approach, regardless of their background.

As the Ritualist in the following rite, you will make a sacrifice of part of yourself. One of the goals of this work is to help you move beyond your attachment to superficial appearances, and so the sacrifice in this rite revolves around removing something that significantly alters your physical self-image. You will choose the exact nature of the physical change, but keep in mind that there has to be sacrifice involved for it to have meaning.

One option is to cut your hair. This allows you to sacrifice a part of yourself without causing any real damage. Although a lot of our self-image can be tied to our hair, it doesn't really hurt us to have it cut away. Shaving your head completely is especially potent, because it has such a radical impact upon your appearance. If you choose to go this route, not only will it change the way you look at yourself in the mirror, but it will also change the way people see you and respond to you. Shaving off all of your hair is extreme and may not be entirely practical. While many men can get away with shaving their heads, the practice is not as accepted among women. Depending upon your career, such a radical change might cost you your job.

If, for some reason, cutting your hair is not an option, what other aspects of appearance could you sacrifice for this rite? If you are male, and you tend to wear a mustache or beard, consider cutting this away. Although the change is not as marked as shaving off all your hair, this can still significantly alter your appearance. Like the hair on your head, facial hair easily replaces itself, so you are doing no lasting harm beyond changing your habitual appearance. If you like to grow your nails long, this provides another option for sacrifice. You can cut away your beautiful nails and offer them up in the spirit of change. Although getting a piercing or a new tattoo is another way to make a significant change of appearance, I do not recommend these for this ritual. The second half of the rite involves discarding the detritus generated by the change. Cutting your hair or nails will give you something to cast away. A piercing or a tattoo does not generate much of yourself that you can throw away.

The Ritual Bath

To perform this ritual, you will need to decide what part of yourself you are going to offer up: hair, nails, facial hair, or something else. You will want a quiet place to make the sacrifice, and you should have a bowl or other receptacle to catch the shed hair or other items in. In addition to the bowl, you should have a cloth or towel to lay under the bowl, a burner with incense, and scissors or a razor. The bowl should be black or some other dark color. The cloth should be black, purple, or red. There are suggestions for incense in Appendix I, but any appropriately dark scent will do. Scents that contain myrrh are ideal, but if this is unavailable, you can substitute something else that appeals to you. Set these items aside, keeping them near to wherever you have decided to perform the ritual.

Prior to performing the sacrifice, you should make yourself ritually pure. Many religions around the world have a standard or ritual purity. Catholics perform a symbolic washing of the feet in a special ceremony leading up to the Easter celebration. Muslims are expected to perform ritual ablutions prior to entering any holy place. As the water washes away dust and dirt from the road, it symbolically cleanses the seeker of spiritual "dirt" as well. In Wicca and neo-Paganism, this process of purification is often achieved through a ritual bath.

You should undertake this bath at least an hour prior to the actual ritual. The best time of day for performing this working is close to dusk, and you should try to time it so that the sacrifice itself occurs as night falls on the world. Draw the bathwater, and as the tub fills up, light a few candles as well as some of the incense, saving some incense for later use. You can arrange the candles and incense along the edge of the tub itself or on a nearby sink. Do not turn on the electric light unless you have great difficulty seeing in low-light situations. Rituals of the Twilight Path are best performed in twilight and in shadows.

Before you get into the bathwater, you should add a sachet containing sea salt, cinnamon, and myrrh. The sea salt is cleansing, and both myrrh and cinnamon will help attune you to the energies of death and rebirth.

The Colors of Death

Black: In Western culture, this has become the color most widely associated with funerals and mourning. If the Grim Reaper is depicted, he is most often portrayed wearing robes of midnight black.

Green: According to certain Irish traditions, green is the color of faeries and the Otherworld, and is thus related to the spirits of the dead.

Purple: In Victorian times, the horses in a funeral procession wore purple plumes upon their heads. Elements of this practice still linger in the purple color of the flags used to designate the cars in a funeral procession.

Red: The crimson color of fresh blood, red has associations with violence, death, and passion.

White: The color of the funeral shroud. In Eastern cultures, white—not black—is the color of death.

Chapter One

The sachet is very easy to make, for it is simply a small swatch of cloth wrapped around a few teaspoons of each of these ingredients. Ideally, the cloth should be of natural fibers, such as cotton or linen. It can be a natural color, but it can also be red. Red not only evokes the color of blood, it also evokes the color of fire. Fire purifies through destruction, and in the myth of the phoenix, what is destroyed by fire is also renewed.

Cinnamon further evokes the imagery of death and rebirth associated with the phoenix. According to the ancient Greeks, once every five hundred years, the mythical phoenix would build a pyre and burn itself to ashes. Only from the ashes of the previous phoenix would the next phoenix be reborn. The bird was said to favor cinnamon branches for its unconventional "nest." The cinnamon included in this sachet is intended not only to evoke the energies of fire and renewal but also to bring the energy of the mythic phoenix into the working.

Sea salt is probably a no-brainer. This substance is used for purification in practically every magickal system today. Salt is used to ground and clear energy, and its inclusion here will help bring your energy to a neutral state so you can better soak up the attuning energies of the cinnamon and myrrh.

Myrrh is often used for cleansing and purification, and in fact this bitter resin has natural antiseptic qualities, which has led to its inclusion in substances such as toothpaste. However, this self-same antiseptic quality is one of the reasons the ancients used myrrh extensively in embalming. This use irrevocably connected myrrh with death, at least in the minds of the ancients. Consider a verse from the traditional Christmas carol, "We Three Kings of Orient Are," written by Rev. John Henry Hopkins in 1857:

Myrrh is mine, its bitter perfume,
Breathes of life of gathering gloom.
Sorrow, sighing, bleeding, dying,
Sealed in the stone cold tomb.

This is definitely not as upbeat as "Jingle Bells." The verse recalls the ancient connection between myrrh and the funerary arts, and, in a Christian context, this gift mythically presented to the infant Jesus was a presentiment of death.

The important thing to take from this is that myrrh, although mainly used in purification, still retains some of that lingering energy of the tomb. Its presence in this sachet, and in many of the recipes you'll encounter in this book, harks back to its use in funerary preparation. Water with myrrh and salt is the perfect substance for washing a corpse, and this image, too, should be on your mind when you prepare this sachet—and when you soak in the tub with these scents mingling around you. You are preparing your body for death, washing it like a corpse that has yet to receive its winding sheet, but adding a hint of the phoenix as a promise that death is not the end.

As you bathe in the waters scented with cinnamon and myrrh, allow yourself to soak for a little while. Breathe in the scents of death and rebirth, and let them permeate your body. As you soak, concentrate on all of the things that have distracted you throughout your day. Think of any emotions or inner turmoil you wish to be free of prior to beginning this ritual. Imagine that these unwanted things are like dirt caked upon your body. With a sponge or washcloth, soak up some of the scented water and carefully wipe everything away. Wash yourself from head to foot, allowing the act of washing to cleanse you of not only physical dirt, but also emotional and psychic dirt as well. Call to mind the idea that you are washing your body just as the ancients might wash a corpse, preparing it for what is to come.

When you are satisfied that you have wiped away all the things that would detract from your ritual and gathered in all the energies that will help tune you to your purpose, open the drain and let all the water run out before you get out of the tub. As the water slips away, get on your knees and focus on any last things that might still distract you. See them sluicing from your body and running down the drain.

When you feel clean and focused, stand and towel yourself dry. Be certain to put out the candles and incense before you leave the bathroom. You may opt to perform the sacrificial ritual naked, but if you prefer clothes, you should make certain to put on something fresh and clean. Dark colors are preferable for any kind of death work, but if you resonate more with Asian culture, pure white is also a funereal color, and is appropriate as well.

The Sacrifice of Self

Set up the bowl, cloth, scissors, and incense in an open space. The floor in the middle of a room is ideal, provided this is a room where you are sure to be undisturbed. If there are windows, open the drapes so you can see night descending on the world outside. The room should be dark, ideally lit with only a few candles. If at all possible, the candles should be black or red, or some combination of the two. Try to set up everything so you are facing west. Because the sun dies on the western horizon each day, many cultures associate the west with the land of the dead.

Spread the cloth out beneath the bowl so that it may catch any stray hair or nail clippings. Light the incense and set it to the right of the bowl. Set the scissors or razor on the opposite side, even with the incense burner. Kneel before the bowl and make the following salutation:

> RITUALIST: I welcome the night and the silence it brings. I welcome the stars and the cool, soothing shadows. I call to the darkness, for I seek release. May the powers and spirits that walk the dark places attend me now and bear witness to this rite!

Pass the scissors or razor three times through the incense. As you cleanse them in the scented smoke, say:

> RITUALIST: These are the blades of sacrifice, instruments of my destruction. May they be clean and sharp so they cut true, severing who I wish to be from the person I once was.

Once you have cleansed the instrument, then begin to cut the chosen sacrifice away. If you are cutting off a portion of your hair, be certain to cut so it falls into the waiting bowl. If you are shaving away a mustache or beard, lean over the bowl so the shed hairs fall within. If you are offering up a sacrifice of your fingernails, carefully cut these over the bowl so none of the parings are lost. Cut away everything that you wish to sacrifice and place the entire offering within the bowl. When you have finished making the sacrifice, set the scissors or razor down. Then take the bowl in both hands and raise it up as an offering to the spirits and powers you have called to bear witness to the rite.

> RITUALIST: This is what I could have been. This is who I was. As I cut these things away from me, so do I cut the ties to my previous self. I have descended into darkness, and I have emerged. Like the dead, I seek change and rebirth. May the spirits who stand and attend this rite accept my humble sacrifice. This is a past that is now behind me. This is a self I willingly let go.

Set the bowl back down. If you have sacrificed hair of any sort, wipe your hands over your face or head to dust off any stray cuttings. Try to sweep these off into the bowl. You may wish to take a moment of silence, contemplating the sacrifice you just made. Consider what your self-image means to you and reflect upon how you are changed by this loss. When you are ready, you should take up the bowl and prepare for the final portion of the rite.

Casting Off the Dead Self

When a person dies, the body is traditionally offered up to one of the four elements for disposal. Which method of disposal you choose will be up to you, but your next task is to discard the objects of sacrifice, making a clean break between who you were and who you have become. Whenever I have performed this rite (and it is a useful rite to perform whenever you really need a change), I have preferred burning the hair thus offered up. There is something very potent and inspiring in seeing the discarded hair consumed utterly by the flames. Fire is not always a safe option, especially for those who live in apartments in the city. If you happen to occupy a large apartment building, consider climbing up to the roof and scattering your offering to the four winds. You may also live near a body of water, and you may wish to take your offering there, allowing the sacrifice to be claimed by the deep. Finally, you can dig a small hole and bury your sacrifice, committing it to the earth in much the same way we Westerners bury our dead.

Whichever method you choose, you should perform the act in silence, contemplating what you have given up throughout. Once you have dumped the contents of the offering bowl into the water or the flames, cast it to the winds or into the earth, you should call upon the spirits again to bear witness. These words will conclude the rite:

> RITUALIST: Spirits of the air! Ancient beings and powers that tread the dark spaces between shadow and light! I call to you now to witness this sacrifice. I have died to my former self, and I cast that self away. Gather about me now and lend me the strength and courage to be reborn!

Return to your home and go back to your regular activities. Whenever you look at yourself, remember what you have given up, and what this sacrifice means. You have taken the first step toward embracing the transformational energies of death. This rite opens the door to let that power flow through your life. You have changed, and you have survived. You are now ready to walk further down this powerful path.

JOURNAL EXERCISE: THE ALLURE OF DEATH

Just as there have always been people who fear and revile the very concept of death, so too have there always been people who find death both alluring and romantic. Because it is a universal principle and representative of the "great unknown," death holds a great fascination for many people. Sometimes, as in the modern Gothic movement, this fascination inspires great art and poetry. Sometimes it leads to morbid obsessions and self-destructive behaviors.

It is imperative, before you embark on a journey that takes you intimately into the realm of death and the dead, to determine from where your particular interest arises. A fascination with death can be healthy, if it is given the right outlet and expression. An obsession with death is something you should avoid. The line between the two can be very fine indeed, and only you can know your own heart and soul on the matter.

Consider the following questions before you proceed. Take a good, hard look at your attitudes toward death and the dead, and try to determine where in your psyche they come from. If there are traumatic events in your past, if you have a history of mental illness, or if you are grieving for the loss of a loved one, this is probably not a good path for you. Furthermore, if you are seeking to follow this path just to shock people or to delve into something sensational and forbidden, find your cheap thrills elsewhere. The material in this book is intended to help guide you in your discoveries of a mystical path, and as such it requires much dedication and hard work before you see any significant benefits. Keep this in mind as you answer the self-analytical questions below.

1. What initially attracted you to this book? Why did you finally purchase it? How do you think it can help you? What lessons are you seeking to learn?

2. How sincere do you think you are in these interests? Has this subject fascinated you for a long time? Do you feel you are willing to apply yourself to a long and demanding process of learning?

3. If you are one of those people who has always found death beautiful and fascinating, where does this fascination come from? Take a moment to explore your feelings, and try to explain what they say about you.

4. If you are one of those people who has always found death disturbing and frightening, why do you feel this way? Take a moment to explore these feelings and try to explain what they say about you.

5. Are there events in your life that have influenced your attitude on death? Describe these events, and explain how you think they have changed you. What lessons are these experiences trying to teach you?

6. What do you think your interests and desires say about you to other people? How would you defend your beliefs if they were called into question? Do you think your response would

Statue showing the juncture between life and death. Woodlawn Cemetery, the Bronx.

be reasonable or fanatical? Which do you feel is the healthiest response?

7. In what ways do you expect this book to spiritually and emotionally enrich you? What impact does an investigation into the metaphysics of death hold for your life now? Will this material be of use to you? Do you think it will answer questions you have not been able to answer for yourself?

8. Finally, how did the sacrifice of self affect you? What has this ritual taught you about your relationship with death and change? Are you as willing as you thought you were to embrace radical change in your life? What does this tell you about your real relationship with death energies?

Take a few moments to read back over your answers. If you are satisfied that you have not undertaken this path simply for shock value or out of morbid curiosity, but from a sincere desire to understand death as the essence of change, you are ready to move on.

BEAUTIFUL DEATH

We come to the cemetery in winter, the season when snow blankets the land like a funeral shroud. All of nature lies sleeping beneath the cold, bitter snow and yet there is a beauty and elegance to the stark white of the landscape. As we stroll along the cemetery path, gravel crunching beneath our feet, we come to a gorgeous and striking memorial cast in weathered bronze. The years have imbued the statue with a rich green patina, bringing the statue's features and the folds of her flowing dress into greater relief. She stands, arms outspread, as if in invitation. Her beautiful features are inviting and serene, and there is a proud lift to her strong chin.

Here is death, portrayed as a beautiful woman. She may be a lover beckoning from beyond, or perhaps she is a young mother holding out her arms to provide a beloved child with a nurturing embrace. Many people in this day and age see death as something terrible, a sere specter that waits at the end of life to take all of our favorite things away. And yet, there is nothing grim or frightening in this statue. The woman here, who can be seen as a personification of death, is simple and regal.

Consider the romanticized ideal of death embodied by this statue. Can death be seen as a lover who steals us away to a better, more beautiful place? Is death less like a Grim Reaper who cuts us off from our lives and more like a loving mother who takes us in her arms to carry us gently away from the source of our distress? What mysteries might be revealed to us, if only we accepted the invitation implicit in this statue's stance, took those outstretched hands, and stepped into the world beyond? Take a few moments to contemplate this image, and record your impressions in your journal.

2.

BRINGING DEATH INTO YOUR LIFE

You have dedicated yourself to this path, reaching out for your very first taste of transformative death energies. Having made a sacrifice related to your appearance, you have learned that change can be both painful and liberating. You have learned that the energies of death are in fact the energies of change—now it is time to bring these energies more fully into your daily life, allowing them to make a presence in your living space. The easiest way to bring these energies into your space is to erect an altar dedicated to deathwork, creating permanent space in your home or bedroom focused on the energies of death. This altar will become a threshold between the worlds of the living and the dead, a sacred space where you can safely and intensely pursue the challenges of this path.

In Catholicism, an altar is often an immense and elaborate affair located front and center in a church. During mass, the priest stands at the altar, performing all the actions pivotal to the ritual right there for all to see. In modern Pagan practices, an altar is a somewhat different affair. First of all, one does not need a church or a temple in order to maintain an altar. An altar can be set up anywhere in one's home, though it often helps to place it somewhere away from the normal bustle of the household. It's helpful to be able to control the space around the altar, and that can be difficult if you place your altar near a busy walkway, or right next to the television. Also, it's best to separate the altar from your more mundane furnishings so there's no temptation to drop the afternoon mail smack dab in the middle of your ritual tools when no better space presents itself. The altar represents a space that is separate and distinct from your ordinary, mundane space. It is a bridge between your everyday reality and the world of spirits and the divine, and thus it should be in a location conducive to the act of moving beyond your ordinary routines.

Most home altars are constructed of nothing more than a table or even a bookcase. Usually, a cloth is draped over the base structure so focus shifts to the surface of the altar itself rather than the item the altar is constructed from. Your altar is a little piece of sacred space in your living space, and its surface serves to store ritual tools, symbols of the elements, statues of gods and goddesses, or other sacred items. You should make an effort to keep only these items on your altar and resist the temptation to lay anything down on the altar's surface that is not dedicated to sacred work. Coffee cups, soda cans, and the stack of magazines that just came in the mail have no business being on your altar. Find some other place to put such clutter, and have words with anyone in your household who cannot respect the purpose of this sacred space!

We've covered a little of what should not be placed on an altar, but what items normally get placed on this representation of sacred space? A typical Pagan altar has, at the very least, a representation of each of the four elements. It also contains ritual tools as well as statues or other items, such as stones or fresh flowers, that serve to represent the concept or deities to which the altar is dedicated. In our case, we will construct an altar devoted more to a general idea than to any specific god or goddess. Our altar will be a focal point for the concept of death and its identity as the essence of change in our lives.

This brings us to a salient point on altars and the Twilight Path. Altars, for many people, are necessarily connected with religion. However, an altar is really just a focal point for sacred space, a threshold you erect in order to come closer to something that does not easily cross into ordinary reality. The concept of a threshold does not belong to any specific religion. You can erect an altar to an idea or a concept just as easily as you can erect an altar to a specific deity.

Do you have to worship a god in order to use the threshold space represented by an altar? No. Not everyone who follows the Twilight Path will be comfortable with the idea of working with deities. Fortunately, death is such a universal concept that there is no need to invoke specific gods or goddesses when doing this work. If you prefer to deal with anthropomorphic personifications when invoking certain powers, there is a list of gods and goddesses connected with death and deathwork in Appendix IV. However, you should not feel obligated to include deities in your practices. You can call upon gods and goddesses to act as guides or guardians as you perform the exercises and rituals contained within this book. You can summon spirits and powers to bear witness to your work. But all of these are helpers only. If you succeed in this path, you have succeeded through your own will, alone.

Elements of the Altar

In its most basic form, an altar is merely a table or raised structure that provides a specialized space where matter and spirit converge. For our purposes, the altar will become the focal point of death energies in your home, creating a threshold between the world of the living and the world of the dead where you can more effectively pursue the Twilight Path.

The first and most basic step is to find a table, desk, or similar structure that can serve as the base of your altar. This can be an item that you already have lying around your home, or it can be something purchased specially for this use. If you are working on a budget, a side table or even a small bookcase can do the trick. If you don't like the way the item looks, consider buying a piece of cloth to drape over it. Good colors include black, purple, and red. Black is a color connected with funerals in the West, and it also has associations with night, mysteries, and the hidden. Purple is another color with funereal associations, and it has additional connections to power—especially magickal power. Red is, of course, associated with blood, and through blood, it has further associations with both life and death.

If none of these three colors has a particular appeal to you, a deep, midnight blue can also work. Especially if it has little flecks of silver or gold, this color can be equated with the star-strewn vault of heaven that overlooks the world at night. The night's sky has deep cultural associations with numinous mysteries. In ancient Egyptian mythology, one of the paths to the afterlife allowed the blessed dead to ascend to the heavens and become an immortal star. In accordance with this belief, Nuit, the female embodiment of the starry skies, was painted stretched across the ceiling of the tombs and occasionally also on the inside of the coffin.

Set up the base of the altar in a room that you can close off, so you will not be disturbed in your work. If your living space allows, you may want to set the altar against a western wall, so each time you approach the altar, you will be facing the land of the setting sun. In the mythology of several cultures, and particularly the ancient Egyptians, the west was the traditional realm of the dead.

You may place the altar in any room of your home or you may devote an entire room to the altar, thus creating a kind of personal temple to the energies of death. One option is to convert a walk-in closet to an altar room, draping dark fabric along the walls to hide the room's original intent, and setting the altar itself up against the far wall, away from the door. Provided this is a large closet and you do not have to use it for anything else, this can create a cozy and very intense space, and you can close it off from the rest of the house with relative ease.

Once you have a base that you find visually appealing, your next step is to find representations of the four elements: earth, air, water, and fire. To represent earth, most traditional Pagan altars will have a bowl of salt or possibly dirt. Because we are tuning this altar specifically to invoke death energy, you should collect a small handful of dirt from a nearby cemetery and use this to represent the element of earth. Ideally, this should be taken from a freshly dug grave, but you can also take a little earth from an older grave. You do not want to take so much that you leave an ugly, bare hole over the grave; this would be disrespectful to both the cemetery and the memories of those interred in it. One option is to take a spoon to the graveyard and dig just a little dirt up from a number of graves. You don't need much—just enough to serve as a token reminder that we are all, eventually, dust.

The element of air is traditionally symbolized by the smoke from incense. Because this altar is dedicated to drawing in the energies

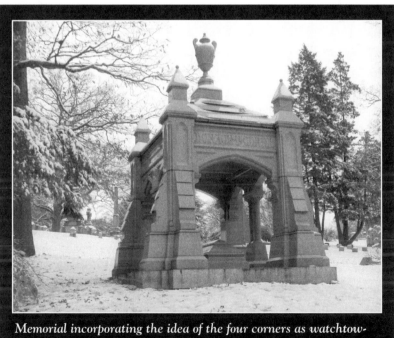

Memorial incorporating the idea of the four corners as watchtowers protecting the deceased. Located in Woodlawn Cemetery, the Bronx, New York.

of death, you will want an incense that resonates with those energies. Any of the incenses discussed in the previous chapter will work. It doesn't hurt to experiment with scents until you find one that you really like. There is no sense in having an incense that is ritually appropriate if you cannot stand the smell! You can also consult Appendix I at the back of this book. This contains further suggestions for incenses, as well as recipes for scents you can make on your own.

In addition to deciding what scent you will be burning on your altar, you need to decide what form of incense you will burn. There are three main types of incense: sticks, cones, and granules. The type of incense will determine what type of incense burner you will keep on your altar.

Incense sticks are perhaps the most common form of incense available today. These are relatively inexpensive and easy to burn. Holders for incense sticks are also very common and appear in a wide range of shapes and styles. Incense cones are the next most common type of incense. Cones burn all the way down, making the area immediately beneath them quite hot, and for this reason they are typically burned on a fire-proof piece of pottery or in a small bowl of sand. The final, and most challenging, type of incense is loose incense. This usually takes the form of unprocessed wood or resin, either in granules or ground to a fine powder. Frankincense, myrrh, benzoin, dragon's blood, copal, and sandalwood have all been used as incenses since ancient times, and many of these are available online or at specialty stores in whole or powdered forms.

The trick with loose incense is that it does not light or stay lit on its own. Both cones and incense sticks are designed to smolder once you light them, but loose incense must be burned over a hot plate or a coal. Self-lighting charcoals are almost always sold alongside loose incense, but these are a little more dangerous to have around than simple incense cones or sticks. You need a well-insulated bowl of either pottery or metal—never wood! This should be filled with several inches of sand to absorb the heat of the self-lighting charcoal. Even with the sand, the charcoal throws a lot of heat and should be kept away from dangling cloth or other things that are extremely flammable. Loose incense does have a very dramatic touch, for it produces large clouds of heavily-scented smoke, harking back to the smoking brazier of an ancient temple. However, safety and convenience, as well as expense, are all concerns, so you should consider your situation carefully before choosing this route.

After the considerations of safety and expense, the main factor in your choice of incense and incense-holders is an aesthetic one. You want an incense-holder that looks good on your altar and resonates with the overall image that altar is intended to represent. To this end, an incense-holder in the shape of a happy, prancing unicorn is probably not the best choice, whereas something made to look like a skeletal hand would fit the altar quite nicely. Another option is to just stick with something simple, preferably in a darker shade that fits the color scheme of the altar. Suggestions for smokeless alternatives appear in Appendix I.

Once you have solved the quandary of what scent and type of incense to choose, you can move on to the rather simpler issue of water. A traditional altar typically has a chalice or goblet to hold the element of water. The water is periodically refreshed so it does not grow stale. Some Pagans will use rainwater for a natural touch on their altars, or they may draw water from a nearby lake or stream. For the altar devoted to deathwork, you should have water mixed with a little salt. The water is then symbolic of both tears and blood. You should refresh this water about once every week, and you should ideally keep it in a glass goblet or bowl, as the salt will corrode most vessels of metal.

To represent the element of fire, you will have two candles, one of black and one of white. These candles will actually serve a dual symbolic purpose. The lit wicks will represent the element of fire upon your altar, the element that both destroys and renews. The candles themselves will represent the forces of life and death. Place the white candle on the far right corner of your altar. Place the black candle opposite this, on the far left. Together, these represent the pillars of the threshold between life and death, and this is the conceptual space ultimately evoked by your altar.

The centerpiece of your altar will be a mirror. This should be a relatively large mirror, at least large enough so you can look into it and see your whole face. The mirror represents the Otherside, the realm of spirits, which is the energetic echo of our own physical world. The mirror is traditionally the centerpiece of the *psychomanteum*, an ancient Greek word for a place where one goes to commune with the dead. The use of a mirror for communication with spirits goes back at least to ancient Greek times, but also appears in necromantic work outlined in *The History and Practice of Magic*, by Paul Christian. In the 1980s, Dr. Raymond Moody brought the psychomanteum back into popular practice, converting a closet in his home for his spirit work. A blackened scrying mirror was the focal point of this space.

The design of the mirror should appeal to you visually, and you should be able to hang it securely on the wall above your altar. Place it so it hangs in the middle of the altar space, directly between the candles of life and death. You will also need a piece of lace or a sheer piece of cloth large enough to completely cover the mirror. This veil should be black or some other appropriately dark color, but it cannot be opaque. When you drape it over the mirror, it should obscure the reflection slightly, but you should still be able to see partial images through it. The veil represents the point of separation between the world of spirit and the world of flesh. In many spiritualist circles, this is known literally as "the Veil," and so a veil of lace or sheer material partially obscuring your mirror is an ideal symbol.

With the mirror, veil, candles, and the four elemental representations, you have the basic structure of your altar. Now you are ready to personalize the altar a little further, adding statues or other items that speak to you deeply about the mysteries of death.

Memento Mori

Memento mori were objects or symbols used in the Middle Ages and beyond to remind people about the ever-present reality of death in their lives. The phrase is Latin and is generally translated, "Remember that you must die." As much as modern people may shrink from every reminder of death they encounter, the Christians of Medieval

Europe often carried personal symbols of death so the brevity of life was never overlooked. Mary Queen of Scots, for example, owned a large watch that would have been the envy of any modern Goth. Featuring a large, silver skull, the watch was also inscribed with thought-provoking lines by the classical writer Horace. Skulls, such as the one carved upon Mary's watch, are one of the most widely recognized memento mori. Their relation to death is almost universal, and their appearance is visceral and hard to mistake. Other mementos with meanings that are similarly direct include coffins, tombstones, and bones of any sort. Funerary urns are another potent symbol depicted as mementos of death.

The connection between the above symbols and what they represent is fairly clear. Other symbols have slightly more obscure associations. Willow branches or branches of cypress are sometimes depicted as memento mori, because these two trees were often planted in graveyards. The willow has even older associations with darkness and death, for in ancient Greek times, it was sacred to the goddess Hecate. From this same association with the dark goddess of the crossroads, toads are sometimes used in images representing death. Both toads and frogs have connections not only with death but also with rebirth and renewal. In ancient Egypt, Heket was a frog-headed goddess who assisted with childbirth, and amulets carved in the shape of frogs were used to help ease the pains of birth.

Hourglasses, because they symbolize the fleeting nature of life, are also appropriate. In many traditional memento mori, hourglasses were depicted with wings to further underscore the idea of how time "flies." Scythes, the traditional tool of the Grim Reaper, appear over and over again, serving as reminders that one's life may be cut short at any time. Using implements like scythes and sickles to depict death as a harvester of souls also neatly embodies the natural, cyclic, even necessary qualities of this much-feared process.

Bats, at least in Western lore, have symbolic associations with night and sometimes also with the dead. Although most researchers cite Bram Stoker as the originator of the myth that bats are connected with the living dead, associations between bats and night

symbols of death

In Western funerary art, there is a wide variety of images used to symbolize death and mourning. Some are not as immediately comprehensible as a coffin or skull.

Anchor: A symbol of hope that one can cling to through troubled times. Typically appears on Christian graves.

Book: The Book of Life, wherein one's destiny is written. Also has Biblical overtones.

Broken Chain: When this symbol appears upon a memorial, it represents the bonds of family that have been sundered through death.

Circle: A symbol of eternity. When complete and whole, the circle represents the hope for unending life in the next world. A broken circle signifies that life has ended.

Covered Urn: A symbol of death and mourning used from Roman times onward.

Crown: A symbol of glory in the afterlife and victory over death.

Lit Torch: The flame of life. When upended, the torch indicates that life has been snuffed out.

Tree Stump: The severing of life, often before its proper time.

demons existed as far back as early Jewish lore. A passage in the Talmud describes the genesis of a certain type of demon that is said to start off as a hyena. After seven years, it transforms into a bat, and after another seven it transforms into a type of night-creature that is translated as a "vampire." In keeping with the dual nature of many traditional symbols, although bats have a dark reputation in Western lore, Eastern traditions see them as guardians that ward evil away.

The death's head moth, whose body appears to depict a human skull, also came to be viewed as a reminder of death, especially in Victorian times. The pupae of this particular moth are potent symbols of death and rebirth. To the ancient Greeks, the asphodel was a flower of the dead. One of the realms of the afterlife was referred to as the "Field of Asphodels." Poppies are another item that developed strong thanatological associations, particularly in Victorian times. The plant, which is the source of opium, was often used to symbolize dreams and visions, as well as the sleep of death. The poppy's association with

MYN GLAS LOOPT RAS

This Dutch image, a 1651 printer's device belonging to Amsterdam publisher Joost Hartgers, says, "My glass runneth quickly."

death changed slightly after World War II, as poppies often grew over the fields that had once seen some of the bloodiest battles. In addition to their connections with sleep and death, poppies now also have an additional association with the courageous dead of Europe's great wars.

Making Your Choices

Because you are dedicating your altar to the energies of death, you will want at least one memento mori to serve as an engaging, visual symbol of your intent. You are by no means limited to just one item, and you may consider changing items or adding new ones as you progress along this path. You are also not limited only to the symbols and images discussed above. The real potency of a symbol is with the meaning it holds for you. Sometimes a symbol just does not seem to speak to you, no matter how time-honored its meaning may be. When such a case arises, experiment with different objects, items, and symbols until you find something that really evokes the state of mind you want to experience when you approach your altar.

The more visually and emotionally stimulating you find the altar, the more you will find that it draws you into the proper frame of mind for the work ahead. If you have chosen to work with deities or tutelary spirits for your journey, you may want to include a statue or other representation of these beings on the altar (a photograph of an ancestor, for example). Even if you are not directly working with deities, consider that certain gods and goddesses have such a traditional connection with death that their image alone evokes a funereal theme. The Egyptian god Anubis, mortician of the gods, is one of the many deities who carries a weighty symbolism that extends beyond his identity as a deity. Hecate is another deity whose associations with death and darkness have become stamped upon the collective imagination. Other gods and goddesses traditionally associated with death are described more completely in Appendix IV, and you can choose from among these should any have a strong appeal for you.

Because the mementos that you choose are intended to help put you in the proper frame of mind, you not only want items that are deeply symbolic, but you may consider items that you can pick up and handle, allowing the tactile interaction to help you meditate on the energies you wish to evoke. Bones or small stone carvings are perfect for this, and bones especially contain the lingering energies of both life and death.

Do not kill anything simply to include its bones on your altar. Remember that nothing should be sacrificed that isn't yours to give. Rather, walk along the side of a busy road and search through the gravel there. You will inevitably find bits of dry and weathered bones left over from animals killed on the road. You could harvest bones from fresh roadkill, but this is a messy, involved process that also carries with it a risk of disease.

A much easier route is to purchase bones online. There are a number of specialty stores that sell bones legally over the Internet, including human bones. The Bone Room (www.boneroom.com) is a reputable source for a variety of bones. You may also consider the Anatomy Warehouse (www.anatomywarehouse.com), which provides skeletons for medical students as well as the public. Skulls Unlimited (www.skullsunlimited.com) specializes in human skulls and, finally, the artist Columbine, who was featured on an episode of *Ripley's Believe It or Not*, crafts jewelry from bone. You can find her work at http://shadegarden.blogspot.com/ which will lead you to her site, hosted by Apocalypse.org.

Services like the Bone Room acquire their human bones legally. However, many of their bones come from sources in China or India where the remains have been removed from their original resting places, typically to make way for new building projects. If there are spirits attached to these bones, they may not be entirely happy about this development. Therefore, it is a good idea for you to make peace with these remains before using them in your ritual work. I've met Columbine, and she often reaches out to communicate with the energy of the bones that she crafts, whispering to them of what they are destined to become through the application of her art. As she makes them into something beautiful and new, she is certain to extend her gratitude for the part they play in her projects.

Taking a page from Columbine, when you first acquire bones of any sort, you should spend a little time with them before using them in ritual. Reach out to the energy contained in the bones and make contact with what resides there. Even if there is not a full-blown spirit attached to the bones, there is likely to be an echo of what once was. Out of respect for whatever once resided in these bones, you should at least introduce yourself, explain the purpose you envision for the bones, and extend your gratitude for the role they will play in your rites. You can develop this into a full ritual or, like Columbine, you can simply whisper your intentions while you work.

Human bones are very evocative of death energy, not only because they resonate strongly themselves, but the very fact that you know these bones came from another human will remind you deeply of your own mortality. Some people may find the idea of keeping human bones on an altar creepy and morbid, but consider that in Tibetan Buddhist practices, trumpets are made out of the femur bones of dead monks, and skulls are used either to create goblets or special drums. The physical remains of the monks are used this way, not out of any disrespect, but to remind the living that bodies are just things we should be ready to discard when the time comes.

Whatever items you choose to include on your altar, make certain that they are personal and meaningful to you. For additional help in making the right decisions, there are questions at the end of this chapter. These journal questions can be used as a kind of workbook exercise to help you design an altar that is perfect for you.

JOURNAL EXERCISE: AN ALTAR FOR THE DEAD

1. Look over the options for symbols of death that you can place on your altar. Make a list of the ones that seem most appealing to you. Are there any images or symbols that you personally associate with death that are not described in the previous chapter? Add these to the list. For each item, write a short description of what it inspires in you. How does thinking about each particular image make you feel? When you

are finished writing a short response for each item, look over what you have written. The items you have written the most about are probably the ones that profoundly speak to you. Consider seeking out representations of these items and giving them a place upon your altar.

2. Consider the idea of having a statue dedicated to a particular god or goddess on your altar. Does this idea appeal to you? Why or why not? Now think about any friends or relatives you had who have passed away. Is there one person among the dead who really means something to you? What do you think about the idea of keeping a photo or other memento of this person on your altar, instead of the image of a deity? Deities, ancestors, or other spirits can act as guides as you walk this path. Not everyone likes to have someone helping them along their way, but if you feel more comfortable having a guide, make a careful decision about who this guide will be and include an item representative of the guide among the other objects on your altar.

3. How much money do you have to devote toward the items on your altar? If you are working on a budget, what options are open to you? Make a list of the items you need to purchase. Do you have things already lying around the house that can be substituted for these items? Consider that you do not need to go out and buy an expensive crystal bowl to serve as a receptacle for your grave dust. A bowl from your cupboard could work just as well. You may also consider using certain items you already own in a temporary capacity, planning ahead in your budget to purchase something you feel is more appropriate.

4. Go back to the list of items you need for your altar. Number this list in order of importance. How significant is the item to you? How fancy would you like that item to ultimately be? If you are working on a tight budget, pick one or two items that you absolutely feel you should spend money on in order to get

the best and most appropriate item possible. If you still need to purchase the other items, consider going to a thrift shop or second-hand store before looking to make a more expensive purchase. You can always upgrade later; the essence of the energies you are working with, after all, is change.

Mausoleum gate separating the world of the living from that of the dead.

5. Take a good, hard look at the space you have to work with for your altar. Before you set up the altar, consider all the possibilities open to you. Also consider all the difficulties that may be connected with each different location. You probably do not want to place your altar next to a phone, for example, unless you intend to unplug that phone each time you sit down to perform any work. You also do not want an altar in a main thoroughfare of the house; many of the exercises and rituals you will be performing require that you be undisturbed.

6. Consider the pre-existing energy of the location you intend for your altar. Does this energy fit with the energies you wish to invoke? If not, how would you have to change the energies of that location in order to make them more conducive to deathwork? If you are setting your altar up in your bedroom, for example, consider adding some decorations on the walls in the area immediately around the altar that also help to evoke the right frame of mind.

7. Make a rough sketch of the top of your altar. Beside it, make a list of the items you will need to fit into that space. Take some time to play around with different layouts for your altar. Keeping the candles of life and death on opposite ends, experiment with the placement of everything else. Make certain to consider issues of safety in the placement of your incense burner, especially as this is a brazier that will hold live coals. If you are having trouble visualizing everything on the altar on paper, sit down with the items themselves and play around with different setups on the altar itself. Adjust things as necessary until the altar looks and feels right to you.

Back to Life

You have spent some time designing an altar dedicated to the energies of death. Once you are satisfied with the layout of your altar, take a break. Make a point of going out to a park or other space that reminds you not of death, but of life. The poet Henry Wadsworth Longfellow suggested that nature presents a grander cathedral than anything constructed by the hands of humans, and there is wisdom in his observations. Give yourself at least half an hour to walk near a lake or stream, or to hike the paths of a nearby forest. Immerse yourself in the immediate, sensory experience of this place, and make an extra effort to pay attention to all the life teeming in this natural habitat. Everything must die, but before that, it must live. These two inseparable forces, life and death, complement and empower one another in an elegant synergy. Consider the contrast between the energy of this living, vibrant, natural space and the energy of your home altar. When you have taken some time to enjoy and explore this place, write your reflections in your journal.

3.

ERECTING THE THRESHOLD

You have already performed one ritual as part of your initial dedication to the Twilight Path. With your altar in place, you are ready to perform more. The next rite is going to be a consecration of your altar. This rite will allow you to better harness the altar as a focal point for opening a threshold between the world of the living and the world of the dead. Before we engage in another ritual, however, we should take a little time to consider what ritual really is, exploring the best ways to get into a ritual mindset in order to achieve the most potent experiences possible.

Ritual Preparation

A ritual is any specific set of actions that you perform in order to achieve a higher, spiritual state. Ritual belongs to the sacred part of our lives, as opposed to the too-often more prevalent secular aspect of our lives. In order for ritual to succeed in connecting us to the sacred and moving us toward mystical experience, we must achieve a certain frame of mind before and during the ritual. This frame of mind involves thinking and acting in ways that differ from the ways we think and act on an ordinary day-to-day basis. It helps to think of ritual as a sacred space we build for ourselves starting from within our minds and moving outward. Some of us need stricter, more dramatic rituals to help us move beyond our ordinary way of thinking because we find it hard to separate ourselves from the secularity of everyday life. Others of us tread the line between the sacred and the secular every moment of our lives. For these few, ritual may be a very informal, spontaneous thing. It really differs from person to person, and the most difficult and time-consuming part of following any mystical path is exploring all the possibilities and finding out exactly what is right for you.

So how does one prepare for ritual so the proper frame of mind is achieved? There are a number of different ways, but essentially all of them serve to make a distinct separation between your ordinary get-up-and-go-to-work reality and the sacred reality of mystical experience. It helps to think of things in a dualistic manner. There is ordinary reality in which we live most of our daily lives—eating, working, socializing—and then there is non-ordinary reality. Non-ordinary reality is the realm of dreams, the realm of mystical experience, and the realm of ritual. Non-ordinary reality verges on the subtle realm. It does not have the same boundaries as ordinary reality and it does not follow the same strict rules. In ordinary reality, we rarely have time to think of things such as spirits and magick; it is in non-ordinary reality that we may encounter spirits, speak to them, even work magick. The difference lies not only in our perceptions between the two forms of reality but also in our experiences and our ways of thinking in the two realities.

Threshold States

Ritual, ideally, takes place in non-ordinary reality. But how do we get into non-ordinary reality? Anything that elevates us or separates us from our ordinary existence helps us to get there. Meditation takes us into the realm of non-ordinary reality, as do trance states that can be induced through repetitive chant, ecstatic dance, fasting, and other ascetic practices. A more subtle way of entering non-ordinary reality is to simply separate yourself from ordinary reality. Consciously remove yourself from your ordinary existence and cross over into a more magickal, potent, and ritualized frame of mind. We can do this by consciously altering our dress, our appearance, and our surroundings in ways that make it clear to us that a change has taken place and a threshold has been crossed.

It is this sense of threshold, really, that serves to delineate between the two realities. In truth, both aspects of reality exist simultaneously and in the same space. Thus, of course, we are constantly moving through both ordinary and non-ordinary reality. Our perceptions alone keep them separate, and when we wish to cross over or become more aware of the subtler aspect of our existence, all we really need to do is make a conscious effort to do so.

Exactly how you alter yourself and your surroundings is primarily up to you. Most practitioners of magick and ritual have ceremonial robes that they wear before and during ritual work. Priests, rabbis, and priestesses all have certain costumes that indicate when they have entered the realm of ritual. You may not want something as elaborate as a robe, though most prefer something loose and flowing. Your ritual garb should be impressive to you—impressive enough to really drive home the point that you are not simply going out to eat in these clothes. Impressive does not necessarily mean expensive, however, and it is important that you design a ritual costume that you will not have problems lying down on the ground in and possibly getting muddy. Your clothes are not going to help your ritual frame of mind if all you can think about are dry-cleaning bills!

In general, a solid color is preferred. For our purposes, black is ideal, though white will also work. Both are colors associated with funerals and death. White represents the pallor of the corpse and the white of the funeral shroud. It is the white death of winter as snow blankets the land, when all life has been erased, pushed back, or cleared away. Black represents the shadow of death, the great, impenetrable unknown. It is the color of night, when the laws of daylight weaken and spirits are more likely to be wandering about. Red or purple may also be used, either by themselves or to complement and accent a foundation of black or white. Both red and purple have represented blood in the past, and purple, as the color of the adept, the color of majesty and power, adds a regal aspect to any ceremonial robes.

Silver jewelry may be added, but if you are going to add something with color, stick to deep reds or purples. Jewelry with onyxes, garnets, or amethysts is best. The amethyst, the color of wine, is traditionally a sacred stone of Dionysus, and in the mystery religions of ancient Greece, he was associated with a dying and rising cult. Further, through its association with Dionysus, the amethyst has also come to be seen as a protection against drunkenness and intoxication. Its name means literally "not drunken." Amethyst induces a clear mind in its wearer, and for this reason it is the stone worn by bishops in the Catholic Church. The garnet, a gem the color of clotted blood, has, through the doctrine of self-similarity, often been associated with sanguinary concerns. It is further a gem of mystery and of secret revelations: to dream of a garnet indicates that a mystery will be revealed to you. Black onyx, and in fact nearly every stone with an ebony hue, is associated with protection. Its color allies it with darkness and negativity, and thus it draws these forces into itself and away from the wearer. Clear crystal may also be used. It is a gem of high, clean resonances, and it is easily used as a focus in most magickal workings, but especially those that deal with the spirit realm.

You may also wish to add scent to your ritual attire. Consider anointing the space over your heart and the insides of your wrists with an appropriately scented oil or perfume. As we have seen before, scents and perfumes that are associated with death and spirits include myrrh, lilies, wormwood, mugwort, and chrysanthemums. Chrysanthemums have long been a traditional flower of death in France, as anyone familiar with the works of Anne Rice may know. The scent of burning mugwort is said to summon spirits and a visionary state. Wormwood may also produce a visionary state in those who partake of it. It was once the main constituent of a liqueur known as absinthe. An anise-based liquor, absinthe was emerald-green in color and an immense favorite of many artists and poets. Known as the "green fairy," absinthe's fervent fans included Arthur Rimbaud, Toulouse-Lautrec, Oscar Wilde, and Ernest Hemingway. In addition to the alcoholic effects of the drink, the absinthe induced a dreamy, almost hallucinatory state in those who drank it. A bitter pleasure, absinthe was also believed to slowly poison those who partook of it. For this reason, the drink was outlawed in the United States for nearly a hundred years, although it has recently come back into vogue.

Cypress and yew are also associated with death and the grave, and ancient specimens of these trees can be found spreading their dense branches over graves in many of the grander cemeteries of Europe. Willow, a plant sacred to Hecate, also draws on her associations with darkness, night, magick, and secret operations.

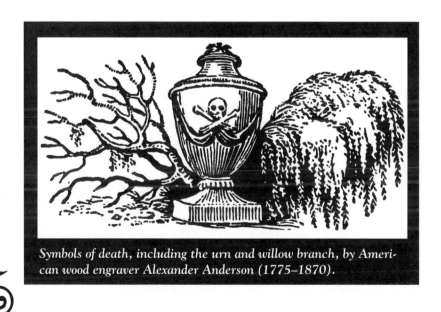

Symbols of death, including the urn and willow branch, by American wood engraver Alexander Anderson (1775–1870).

ꝺꝷ MAN'S ꝼARꝺꝷN

Trees and Flowers Associated with the Dead

Anemone: Sometimes depicted on a memorial to symbolize the brief flowering of life and an early death.

Asphodel: Believed by the ancient Greeks to be the favorite food of the dead, these flowers were thought to grow in one of the fields of the underworld.

Chrysanthemum: In many European countries, including Italy and France, this flower is associated with death.

Horehound: This plant was one of several listed as sacred to the ancient Egyptian god Anubis and is useful for summoning the spirits of the dead.

Lily: Associated with resurrection, lilies were used widely in Victorian funerary iconography and can be found decorating many modern tombstones as well.

Poppy: A plant sacred to the god Morpheus, the poppy is the source of opium, which relieves pain and induces dreams. Its association with death is two-fold: First, it presents death as a relief from pain. Second, it presents death as a great sleep or dream.

Willow: Sacred to Hecate, the willow has ancient ties to the dead in both Western and Eastern traditions.

Yew: A poisonous tree whose dark, brooding greenery seems perfectly at home looming over a lonely grave.

In general, dark floral scents, earthy scents, or scents with bitter, resiny undertones are appropriate. These are guidelines only, however. Your final decision should be based upon what feels right to you.

Putting On Your Face

In addition to your other ritual preparations, you may also wish to adopt a ritual mask. The purpose of the mask is to alter your ordinary appearance and move it into the realm of non-ordinary reality. Death masks also have a long tradition with roots in ancient Egypt and Greece. In some traditions, the death mask is made shortly after the moment of death. It may even be molded directly from the visage of the deceased, thus capturing their final expression for all time. In the funerary practices of ancient Egypt and Greece, the death mask more often resembled the dead person in his or her prime, and thus it served almost as a guide for the spirit to build its likeness upon lest it forget who it was. Among the Romans, death masks were made when famous people died, and during certain public rites, the descendants of these great people wore the masks, invoking the spirits of their ancestors in a grand procession.

Your ritual mask may be an actual physical mask that you made (or had made for you) and wear during ritual, or it may simply be a certain pattern of facial make-up you apply as part of your ritual preparation. If you often wear make-up, the "mask" may be the absence of any make-up at all. Consider that the mask or make-up does not have to be elaborate in order to have meaning. As you are working to call upon the energies of death, powdering your face to make it pale as a corpse may be one simple way to prepare for your ritual work. One such "mask" that I have used to great effect involves a foundation of pale powder, followed by a streak of ash that I draw with my finger from the middle of my forehead, down the center of my nose and lips, all the way to the underside of my chin. This very simple ritual mask creates a striking visage that recalls at once the threshold state of the ritual space itself, as well as the traditional appearance of the Norse goddess of the Underworld. Hel, a daughter of the trickster god Loki, was believed to have a face that was half formed and half unformed.

On one side, she looked like a normal, living being, while the other half of her face was caught in potentiality, forever unfinished and incomplete.

Masks have been used in ritual the world over, in nearly every culture and tradition. At the core, the mask holds something of you, especially if you make it with our own hands, and yet it is something else entirely, a semblance that you take up or set aside. In this respect, it is symbolic of your entrance into or departure from the reality of ritual space. Remember, the goal here is to create a distinct break from your ordinary reality. Experiment with methods that will help to wipe away the traces of your mundane life so you can elevate yourself into a new and different existence for the duration of the ritual.

Final Concerns

The first few times, you may want to experiment with your ritual preparations. After a while you will learn what works best for you. *Don't ever do anything that makes you feel uncomfortable or awkward.* All of the ritual items and preparations I have discussed are guidelines only. They are designed to be used as a focus, to help you concentrate on the essence of the ritual itself. If at any time the items or costumes used in a ritual detract from the ritual itself, you are doing something wrong. You have lost sight of your purpose. The idea is not to become so bogged down with toys and tools that you no longer recall why you were holding the ritual in the first place. The idea is to help the ritual have as much profound, personal meaning for you as it can possibly hold. The ritual itself, even, is only a tool, and should be used as such. You and the goals you seek to achieve through the ritual are the real essence of the ritual actions; ultimately, however you choose to perform your ritual is fine so long as you never lose sight of yourself and your goal.

Sometimes, once you've gotten comfortable with a certain way of doing things, you suddenly find that this no longer works for you. Don't panic. Everything changes. You change, your needs in ritual change. This is the essence of the energies you are seeking to work with, after all, because transformation and change is the essence of

46

death. So don't be afraid to change and grow, to alter your approach, to take up a certain tool or focusing device one month only to leave it for another a few months down the line. Your ritual should be alive. It should be vibrant, it should speak to you, with you, through you. The minute ritual becomes static, it is nothing more than a cage that obscures the real magick, which comes not from any actions or items, but from within you.

JOURNAL EXERCISE: GETTING INTO RITUAL

1. Go back through this chapter and make a list of all the methods suggested for making a distinction between your ordinary reality and ritual. Can you think of other methods not discussed that you can add to the list? Write a brief response to each method, discussing why you think it would or would not work for you.

2. Go back over your responses from question 1. Make a second list of the top three methods that, from your responses, you feel will work best for you. Of these three methods, are there any that are impractical given your current circumstances? Consider what it would take to incorporate these into your ritual practices. Carefully assess issues like expense, practicality, and long-term appeal. Is there anything you could do to make the technique a little more practical? How can you adapt it to your particular circumstances? What other ideas occur to you?

3. Before you engage in ritual, pick at least one method for creating a break between your ordinary reality and your ritual frame of mind. Experiment with this method, preferably in front of a mirror. How does the technique make you feel? Do you feel different from your ordinary self, or do you just feel silly? Once you put a specific technique into practice, you may find that it does not work as well in reality as you thought it might in theory. Look back over the other methods you listed

in your top three. Experiment with these as well. Record your reaction to all three in your journal.

4. Describe your ideal ritual experience. How can you apply the ideas and information gained from the previous three exercises to achieve this ideal experience?

4.

WALKING THE
SPACES BETWEEN

As your ritual frame of mind will help you enter an internal threshold state, walking more completely between the world of flesh and the world of spirit, your altar is to be a focal point for an even more potent threshold. The altar you have constructed is a physical representation of the transformational energies of death. Between the candles of life and death stands a threshold, and every time you approach the altar, you will pass into this liminal space. The following ritual empowers you to initially open that gate, formally dedicating your altar to the work ahead.

As a part of this rite, you will be invoking the elements. Among Wiccan and Pagan rituals, this is a fairly common method of consecrating sacred space. In traditional witchcraft, the elements are typically called in the following order: earth, air, water, and fire. As you read through this ritual, you will note that the order is not followed, and if you are coming from a more traditional Pagan background, you are probably wondering why.

The Twilight Path is a syncretic system, and it owes a great deal to the Bardo tradition of Tibetan Buddhism. As we will see later in this book, the Tibetan Buddhists have a very interesting take on the process of death as it relates to the five elements (the fifth, in their system, being "void"). They feel that, as a person is dying, five nadi-wheels—energy centers that are comparable to Western chakras— begin to unwind. These nadi-wheels can be seen as locks that bind the body and spirit, literal knots that tie us to the flesh. Through their careful study of this process, they have come to recognize five specific stages in the process of death. At each of these stages, another one of these knots is believed to unravel, releasing the spirit one more step from the flesh.

In traditional works devoted to the Tibetan Bardo, such as *The Mirror of Mindfulness* and *The Bardo Guidebook*, each of these five stages of death are associated with an element. The progress of the unwinding of the nadi-wheels, in fact, is measured by this elemental progression, which goes: earth dissolving into water, water dispersing into fire, fire dispersing into wind, and wind dispersing into void. This is an elemental progression that will be harnessed in our later work, particularly in the death and rebirth rite. For the sake of consistency, I have retained this progression throughout all rituals of the Twilight Path, in part to help the practitioner adjust to this different way of enumerating the elements, but also because of the process of dissolution into void that the progression represents.

The Ritual of Thresholds

Prepare yourself, as before, with a ritual bath taken about an hour before you begin the rite. After the ritual bath, dry yourself off and don whatever mask or other attire you have settled upon to help make a break with ordinary reality and keep yourself in a ritual frame of mind. Approach the altar in silence and light first the incense, then the candles of life and death. Cross your arms upon your chest and kneel down for a moment, contemplating your purpose and intent.

When you are ready, stand before the altar. Stare into your own eyes behind the veiled mirror. You will do this whenever you do ritual work at your altar, for your veiled reflection represents the spirit aspect of you. When you work at this altar, you are trying to bring both spirit and flesh together, to allow yourself to walk and work as one, so identification with this veiled self is important.

Take three slow, deep breaths and feel the power begin to flow throughout your body. Place your fingers in the vessel of earth and invoke the first element.

> RITUALIST: I call upon the earth, which gives and then takes back! You are the foundation of all life, nurturing the young and welcoming the dead with open arms. Lend your power to this space and consecrate it to the element that grounds.

Scatter a pinch of earth across the altar. When you are finished, touch your fingers to your forehead, leaving a streak of dust. Then place your fingers in the vessel of water and invoke the second element.

> RITUALIST: I call upon the water, which cleanses and renews! You are my blood and my precious tears, and in the form of the great ocean, you take everything into yourself so it is transformed. Lend your power to this space and consecrate it to the element that flows.

Scatter the water clinging to your fingers upon the altar. When you are done, touch your fingers to your lips, tasting the salt of blood and tears. When you are finished, pass your hands over the candle flames, both at once, so there is a balance between life and death. As you do this, invoke the third element.

> RITUALIST: I call upon the fire, which illuminates and consumes! You are the shifting flame that shines and then destroys. You are capable of devouring everything, reducing

it down to its most basic parts. Lend your power to this space and consecrate it to the element that burns.

Press both of your palms together in front of your heart. Smell the lingering scent of the flame as it clings to your flesh. When you are finished, waft the smoke from the incense toward you, so it billows up and around you. As you do this, invoke the fourth element.

> RITUALIST: I call upon the air, which is both breath and life! You are the essence of a sigh and the voice of a mighty storm. Invisible to the naked eye, if you are absent, all life comes to an end. Lend your power to this space and consecrate it to the element that breathes.

Hold the incense holder in both hands and present the smoke to the left of the altar and then to the right. Finally, present the smoke to the veiled mirror, so curls of incense waft up past the centerpiece of your altar. Put the incense holder back down in its proper place. With the scent of the smoke still clinging to your skin, fold both hands over your belly, just beneath your navel. When you are finished, hold your hands out at your sides, palms turned upward. As you do this, invoke the final element.

> RITUALIST: I call upon the spirit, supreme force that binds the rest. You are the essence that remains when the wind falls still. You are the light that shines when the fire has burned down. You are the force that flows when the water has gone dry. You are what remains when all the earth crumbles into dust. Lend your power to this space and consecrate it to the element that survives even death.

Lift your hands before you and feel energy gathering in your open palms. Radiate this from your hands and your heart into the altar. Still summoning energy and infusing it into the altar, imagine a gate opening up between you and the veiled mirror, a threshold that stretches between the candle of life and the candle of death. Call upon the spirits to help open this gate from their end.

> RITUALIST: I call to you, spirits and unseen powers! I invoke
> the shadows and the creeping arms of night! Come, stand at
> this threshold and bear witness to my rite. Lend your power
> to the gate I now throw open. Join me here in the space
> between death and life.

Point the first two fingers of your right hand out. Concentrate all of
the energy you have been building in the ritual thus far into the tips
of those two fingers. Starting at the floor directly beneath the left
candle, begin to draw the outline of a gate in the air just in front of
the altar. Move up in a line parallel to the left candle, arching over
the altar, then drawing a line on the other side all the way to the
floor, in line with the candle burning on the right.

As you do this, continue to concentrate the energy into your fingers, summoning the power of all five elements you have just invoked.
Use this power to cut a gateway in the very fabric of reality, opening
a gate between flesh and spirit.

> RITUALIST: I consecrate this altar as a space between. When
> I stand here, I stand between life and death. When I stand
> here, I stand among you, my spirits, guardians, and friends.
> This is my threshold, and my will is my key. When I call for
> this gate to open, nothing will stand in my way.

Stand before the gate, spreading your arms wide. Briefly invoke each
of the elements again, calling the memory of their energy to your
hands and imbuing this energy into the space of your altar.

> RITUALIST: By flesh and spirit, by earth and air, by fire and
> water, I open this gate and bind it to me.

Cross your arms upon your chest and kneel before the altar once
more. Silently thank the spirits, elements, and powers for attending
your rite, and silently bid them to depart. Continuing in silence, blow
out the candles, snuff the incense, and remove your ritual attire. Do
not speak until you have left the space of the altar. You may want to
eat a small meal to help yourself ground and return to a normal frame
of mind.

Daily Meditation

Once your altar is consecrated and it stands as a door between the world of the living and the world of the dead, you want to immerse yourself in the energies it represents. The best way to do this is through simple, repeated rituals that invite the energy you are seeking to connect with into your life. The following rite is a very basic ritual, almost more of a daily meditation. It invites both the spirits and the transformational energies of death to be a part of your daily experience.

Perform this rite each night, during twilight as night descends upon the land. If you have a day job, you can alternately harness the twilight time just before dawn, performing this brief ritual as night gives way to dawn.

Approach the altar and cross your arms upon your chest. Light the candles of life and death and take a moment to gaze into the mirror through the veil, seeing yourself as a being both of flesh and of spirit. Dipping your fingers into the chalice of water, touch them to your forehead, your lips, and your chest. As you do this, say the following:

> RITUALIST: I anoint my forehead, that I may open my mind.
> I anoint my lips, that I may loosen my tongue. I anoint my
> chest, that I may open my heart.

The first step opens you mentally and psychically to a deeper experience of this threshold state. The second step opens you so you may better communicate across the veil. The third step opens you emotionally and energetically to the spirits and the forces they represent. Spreading your arms wide, picture the edges of the gate glowing softly around you. Reach out mentally to any spirits that may be gathering nearby. Silently invite them to attend you. Out loud, declare the following:

> RITUALIST: Standing on the threshold between darkness and
> light, I open myself to the mysteries of death and transforma-

tion. Gather round, ye spirits, and whisper to me the secret names. Open the path before me and show me the way.

Close your eyes and allow your awareness to spread beyond the limits of your body. Listen carefully with both your physical and internal ears for any contact or messages. After a few moments, close yourself so you can exit the threshold state and return to the demands of your ordinary life. To close yourself, touch your forehead, lips, and heart again, saying:

RITUALIST: The door is closed, but I carry it within. If a lesson presents itself to me, may it open again, so I may see and, seeing, learn.

Snuff the candles and return to your normal affairs.

Back to Life

You have begun to firmly establish the presence of death and change in your life, maintaining an altar and performing daily meditations to invite the threshold state. As you immerse yourself more and more in the energies of death, you may find yourself drifting further and further from the pleasures and concerns of the physical world. While it is certainly the goal of the Twilight Path to put you into closer contact with the realm of spirits, one should always remember to walk firmly on both sides of the threshold. Life is precious, and this is a fundamental lesson of this path. To help remind yourself of the other side of things, take a day to treat yourself to a meal with food and drink that you deeply enjoy. You may want to prepare this meal yourself, enjoying the organic, hands-on process of preparing the food, or you may want to indulge your tastes by taking yourself out to a favorite restaurant. Whichever you choose, immerse yourself in the experience, allowing yourself to live in that moment, just enjoying the food, the drink, and the atmosphere of the meal. If there are foods that you like, but which you normally deny yourself, splurge a little with this meal and indulge your tastes. Remember the old saying, "Eat, drink and be merry, for tomorrow we die."

5.

PROTECTING
YOURSELF

Typically, when witches or other Pagans perform ritual, they cast a circle around the sacred space. This circle serves a dual purpose. On one hand, it defines the boundaries within which sacred space is raised, erecting what is essentially a spiritual temple. On the other hand, the barrier exists on both sides, providing walls of energetic force that keep unwanted spirits out. Most traditional magickal workers feel that such a barrier should be erected each and every time a person seeks to bridge the gap between the world of flesh and the world of spirit. It is often perceived as both reckless and dangerous to simply open up a gate between the two and invite in anything that answers.

I do not immediately suggest falling back upon this practice of circles and barriers when following the Twilight Path. One of the main points of building an altar dedicated to the energies of death right there in your living space is to invite those energies, and the spirits and other forces that come with them, to cross into your daily realm of experience. In many ways, the exercises in this book seek to create an environment of total immersion in the threshold state, so there is a constant cross-over between flesh and spirit. There are many magickal workers who will probably object to this idea, seeing it as dangerous. Completely opening your sacred space to spirits, and maintaining this open policy even when you are not actively working in that space has the potential to attract things that you may not want. But I feel that, for the diligent student, the benefits of total immersion outweigh the risks. However, the choice of risk or safety should be left up to each individual practitioner. To this end, I have included this chapter on erecting barriers and driving off unwanted spirits. This is the chapter to fall back upon if you feel you have gotten in over your head.

The Gate of Life

Your altar, once formally dedicated, becomes a threshold space, a point where opposing energies converge and mingle. The two candles that stand opposite one another on the altar represent not only life and death but also shadow and light, flesh and spirit, mystery and revelation. The symbolic gate that you cut into the space with your energy opens a door to the Otherside. This allows spirits to better cross into your space. There is one drawback to this, however. Not all spirits are beings you want to welcome into your space.

Some of you may already have a spirit—or spirits—in mind when you reach out across the veil for contact. This could be a loved one who crossed over many years ago, or perhaps a friend who has died. For those who are comfortable working with guides or deities, this does not have to be a human spirit at all, but can be one of a vast number of potent beings that exist beyond the Veil. When you are not certain whom you want to invite, however, you first must simply open the door. This open invitation will allow a spirit that is right for you to find you and come. However, other entities can find this gate

ςoδs & ςoδδesses oρ τhe δeaδ

Baron Samedi: Sometimes also known as Papa Ghede, Baron Samedi presides over death as well as the libido in traditional Voodoo.

Dis: A wolf-headed Etruscan lord of the Underworld, later adopted by the Romans.

Itonde: In Nkundo myth, he is the god of death and darkness, as well as of the hunt.

Izanami: A Japanese goddess of both death and creation whose husband failed to retrieve her from the Underworld.

Kalma: Pale goddess of death in Finnish myth.

Maerin: A Greek goddess of the dead, her name means "wolf-mother."

Nephthys: Ancient Egyptian goddess who helps to wrap the dead. Wife of the god Set.

Nergal: A fierce warrior from Mesopotamian myth who was also a god of the Underworld.

Oya: In the practice of Santeria, Oya is an Orisha who presides over the hurricane and therefore is associated with destruction and death.

Sedna: Fierce goddess of the frozen Underworld, from the pantheon of the Inuit peoples.

Yarilo: A dying and rising god from Slavic myth.

Yngona: In the myths of the Saxons, she is a crone-like goddess of death.

as well, answering the invitation even though you might discover that you do not like them at all. So if you are trying to be open and inviting to spirits, what can you do when something you don't like answers the call? The gate you have opened remains accessible at all times, and so, even when you are not doing deathwork at your altar, it is possible for something to come through.

If you have at least some idea of what you would like to allow into your space, you can create a selective barrier that will keep unwanted beings out. This barrier is simply a shield of energy, shaped and directed by your will. When witches cast a circle prior to ritual, they are erecting a formal version of this kind of barrier and use it to define the space between ordinary reality and their ritual space. Often, they call upon deities and watchtowers to help them define and enforce this barrier. You can choose to ask other forces for help, but it is entirely feasible to erect a barrier like this through your own power.

The simplest way to create this type of barrier is to first sit down in front of your altar. Close your eyes and gather energy within. Call upon your power and focus on your intent. In this case, your intent is to create a barrier that is impassable for anything malevolent or harmful, a barrier that will nevertheless allow helpful spirits to pass. Focus on working this intent into the energy, calling to mind some examples of what you consider helpful—and therefore allowable— entities, then calling to mind the kind of beings you do not wish to allow. When you feel the power and energy gathered like an intensely glowing sphere in the center of your being, begin to project this out, expanding it into the space. Visualize it as a bubble of force that grows until it envelops your ritual space, incorporating both the altar and the spiritual gate. Because energy degrades over time, especially when we don't reinforce it with our will, repeat this exercise every few weeks to rebuild the barrier.

Not everyone who pursues the Twilight Path is going to want to keep things out. There is some value to learning to take the bad with the good, especially among spirits. Sometimes our initial impression of a being is that it is malevolent, when what we are reacting to has more to do with the intensity of its energy. Keep in mind that many people see death itself as something bad or even evil, but they formulate this opinion largely out of fear. If you really seek to immerse yourself in the realm of spirits when you do work at your altar, you may not feel that a shield is entirely appropriate. However, if you live with other people or even if you live in an apartment building where all of the apartments are connected by contiguous walls, you should consider placing barriers at the limits of your workspace. You may be comfortable with the spirits that come through, but what happens when your unsuspecting neighbors discover that something mischievous has suddenly taken up residence in their kitchen and is busy knocking over the crockery? Unless you have created a very specific gate at your altar, that threshold will be open to anything curious enough to come through. There is ample motivation for many types of spirits to gather round the gate you have erected and use it to enter the rest of your home or as a method of passage into your neighbors' space. Remember that spirits consume energy, and some of the most potent and satisfying energy is the vital energy generated by living people.

The average person is not equipped to deal with an invading spirit, no matter how harmless that entity may actually be. In this case, you want to erect a barrier that will keep the spirits in the space that you have devoted to them, as a courtesy to those around you. Creating a spiritual temple will accomplish this goal.

Building a Spirit-Temple

Building a spirit-temple begins much like the process of building a selective shield. In many ways, it is simply a more concrete way of casting a circle, only this circle is intended to remain standing whether or not you are engaged in ritual.

Sit in front of your altar and gather power within yourself. As you formulate your intent, focus more on a solid, general barrier than something that will allow certain things to pass. When you feel the burning center of energy gather in your chest, stand. Instead of expanding this as a bubble outside of yourself, let the power flow throughout your entire body, but direct it especially to your hands. Walk up to the altar and place your hands on the wall against which your altar stands. Start to infuse this wall with the energy of the barrier, making it something that is real on both sides of reality—a wall of both spirit and matter. As you infuse the wall with energy, say:

> RITUALIST: Brick by brick and thought by thought, I build my spirit-temple.

Spread the barrier of energy to the right and left until you feel that it reaches the limits of your ritual workspace. You need to define the edges of this space clearly in your mind, especially if your altar occupies space in just one corner of a larger room.

Continuing to build the wall of energy, move so you are standing at the far left corner of the ritual space. Still weaving the energy of the barrier, walk the edge of the ritual space on this side of the altar. Imagine the energy flowing from every portion of your body, stretching above and below you to make an invisible wall. Continue to visualize this as the wall of an ancient temple, a temple that will now house your private ritual space. As you trace the left wall of this spiritual temple, say again:

> RITUALIST: Brick by brick and thought by thought, I build my spirit-temple.

Continue until you reach the next corner that defines the limits of this space. At the corner, turn and build the third wall. This should be the wall opposite your altar. In the middle of this wall, you should envision a door—a very heavy door with an intricate lock, to which you have the only key.

> RITUALIST: This door stands as a barrier to all but me. With each brick and with each thought, I build my spirit-temple.

From now on, when you approach your ritual space, you will do it only by walking through this conceptual door.

When the door is in place and tuned only to you, continue to the next corner, then turn back toward your altar. You have one wall left to build. Create this barrier the same way you have built all the rest, walking the line straight back to the back wall of the altar. As you build this fourth and final wall, say once more:

RITUALIST: Brick by brick and thought by thought, I build my spirit-temple.

Once the fourth wall is finished, you will stand once more at your altar. As you stand there, close your eyes and envision the walls stretching up around you. Clearly imagine the substance they are made of. See their color in your mind, the style of the walls and any decorations. Make these barriers as real as possible on the level of spirit.

With the four walls firmly in place, you now have only to add a floor and a ceiling. As you stand in the middle of this newly constructed spiritual room, reach up and down with the energy.

RITUALIST: A ceiling above, a floor below, my temple stands complete.

From the central point before the altar, make certain that there are no holes or cracks in the barriers. Behind you, there is a door that opens to your ordinary space, and this door will open only for you. The gate remains in front of you, hanging between the candles of life and death. This gate is a threshold that allows spirits access to your little temple. The energetic barrier will not prevent them from coming through this gate, but once they are within the walls you have erected, the only way they can leave is to go back out through this gate.

Creating this energetic temple neatly separates your altar from your ordinary space. Just as with the selective barrier described earlier, you will want to periodically refresh the energy of the temple, repeating the process of building the walls, ceiling, and floor. Do this about once a month, paying close attention to how these energetic walls change the flow of energy in your ritual space. If you find the barriers to be a little too heavy or if they start to make the energy feel stagnant or trapped, stand in the center of the space and shatter the entire temple as if it were glass. Allow the energy to fall to powder around you, and call upon the elements to sweep the energy away. Wind can scatter it, fire can consume it, water will wash the residue away, and earth will take the used energy into itself, reclaiming anything that can still be used. Then start fresh with the temple, and focus on making the walls not quite as heavy or thick, so the energy may breathe rather than stagnate. Once again, if your goal is total immersion in the threshold state, you may ultimately wish to dispense with this artificial construction, allowing there to be no barriers between the gate and the rest of your space.

Unwanted Visitors

Every once in a while, things do not go exactly as planned. When your work involves the realm of spirits, this means that, no matter what precautions you may have taken, something unwanted managed to get through. So what happens when you end up with something really nasty in your home?

There are a wide variety of techniques you can employ to protect yourself from a malevolent, unwanted spirit. Books like Dion Fortune's classic *Psychic Self-Defense*, Christopher Penczak's *The Witch's Shield*, Kerr Cuhulain's *Magickal Self Defense: A Quantum Approach to Warding*, and others explore these techniques in great detail, but all matters of psychic self-defense come down to controlling your energy and being firm about your boundaries. If you find yourself being attacked by an unwanted spirit, clasp your hands over your heart and hold your energy inside of you. Then concentrate on erecting a barrier around yourself so that the spirit cannot get at your energy. This barrier is exactly like the one you set up around your ritual space, except that it only envelops you.

Do not be afraid of the spirit and do not panic: strong emotion adds flavor to the energy, and your fear is likely to make the spirit try even harder to get at you. Remind yourself silently that this spirit has no power over you, and if you choose not to interact with it, it cannot touch you. Out loud, firmly tell the spirit to be gone from your presence. Do not let fear or anger into your voice: just be clear that you want it to go. Most spirits, confronted with strong personal bar-

SIGNS OF PSYCHIC ATTACK

Not every entity is out to get you, but that does not negate the reality of psychic attack. Psychic attacks are real, though rare. If you suspect that you may be the victim of an attack, here are a few things to watch out for:

- You suddenly feel exhausted or lethargic for no known reason
- You have an inexplicable sensation of dizziness or nausea
- You experience unpleasant tingling or shooting pains with no obvious source
- The atmosphere of the room you are in feels suddenly oppressive
- You experience sudden chills or a sudden rush of heat
- You develop a headache with no obvious cause
- You feel drained of energy
- You feel overwhelmed by negative energy and/or negative emotions
- You feel an unfriendly presence when no one is there

riers and this kind of resistance will just give up and move on. If it persists, simply reach out and attack it back. This is done purely with your energy, directed by your will. As the spirit itself is pure energy, any attack you make will be keenly felt. Very few spirits will continue an attack once it has been returned in kind. Fear is the main thing that makes us vulnerable to spirit attacks, and a weak sense of our own barriers allows those attacks to succeed. Be firm in the knowledge that you are not a victim and that your will can triumph over the will of anything seeking to do you harm, and you'll have the power to keep yourself safe. Failing that, call upon a higher power that you trust.

Spirit-Chasers

Aside from directly attacking a spirit, how can one drive off such an unwanted entity? Every culture the world over has had traditional tools and objects intended to protect the living from unwanted spirits. Gargoyles and grotesques on old churches function on the notion that spirits can be scared off with ugly, hideous faces. Tribal masks from the Inuits to the various African peoples demonstrate this notion very nicely, with their distended faces, enlarged mouths, and protuberant eyes. Similar masks used to frighten away evil spirits can also be found among a number of Asian cultures, with quite a few of these recently finding a receptive market here in the West as decorative pieces.

The jack-o'-lantern, such a common sight in the United States around Halloween, also functions on this principle. Originally used in Ireland (and made out of a potato or turnip before it was ever carved from a pumpkin!), the jack-o'-lantern was placed outside of a family's home with the hope that its distorted face, lit by a candle from within, would frighten unwanted spirits away.

I have found that a grotesque, be it a gargoyle or other mask, functions very nicely as a guardian over a doorway. You may coax a spirit to inhabit the item, or you may work an energetic construct into the item with the specific intent of using it as a guard. Either way, placing this object just over a door has the effect of scaring lesser entities away. Think of the item as a sort of keeper of the threshold, and remember to charge it with energy and intent fairly regularly in order to maintain its function.

Bells

Another spirit-chasing item that the old churches employed is the bells. Like masks and grotesques, the use of bells to clear the air of negative energies and to scare away spirits crosses the boundaries of culture and time. In the Catholic mass, for example, when the host is solemnly raised for the moment of transubstantiation (the transformation of bread and wine into the body and blood of Jesus), a small set of four bells is often rung by one of the altar boys. This ritualistic ringing is only partially meant to draw attention to the mystery unfolding within the priest's hands. The high chiming tone of the bells, ringing throughout the silent church, was at one time also intended to chase off any unwanted spirits from the place. Furthermore, it was a common belief in the British Isles that the sounding of church bells would drive faeries away.

A lot of folk-beliefs are founded on some grain of truth, although in many cases that truth has become greatly distorted. For example, the ringing of church bells was believed to keep faeries away because it was a sanctified and holy sound. Since the fey weren't part of the Christian belief system, the medieval church automatically identified them as "evil" spirits, in league with Satan. Therefore, anything that was holy or blessed by the church was believed to repel the fey (or anything evil, for that matter).

In Eastern countries where bells were employed to ward off spirits, the effectiveness had little to do with what god was in charge and more to do with the actual tone of the bells. The vibrations of the bells were thought to clear negative energies and to disrupt the energy of spirits. From many personal experiences, I am inclined to agree that it is the sound of the bells—very specifically their vibration and resonance—which has the greatest impact on clearing energies and chasing spirits away. To clear energy, a resonant, deep-throated bell seems to work best, while for most spirits, bells with high frequencies or a slightly dissonant tone seem to irritate them and drive them away.

Drums

Drums, cymbals, and other percussion instruments are thought to work along the same lines as bells. Typically, the loud and dissonant playing of percussion and other instruments is used to chase spirits from an area. By this reasoning, the claims of some conservative Christians that heavy metal music is used to summon demons are completely off base. Instead, such ear-splitting tunes blasted at loud decibels are much more likely to disrupt spiritual energies, sending entities—both good and bad—packing.

Rhythmic drumming is used by shamans to aid them in achieving an altered state for working with spirits and with the dead, so be certain not to get confused. Generally, for the effect of chasing spirits away, the sounds you make on drums and other percussion instruments should be disruptive and unpleasant. As with many other spirit-chasers, this functions on the logic that if it makes your mother-in-law want to flee from the room, it will likely chase away any other nasty entity that's out there.

Tibetan Ritual Tools

The Tibetans, who had a highly evolved spiritual "science" before the Chinese invaded and drove them out of their homeland, developed a number of tools for driving off unwanted spirits. The *phurba*, a three-edged ritual blade, was used as a tool for exorcism. The phurba is essentially a spirit dagger, and it is used to symbolically "nail down" spirits. The three sides of the phurba's blade cut on the physical realm, the spirit realm, and the spaces between. The handle of many phurbas is usually constructed of a *dorje*, another traditional Tibetan item that symbolizes a lightning bolt. The dorje represents energy, and in some more elaborate phurbas, it is capped with a head with multiple faces. These faces snarl in demonic fury, peering out into both the physical and spiritual worlds, frightening evil away.

The phurba can be used to literally strike out at a spirit as if it were a physical entity, for the way the phurba is constructed, it is intended to exist and impact both matter and spirit. As a tool for exorcism, the phurba can be used as a spirit nail, pinning down something you don't want in your space, and holding it helpless until you can bind or otherwise clear it.

In addition to the phurba, another ritual blade, known as the *dargu*, is intended to cut spiritual attachments. This is the sacred blade of the *dakinis*, feminine spirits that are sometimes equated with angels. The dakinis are not passive beings that hang out on clouds; they are fearsome, erotic, blood-drinking women who, in their peaceful aspect, can serve as guides, but who, in their wrathful aspect, will use terror to inspire individuals to follow the proper path. While the dargu is intended to sever the attachments a soul may have for things in this life, I have found that this blade works nicely for severing the links that some entities will form to attach themselves to people in the here and now.

Dreamcatchers

A very popular Native American device, the dreamcatcher, has gained widespread usage in recent years. Originally woven of sinew within a circle of wood or vines, the dreamcatcher is symbolic of a spider web. Typically, there is a small, polished stone suspended from the web at some point within its design. This stone is said to represent Grandmother Spider, a Native American goddess of wisdom who watches over any who use her dreamcatchers.

The purpose of a dreamcatcher is to capture nightmares while allowing good dreams to pass through the spaces between the web. Dreamcatchers are traditionally placed on the walls just over the head of the bed, where they are supposed to encourage restful sleep. In recent times, dreamcatchers have been employed to capture any manner of negative energies, while presumably allowing more positive forces to pass through the web.

Fumigation

Just as the nasty-looking faces of gargoyles and grotesques were thought to drive spirits away, so, too, were nasty-smelling substances thought to repel visitors from the Otherside. This is where we get the belief that garlic can keep vampires away. Garlic has a strong and very pungent odor, and if one is wearing a string of garlic around their neck, it is likely to keep not only vampires, but also friends, family members, and perfect strangers at a safe distance.

Moving beyond garlic, there are a number of incenses that were traditionally burned to dispel spirits and drive them from a place.

Head covered, this expertly carved mourner places a laurel wreath upon the tomb of the deceased. Woodlawn Cemetery, the Bronx.

The ancient practice of fumigation—that is, filling a room up with a thick cloud of pungent smoke—was used to dispel negative energies as well as physical pests and vermin from a home. Fumitory is one incense that was traditionally used for this, as was the herb asafetida. The word *fetid* is part of the root for *asafetida* and this is very apt, for the herb has an exceptionally strong and amazingly unpleasant odor. Although it is employed in some forms of Indian cooking, asafetida, in my book, is best reserved for exorcism, and even then, it should only be employed when a situation calls for the "big guns."

Fire

Nearly every religion and spiritual tradition recognizes the purifying qualities of fire. Returning to medieval days, peasants would erect huge bonfires, called "need-fires" during certain festivals or in times of calamity, especially during outbreaks of plague. The fire was allowed to blaze up, and when it had burned down a little, sheep and cattle were driven through the smoldering coals. This was thought to burn away any harmful magick or negative forces that were causing the plague. Sometimes infants or those afflicted with the disease were also passed through the flames for cleansing and purification.

In a ritual setting, fire can be used to dispel unwanted forces from a person or from a place. If the name or sigil (sign) of a spirit is known (especially if it is something you have called up yourself), this spirit can be dispelled by inscribing the name or sign on a piece of paper and committing it to the flames. You can also create your own sigil, something that is a kind of personal, symbolic shorthand that encodes the energy you associate with the unwanted being. As the name or sigil is burned to ash, the spirit is banished from your space.

DEATH AS A JOURNEY

Once again, we walk through our private cemetery when winter blankets the land. We allow our feet to take us where they will, and soon we find ourselves standing before twin statues. These monuments, identical memorials for two members of the same family, are worn and weathered with the passing of the years. The features of the twin angels have become softened in much the same way that the snow now softens the details of the land. Lichen has taken root in the folds of the robes, and in all this stretching landscape of gray stone and white snow, it is one of the few touches of brilliant green, a subtle reminder of the life still slumbering at the heart of winter's chill.

These twin angels with gossamer wings step forth in tandem to the great beyond. They lift their faces to a glory that only they can see, and if we look closely we can see that their feet are already treading on the clouds of another realm.

They are companions traveling a road that can only be found once life has come to an end. We see them, now, in transit, but only their upturned faces seem to capture a glimpse of their final destination.

If death is a journey, where might it lead? The first step, of course, is to move beyond the world of the living, and yet is that the only step along the road to the realm of the dead? What adventures lie ahead of these two companions who move beyond this world in perfect tandem with one another? And if we followed closely behind them, what mysterious vistas might we see?

Consider death not as the end of life, but as the beginning of a process, a long journey whose ultimate destination may never be clearly known. Allow yourself to reflect upon the meaning of this image, and then record your thoughts in your journal.

PART TWO

The Way of All Flesh

"Thou hast conquered, O Pale Galilean,
and the world has grown grey from thy breath.
We have drunken of things Lethean,
and fed on the fullness of Death."
— *Algernon Charles Swinburne*
"Hymn to Prosperine"

6.

ACCEPTING IMPERMANENCE

You have dedicated yourself to your path. Your altar is set, and the threshold inviting death into your life has been thrown wide, with spirits and other powers bearing witness to the act. Now it is time to further delve into the mysteries of death, exploring it not just as some nebulous energy, but examining the very physical reality of death. In the next few pages, we are going to look at what happens to the body in the wake of death. It is an unsettling but wholly natural process, something that most people seek to deny and hide away. You must learn not to shrink away when confronting this aspect of death, even when you stare deep into its gaping, decayed eyes.

Death, although it may fascinate some, is by no means a pretty process. Dying is not only painful and frightening for most people, it is also a nasty, messy ordeal. These bodies we live our lives in are corruptible, impermanent containers for our vital spirits, and once that spirit has fled, the body rapidly decays. Anyone who has worked in a hospital or a nursing home, or anyone who has been at the bedside of a terminally ill friend or relative knows death for the bald and unattractive reality that it is. Death stinks, oozes, and leaves behind nasty stains, and everyone, regardless of how beautiful or noble they may be, is eventually reduced to that unsightly state.

There are aspects of death that are outright disgusting to anyone with traditional sensibilities. Death has been painted as beautiful, as in Henry Wallis' pre-Raphaelite work "The Death of Chatterton." Thomas Chatterton was a brilliant but tragic young man. Born in 1752 to a large and impoverished family, he was a poet and forger of pseudo-medieval poetry. At the age of seventeen, he committed suicide by taking arsenic, rather than die of starvation. Decades after his death, he became a Romantic icon of unacknowledged genius. In the most famous painting of this tragic young figure, the suicide's face is pale and serene, with an ethereal beauty one might expect to find only on the visage of an angel. Yet the artist does not portray the inevitable effluvia of death: the spreading stain of urine and feces that occurs as all the muscles relax their hold on bladder and bowels. The painting cannot capture the unmistakable stench of death, nor cannot it convey the waxen, not-quite-right feel of flesh that was once alive and now is not. The corpse in the painting is the ultimate *tromp l'oeil*, captured in that one perfect moment where death appears transcendent and serene. But the beauty of the dead man is fleeting: most corpses will visibly begin the process of decay within forty-eight hours of the time of death.

For those who wish to embark on this path, it is important that they see death in all its gruesome reality. In the East, various religious traditions have ascetic monks who have dedicated themselves to death as a symbol of physical impermanence. Members of the Aghori sect, for instance, are known to make their residences in cremation grounds. Some will even smear themselves with human ash. This sect, a very secretive and often maligned branch of Hinduism, seeks to prove the illusory nature of all things by wallowing in death and those things associated with death. Many of the things the Aghori hold sacred are things that a Brahmin of traditional Hinduism would avoid as impure. And yet the point of the Aghori is that "pure" and "impure" are as illusory as anything else: they are artificial concepts constructed by humans, often inspired by human revulsion and fear. To achieve true non-attachment, one has to transcend even these primal, visceral human fears.

We in the West have gotten a sanitized view of death all our lives. Only a hundred years ago, families often laid out their own dead, washing the body and performing a vigil by candlelight the first night beside the corpse. The dead family member was traditionally displayed in the parlor, and the term "funeral parlor" is a lingering trace of this practice. Around 1910, the practice of displaying the dead in one's own home became passé, and fashion magazines around that time portrayed it as both disgusting and old fashioned. Accordingly, they suggested that, in addition to ceasing this morbid practice, people re-name their parlors "living rooms" as an affirmation of life, not death. As anyone with a modern home knows, the name stuck.

Now, in our modern culture, the moment a person dies, officials, who are paid exorbitant amounts to handle such untidy things as corpses, come and take the body away. Far from the sight of family members, the corpse is washed and dressed and embalmed. Morticians skilled in the semblance of life use putty, wax, sawdust, wires, and make-up to make the corpse look "natural"—natural in this case meaning as close to "not-dead" as possible. The embalming staves off putrefaction so the family never has to confront the fact that the face they looked upon so many years with love will ultimately bloat, turn black, and fall away.

For our society, death is not a mystical or religious experience. It is not a revered transition from one state to the next. If anything, death is the province of bureaucrats, and it is certainly not something individuals deal with as a family, up close and personal. The reality of death is hidden away from us and anything that might be unpleasant or unattractive about it is hidden with the mortician's sleight of hand. We see corpses presented through the eyes of Hollywood. We see corpses, distant and unreal, through the lens of the media. Few inhabitants of Western society have ever really looked upon death. However, to understand it and to embrace it, to follow a path that harnesses the transformative energies of death, you have to look at both the beauty and the terror, and you must be able to accept the reality of both.

This chapter is going to explore the face of death that has been hidden from the Western world. In the next few pages, you will learn what happens to the body once life has fled. You will be exposed to the process of putrefaction and decay in blatant, unadorned terms. You will see how different cultures have handled their dead and the attitudes that have grown out of various burial practices. And, if this path is right for you, ultimately you will see the elegant beauty inherent in even the worst of these details.

This chapter is not written for shock value. Nor is it intended to glory in the gruesomeness of death. The point here is to honestly reveal an aspect of death that most people—even those who feel they have already embraced death as a romantic or spiritual ideal—almost never get to see. But all of these processes, however grisly and macabre, are part of a natural cycle, and to deny any aspect of that cycle is to misunderstand the whole thing.

The Danse Macabre

In our sanitized culture, we are largely protected from the gruesome realities of death. However, in the not-so distant past, people had a much clearer idea of what happened to the body once the soul had fled. In Europe's Middle Ages, there existed a number of manuals on death and dying. These were called *Der Totentanz* in German, although they are more widely known by their old French name: *Danse Macabre.* Both of these terms mean "Dance of Death." Filled with manuscript illuminations and woodcuts that are at once gruesome and humorous, these texts typically reflect upon the fact that death comes to all people: merchant, pauper, bishop, and king.

The French *Danse Macabre of Women* is an excellent example of one of these books. Written in the fifteenth century, it shows a variety of women from different stations in life as they are carried off by the Grim Reaper. From serving girls to theologians, from courtesans to nuns to queens, Death marches right into the middle of whatever they are doing and drags them away—whether they are willing to join his dance or not.

The religious message of these tomes is that Death comes for everyone in their time, and that time is something none of us can know. And so, it encouraged Christians of the Middle Ages to always be prepared for the end, maintaining a pious and guilt-free soul, lest Death catch them in the midst of sin and ensure their damnation. A lot of the commentary in the verses reflects upon the nature of piety

"Dance of the Dead," woodcut by Michael Wolgemut, printed in Nuremberg, Germany 1493.

european books
of the dead

The ancient "Egyptian Book of the Dead" and the "Tibetan Book of the Dead" are thanatological texts that are widely known. However, there was a little-known movement of death-related texts in the European world following the period of the Black Plague. These European books of the dead served much the same function as their ancient, more esoteric counterparts. Through both texts and images, they sought to demonstrate the proper approach to living so the living could achieve a good death.

Hans Holbein the Younger (1497–1543) produced a woodcut series of the Dance of Death designed by German wood engraver, Hans Lutzelburger.

Michael Wolgemut produced a widely circulated image of the Dance of Death in 1493 as part of Hartman Schedel's *Liber Chronicarum.*

The *Ars Moriendi* ("The Art of Dying") was the first guide to death and dying in the Western literary tradition, anonymously written by a Dominican friar. A long version was produced in 1415 and a shorter version was produced with block woodcuts in 1450.

Bernt Notke (1435–1508) was a Pomeranian-born artist whose Danse Macabre images decorated the walls of churches. His work in St. Mary's Church in Lubeck was destroyed in an Allied bomb raid.

and what distinguishes a truly good life from a life that was lived as a self-righteous façade.

What interests us for the purposes of this chapter is not the Christian proselytizing on the truly pious life but the manner in which Mr. Death is portrayed. Throughout the *Danse Macabre of Women*, Death waltzes in as an emaciated skeleton, desiccated flesh still clinging to his bones. His eyes and ears are gone, and his jaw is set in a permanent grin, the lips worn away and the gums pulled back so the teeth are exposed. His pate is mostly bald, with a few strings of lank hair clinging to the back of his skull. The nose has collapsed into the nasal cavity, and the abdomen is a gaping tear that runs from pelvis to ribs. Tatters of flesh and deflated strings of intestines hang down to his thighs, and long white worms cling to his body. These burrow diligently into the flesh of his torso, arms, and legs, wriggling among what's left of his hair. Sometimes he's shown with a winding sheet, and sometimes he's shown totally nude. In the pictures that are

The bride and the courtesan each being claimed by Death. From Antoine Verard's 1486 printing of the French "Danse Macabre des Femmes."

reproduced in color, Death is an ugly brown color, and sometimes the winding sheet is darkly stained.

This is a horrific apparition, and yet the illustrators of this book are not trying to depict Death as some fantastical bogeyman. With the prevalence of plague and other epidemics during the day, the writers as well as the readers of these books were intimately familiar with the actual appearance of a dead and decayed corpse. At some points during the plague, whole villages succumbed, and corpses were stacked one on top of the other in the streets. People of the Middle Ages knew well the look, feel, and nauseating stench of death.

The Grim Reaper illuminated in these manuscripts, then, is as accurate a portrayal of an actual corpse as the artist could feasibly render. Although these pictures lack some of the anatomical accuracy of drawings later done by DaVinci who was using dissected specimens as models, there is a painstaking realism here that tells us a great deal of what happens to the body after death.

The Diet of Worms

Our physical bodies are dying the moment we are born, and in the intervening years, these shells that we wear are preparing for the moment of our demise. In fact, our bodies are very carefully designed to decompose and return to the earth as soon as our spirits no longer animate them. Recent advances in the field of forensic science have given us a better understanding of how our bodies decay than we have ever had before. Dr. Bill Bass' pioneering Body Farm, located in Knoxville, Tennessee, has taught us that the body technically begins to decay no fewer than four minutes after the onset of death. This is when the cells are deprived of their usual supply of nourishment, and so the digestive enzymes in the cells begin to devour the cells themselves.

Dr. Bass' studies have started to show us that the human body is elegantly equipped for a rapid self-destruct sequence once death shuts down the normal functions. For example, the self-same bacteria that live symbiotically in our intestines, assisting in digestion while we are alive will, upon the moment of death, immediately begin to feed upon our biological material.

This is hardly an appealing image, but it is amazingly efficient. Through the work of such bacteria, the soft internal organs begin to liquefy. The first visible signs of this internal action is a greenish discoloration over the lowest part of the small intestine, that cup of belly formed by pubis and hips. This spreads throughout the abdomen and the abdomen begins to swell soon after. The abdomen can become hugely distended, but eventually the buildup of gases causes the skin to burst, leaving the entire intestinal cavity exposed. This bursting of the abdomen, which can take the form of a violent explosion, has been known to blow the lids off of caskets, and it is the reason that the medieval Grim Reapers are depicted with bellies torn open from ribs to pelvis.

The eyes, our so-called "windows to the soul" are also not long with us after death. During the putrefaction process, the eyes collapse, weeping their aqueous humors like sticky tears down the cheeks and inside the skull. Not long after death, the blood, no longer moved by the beating of the heart, follows the pull of gravity to the lowest portions of the body. Drawn to the areas that are closest to the ground, the blood thickens and congeals, setting in a permanent and distinctive pattern. Because the blood is no longer oxygenated, these areas are a deep purple, the color of a very severe bruise. This discoloration is known as "lividity" and, in the science of forensics, it allows a researcher to know what position a corpse was lying in soon after death. Along with *rigor mortis*, lividity can help to develop a rough estimate of the time of death.

As putrefaction continues, all of the blood vessels start to discolor. As they darken and turn brown, a tree-like pattern emerges throughout the body, visible just beneath the skin. Like the abdomen, all of the skin may begin to take on a greenish color and blisters will begin to appear. The skin can go through several color changes but usually keeps to the colors we see in healing bruises: green or yellow, and sometimes orange or brown.

As the process continues, the blisters burst, weeping fluid. All over the body, the skin is shed in large, irregular patches. This occurs because the dermis and epidermis separate. As part of this process, the nails are shed and the follicles of the hair loosen, causing most of the hair to fall away. Eventually, most of the internal organs are reduced to a semi-fluid state, and blood-stained fluid oozes from the nose and the mouth. It has been theorized that the presence of this blood-like fluid in the mouth of a corpse gave rise to the belief that certain corpses sucked the blood of the living, perpetuating belief in the folk-loric vampire. Given precisely the right conditions, a process known as saponification can occur, where all of the fat from the body essentially turns to soap. Although grotesque in appearance, these so-called "soap mummies" have features that are remarkably well-preserved.

Maggots usually find access to the body and these voracious little larvae help speed the process of decomposition along. Maggots, are, of course, the larvae of flies, and they arise from eggs that have been laid in the flesh of the dead. While flies are hardly high on the ladder of evolved beings, nevertheless, through their action, new life arises from our death.

Mushrooms and other fungi may move in as well, drawing nour-ishment from the decaying flesh. Fungi are *saprophytes*, a word which

Death claiming the Abbot and the Duchess by Hans Holbein the Younger. From Imagines Mortis, *1547.*

translates to "eaters of the dead." It is their job in the natural scheme of things to feed upon decaying biological matter. Fungi break down once-living matter until it is becomes part of the soil, completing an elegant cycle in which all living things return, through death, to the earth that sustained them in life.

Whether through the work of bacteria, maggots, fungi, or other carrion-eaters, ultimately all the fleshy parts of the body dissolve. The membranes and soft tissues are the first to go, and as they decay, the skin, bloated at first, sinks in and shrivels. How long it takes a body to completely undergo this process varies considerably. Reports about both vampires and saints tell of bodies, many years interred, that were dug up and found to be untouched by decomposition. When this lack of corruption happened to the body of a holy person, the body was usually put on display as evidence of a miracle; when it occurred in a body suspected of being a vampire, the corpse was often beheaded, staked, and burned.

When all is said and done, though, the process may take years or even decades. Most corpses eventually are reduced to nothing but yellowed bones. In some burial practices, these bones, once they have been denuded of their flesh, are dug up and interred in ossuaries. Some very old cemeteries would exhume denuded corpses and separate the bones, storing all of the skulls together in one place, all of the femurs in another, and so forth. One monastery in Germany would remove the bones and paint the name of the deceased upon the skull, adding the date of death along with artistic embellishments like ivy or scroll-work. Many of these skulls can still be seen on display. In the Czech Republic, the bones of 40,000 people have been crafted to create ornate decorations in the Kostinice Ossuary—including a chandelier which contains all the bones of the human body.

JOURNAL EXERCISE: THIS LIFE, NOW

1. If you knew that your death was guaranteed within the week, how would you live your life? What would you do differently? What would remain the same? Would your attitudes toward

family or friends change? How do you think this knowledge would affect you emotionally?

2. If there are things that you would rush right out and do if you didn't have much time left, what is holding you back from doing them now? How can you find the courage in your life to do these things without the threat of impending doom?

3. Think about how your attitude toward life would change if you knew it was going to be taken from you in a few days. Think about how each sensation would become precious. Think about the simple things you would do just to do them. How can you gain this kind of immediacy in your life right now? What do you have to change in yourself to make every moment full of precious life?

4. Now think about what it would be like if you died suddenly, right this instant. There is no warning, no time to prepare.

A statue of a guardian angel gazes heavenward, contemplating the fate of the deceased. Woodlawn Cemetery, the Bronx.

How would you feel about the life you have lived? What things would you regret having done? What things would you regret leaving undone? How do you think this would affect your transition? Are there unresolved issues that could keep you lingering in the spirit world? If so, how should you go about resolving them now?

5. Now think about your family and friends. Life for them is just as uncertain. What can you do to help them understand the precious treasure that is this moment, now? How can you help them appreciate the immediacy of life? How would you prepare them if you learned that they were soon to die?

Death as Tragedy

We seem to move back in time as we approach our cemetery, for now the season that has settled upon everything is not winter, but fall. A cool wind emanates from an overcast sky, and the rolling lawns of the cemetery are carpeted with dead, dry leaves.

As we approach this next monument, we see an angel so overcome with grief that she has collapsed upon the tomb of the deceased. With one hand, she holds a wreath intended as an offering to the dead. She holds the wreath dejectedly, as if the carefully woven branches were heavy with the knowledge that no earthly gifts will bring the beloved back from death's embrace. She rests her face against her other arm, too wracked with sorrow to lift her head.

Although death may bring a blessed transformation for those who pass beyond the veil of life, the reality of a loved one's mortality remains a tragedy for those who are left behind. So many of our funeral practices are not performed for the dead as much as they are performed for the living, to allow a sense of closure so that they can move on. In this respect, the powerful force we seek to harness in this book is not all wonder and roses. Death takes things away from us, and even though the soul may live in on another form, it is unlikely that we will ever see that exact combination of flesh and spirit that was once so familiar to our eyes.

Gaze upon the impact that death can have upon the living left behind. Contemplate the depth of sorrow experienced when someone we loved passes beyond our mortal sense. Never overlook the fact that death is a transformation that comes with a price. The toll of the ferry-man Charon is not paid in coin, but with the tears of all those dear to us whom we have left waiting on the shore.

Write your reflections on this image in your journal, then continue with your work.

7.

FACING YOUR FEARS

The Hindu religion has a sort of trinity of gods: Brahma, Vishnu, and Shiva. Each represents an aspect of the realized universe. In the simplest sense, Brahma is the Creator, Vishnu is the Preserver, and Shiva is the Destroyer. Shiva is the divine equal of the others, but he is sometimes approached very cautiously, for his powers make him a very intimidating god. Together with his consort Kali, Shiva represents destruction, change, and, of course, death. Non-orthodox sects of Hinduism, such as the Aghori, devote themselves to Shiva in his aspect as a god of death. They are known to smear themselves with ash from funeral pyres, and some will live in graveyards, conducting rituals there. Human bones and other remains are a part of their worship, and they see their use of such things as an expression of their devotion to the Hindu concept of *moksha*—liberation from the cycle of death and rebirth. The Aghori, a somewhat controversial sect, are not alone in their use of human remains in ritual. Tibetan monks play trumpets that are fashioned from human femurs, and special drums as well as chalices are made from the craniums of monks who have passed away.

These morbid practices are not intended to create an obsession with death and dying. Rather, their aim is to teach us about the mysteries of impermanence and letting go. The body is just a vessel, and so, as the Tibetans see things, its remains may as well be put to good use. Chalices and musical instruments that our culture would find grisly and obscene serve as inspirational reminders to the Tibetans that this life is not the only one we have.

The following exercises and the questions that come after will help you explore your own attitudes on impermanence. The exercises are visualization-intense and emotionally demanding, so you should probably take them in stages. You may find that you have to repeat these exercises several times in order to really get the full impact. The purpose of the exercises and their accompanying journal questions is to help you uncover any lingering doubts or fears you may have regarding death, particularly your own. These exercises may bring some deep-seated psychological issues to the forefront of your mind, so they are not to be undertaken lightly. Once you have run through them successfully at least once, you will permanently alter your perception of yourself, your physical form, and your relation to time and death.

Part One: The Source of Vanity

When you built your altar, you included a mirror as the central item. Ordinarily you keep a veil over this mirror, but for this exercise, you will remove the veil. You will also disrobe for part of the exercise, so be certain your ritual space is even more private than usual.

Prepare yourself as you have become accustomed, taking a ritual bath and then donning whatever special costume you use to pass into a ritual mindset. Stand before your altar. Light the incense and then the candles. As you light the candles of life and death, call to mind the image of the door you cut into this space, willing it to open now. Silently ask the spirits to gather, so they may lend power and bear witness to your work. Stare into your eyes through the veil of the mirror, reminding yourself that you are both flesh and spirit. When you feel the proper mindset settle over you, you are ready to begin.

Remove the veil from the mirror and set it aside, being careful not to catch the veil in the flames of either candle. Stand for a while and simply regard your face in the mirror. Study your features very carefully, occasionally peering in closely to see the minute details like lines and pores on your cheeks and around your eyes. Once you have familiarized yourself with your countenance, begin to study yourself for signs of age. Look for little lines around your eyes or creases that are beginning to form on your forehead. Run your fingers over your flesh to search for rough spots. Test the elasticity of the skin around your cheeks and jowls.

As you stand before the mirror, searching for the stamp of age upon your flesh, begin to disrobe. Take off all of your clothes until you are standing naked at your altar. If you cannot see much of your body in the altar's mirror, look down and examine yourself. Look specifically for those places where things aren't as firm as they once were, where you can see the skin beginning to go soft and perhaps capillaries and spider veins beginning to show through. Run your fingers over your flesh, feeling the damage time has done, and imagining the damage it has yet to do.

Think back to when your appearance was younger, more vital. Consider how the changes you can see make you feel. Then consider how much you attach your sense of identity to your appearance, even after making the sacrifice you did when you started this journey into the realm of death. How much do you still have to let go?

If you have a scar from an injury somewhere, consider what your body looked like prior to that injury. Take a few moments to recall the injury itself and your reaction to the damage done to your flesh. Remember watching the wound heal, then knowing that a scar would be left behind. Put yourself back in that moment of time when you realized that you would be scarred and reflect upon how this affected your perception of your appearance. Were you angry? Were you ashamed? Did you make an effort to cover the scar up for a time? How long did it take you to accept and adapt to this change in your flesh? If people noticed the scar, how did that make you feel?

What do these reactions to scars and injuries tell you about your attachment to your physical form? Have your attitudes changed since the injury you've considered? If they've changed significantly, what influenced this change?

After you have studied your face and your body with a brutal, naked honesty, retrieve your clothes and put them back on. Kneel down for a moment and prepare yourself for the next stage of this exercise. If you feel the presence of spirits gathered about, ask them to help you to be honest and unafraid as you take the next step.

Part Two: The March of Years

Return to the mirror that is the central piece of your altar. As you regard your form in this mirror, start to envision what the progress of the years may do to your flesh. Try to imagine this as vividly as possible. Study your face and the rest of your body very carefully, and with your imagination, overlay what you look like now with what you might look like in ten years. Try to see this projected future self like a double image layered over what you can see with your physical eyes. If you are exceptionally good at visualization, you may even be able to impose the aged image over what you physically see.

Stare hard into your reflected eyes, conjuring the image as completely as you are able. Take your time with this, and once you have a solid image in your mind or in your vision, study that as carefully as you previously studied your current face. As you regard this older you, pay attention to what emotions this inspires in you. After you have studied this version of yourself for a little while, age yourself further. Go forward twenty years, then thirty. Roll the years forward in your mind and watch your face and body age before you as if your life were on fast forward. Take yourself to the very extremity of old age, when you are little more than a shrunken, shriveled shell of your former, youthful self.

Visualize this future self as vividly as possible. Hold the image in your mind so you can study it. Even if there is something that makes you uncomfortable, dare yourself to look at it without flinching. Don't push too hard—if you end up really having trouble with this exercise, you should bring your vision back to the present and step away. Remove yourself from ritual space and save the exercise for a later date. If you really encounter trouble with this exercise, you should also consider halting your progress in this book until such time as you can look at the ancient, withered face without being revolted or shrinking away.

Hold the face you see now in the mirror. Feel the weight of the years pressing down upon you. Call up not just visual effects, but

This image, from T. Carey's 1639 work, "The Mirrour Which Flatters Not," represents the transitory nature of worldy power.

97

aches and pains as your body ages all around you. As you progress further into the exercise, consider carefully how all of this makes you feel, not just physically, but emotionally. Does it disturb you to consider the inevitable impact of aging upon your face and the rest of your body? Do you find yourself shrinking away from more extreme realities, unwilling to place the stamp of illness or debility upon your familiar form? Consider the source of this unwillingness. Plumb the depths of your fear. If there is an image or an idea that you find especially disturbing—such as the way half of a person's face will sag, lifeless, after a severe stroke—make a point of projecting this upon your own face. Make a point of identifying and confronting your fears. Take as long with this exercise as you feel you need. Really explore what disturbs you and work toward overcoming those fears.

When you feel that you are finished and have gotten as much out of this visualization as you can, lock eyes with yourself in the mirror and slowly reverse the aging process. Feel the weight of the years sloughing from your body and bring yourself back to how you now appear. You are finished for now with this exercise. You should put the veil back on the mirror and close the ritual space, snuffing the candles to signify that you are done.

Step away from the altar and take some time to reacquaint yourself with the here and now. You may want to eat a light meal or have a sweet snack to remind yourself of the immediacy of the present moment. This also serves to make you more grounded and present in your physical flesh. When you are ready to think about your experiences in front of the mirror, sit down with your journal and write out your success with this exercise and how it affected you. The questions that follow can help you reflect upon your work.

JOURNAL EXERCISE: THE WEIGHT OF THE YEARS

1. When you took a good, hard look at time's effects on your appearance now, what bothered you the most? How attached are you to an idealized image of your body? How do you think

this affects your behavior and attitudes toward clothing, exercise, food, and interactions with others?

2. Think about how you react to your body on a daily basis. Are you ashamed or troubled by any aspect of your appearance? Is the problem area something you have control over? Are you being fair to yourself in your desire that this part of your appearance be changed? How much of your reaction truly comes from you and how much comes from the perceptions of others?

3. Consider the attitudes toward body, appearance, and age that exist in your culture. How healthy do you think these attitudes are? Do you feel that these attitudes create any kind of pressure that helps to build a negative image toward yourself? If you find these cultural attitudes unhealthy, what can you do to let them go?

4. When you imagined your face and body growing old, what part of the visualization disturbed you the most? Could you identify any specific, significant fears? How realistic are these fears? What can you do to overcome them?

5. When you look at yourself in a mirror, what part of your image do you identify as "I"? Consider every aspect of your face and body. What part of this is you—your thinking, experiencing point of perception? Does this "I" have a specific location in the physical body? What does this tell you about what you really are?

Part Three: The Face of Death

You have made a brutally honest examination of time's effects upon your face and body right now, and you have projected yourself decades into the future, when time's stamp will have rendered your body frail and your features nearly unrecognizable. You have reflected upon the emotional impact of these sights and experiences, recording your thoughts about what this says about you and your attitudes toward impermanence in your journal. Now, after you have taken at least a short break from the first two exercises, it is time to cross that final threshold. In the next exercise, you will go beyond the visualization of old age to confront the truth of what death itself will do to your flesh.

Once again, if you really had trouble with fear, revulsion, or anxiety in the previous exercises, I strongly recommend that you not undertake this final portion until you can perform the first two parts without adverse psychological effects. Furthermore, it is not wise to proceed with the rest of this book until you have resolved any internal emotional issues these exercises have raised. Personal and emotional growth are also goals of walking the Twilight Path.

Seeing Beyond the Grave

Cleanse yourself, dress for ritual, and approach the altar once again. Light the incense, then the candles, and meet your eyes beyond the veil. When you have summoned the proper mindset, once more remove the veil from the mirror. This will be the hardest of all the exercises, and you may want to call upon the spirits to watch over you and help you through the sights that are to come.

In the previous chapter, we looked at death in all its gruesome glory, and now you are going to put what you've learned to practical use. Take a moment to prepare yourself, and then begin by regarding in minute detail the features of your face. Familiarize yourself once more with the things you like, the things you don't like, and all those qualities you associate with *you*. Just as you did in the previous exercises, do this by looking deeply into the mirror that hangs upon your altar, between the candles of life and death.

Now, as you watch, see your features fall rapidly through the stages of decay. It starts simply, with all the color draining away. Your eyes lose their luster, then quickly become cloudy with death. Your jaw goes slack, and you can see the gums pull back from the roots of your teeth. Your lips shrivel similarly, and now the color of your face changes, going from a shade that is almost ashen to progressively darker and blotchier colors. You can see the capillaries burst and the veins grow purple, then almost black. Your eyes, milky white with the pall of death, begin to shrivel in your skull, until you can see thick fluid weeping from your sockets. The fleshy parts of your nose tighten around cartilage and bone, shrinking back until your nostrils are huge, raw wounds in your face. You stare with empty sockets as the decay progresses even further, your skin cracking as it is pulled tight across your features. Your lips are pulled back further, until your yellowing teeth are exposed in the mockery of a grin.

Visualize this progression vividly, and make certain that you continue to identify the face in the mirror with you. If you start to lose your conceptual connection with the face you are seeing, take a moment to remind yourself that what you are looking at is you. This sense of connection is imperative to the success of this exercise; you cannot cushion your psyche with the convenient escape of detach-ment. The point of this exercise is for you to face the certainty of your own mortality, and then to transcend your attachment to your physi-cal form so you are better able to perceive the dance of life *and* death.

As you see your face transform into that of a corpse, extend the visualization further, so you can actually *feel* the process of death and decay. Feel the chill settle in as your life drains away. Your limbs grow heavy and inert. In the next stage, your skin discolors further and begins to bloat as bacteria and other living organisms feed upon your dead tissue. Feel your body as everything beneath the skin grows soft and begins to liquefy. Stare deep into the wet, empty sockets that were your eyes and see maggots squirming in the hollows. You can feel maggots crawling everywhere, in your brain and in your belly. As the process of decay continues, gases build up and your stomach becomes distended until the skin finally bursts. There is a rush of fluid and liquefying organs as the contents of your entire abdomen spill out onto the floor.

Even with no eyes, you still see the progression of decay: the skin discolors further, going through the many sickly colors of an old bruise. In some places, the bloating of the skin is so severe that it cracks and weeps pinkish fluid. Hair falls out in swaths; great patches of skin flake away. Eventually, enough fluids drain away that instead of swelling, the skin begins to shrink, growing leathery and dark as it closes around the thin bones. Everything tightens, dries out, and grows stiff. Ultimately, you peer at a face that is little more than a mask of leathery flesh stretched tightly across a grinning skull. As you look at the shape of the skull beneath the flesh, know that this is you—or at least, the body you wear right now. Understand that all flesh undergoes this process, and reflect upon what quality beyond your fleshly form really makes you *you*. Focus on these other qualities that are not rooted in your flesh. Consider how these are left unchanged regardless of what happens to your physical form. Then, as you regard the grisly corpse-face in the mirror before you, acknowledge that this is just your flesh, and let it go.

Slough off the image of physical death like a mask you were wearing for Halloween. Feel the burden of decay slip away, leaving you light and free of any rotted flesh. In the mirror, you once again see your face as it is, healthy and uncorrupted.

Take a few minutes to regard this face. Consider those non-corporeal qualities that you had called to mind just moments before, and acknowledge that even though this current face is more recognizable and familiar than the previous mask of death, it is still just flesh. The essence of you goes deeper than the skin, deeper even than the bones that shape your frame. As you stare at the image of your current face, make a conscious effort to let go of this attachment as well. The flesh is a costume you wear for a time. It is something you take up and put down once it's worn out and in need of repair. It is a vehicle, a vessel, a seeming. It is not *you*.

When you feel solidly connected to the immortal part of yourself, put the veil back upon the mirror and step away. Thank the spirits and any other forces you invited to attend you, then ask them to depart as you snuff the candles. As with the earlier half of this exercise, you may wish to eat a light meal or have a snack in order to bring yourself more completely back to the here and now. Make a break from the mental space of the ritual, and when you feel you are ready, sit down with your journal as you did before. Record your experience with this exercise, noting any portion that gave you particular trouble. Reflect upon the lesson of impermanence and explain how

successful you feel you ultimately were at letting go of your attachment to your physical body. There are questions after this section that
can help you carefully analyze your experience with this visualization,
so you can develop an accurate measure of your success.

If you don't feel that you've grasped the essence of impermanence
after this portion of the exercise, make time to perform the whole series
of visualizations again. Do this until you are able to look at the reality
of your own death and remain confident that the end of your flesh is
not in any way the end of *you*. Once you have firmly grasped this concept, you are ready to move forward in your pursuit of this path.

JOURNAL EXERCISE: YOU ARE NOT THAT

1. Think back through the entire visualization. Were there
   parts that were especially hard for you? Did you experience
   any severe emotional reactions? Take a moment to describe
   these reactions here. Why do you think the visualization had
   this impact upon you? Are you happy with your reactions?

2. How successful were you in imagining the reality of your
   future decay? Were you able to clearly identify yourself with
   the rotting image you attempted to visualize? If you had difficulty maintaining a sense of connection with the image of
   decay, what do you think was the root of the problem?

3. If you are still having trouble thinking of your body as an
   impermanent thing, how do you think you can fix this? What
   type of an experience do you think it might take for you to
   achieve a true sense of non-attachment?

4. In theory, we all accept that we are mortal and destined to
   die, however few of us behave as if this is truly an eventuality. How distanced do you feel from the acceptance of this
   inevitability? Why do you think we often persist with the
   delusion that our body right now is immortal?

5. How completely do you think you succumb to the illusion that
   your current body is immortal? Seriously assess your lifestyle

and behavior. How many aspects of your life and attitudes demonstrate a sense of invulnerability? Do you feel these attitudes are good or bad in the long run?

6. Think back to the parts of the visualization where you tried to determine where you place your sense of "I" in your body. What were your answers for this part of the visualization? Explain your reasoning.

7. Think back through your experience of the entire visualization. Do you feel that you were successful overall in achieving a sense of non-attachment? Why or why not? What would you need to change for this to work better?

Back to Life

You have contemplated the impermanence of your earthly flesh, and you have made an effort to seek a certain amount of detachment from your physical body. However, the flesh isn't all bad, and even though it will certainly age and decay, there is no harm in enjoying what you have for now. After you have done all the exercises in this chapter, take some time to appreciate your flesh as you have it right now. Stand in front of a mirror and admire yourself. We can all be critical of our appearance, but make a point of focusing on your best qualities. Remind yourself about the parts of your body you feel are attractive. You may want to take a day at a spa and pamper yourself, or you may simply want to go out and buy some new, flattering clothes. Dress yourself up so you look your best and take a moment to admire yourself. It's true that this fleshly beauty will not last, but that should be all the more reason to enjoy your body while you still have it.

8.

THE WEIGHT OF ETERNITY

Humanity's instinctive fear of death has long inspired us to remove the bodies of our dead and hide them away, typically through burial. Removing the dead from regular living spaces is a matter of health and hygiene, but we demonstrate our fear and obsession with death by going well beyond simple corpse disposal to developing complicated rituals of burial and preservation.

Many cultures the world over have employed various techniques to prevent or at least retard the inevitable decay of a corpse. Perhaps the most famous of these funerary traditions can be found in ancient Egypt. The ancient Egyptians believed that a person's survival in the Afterlife was linked to the survival of his body in the physical world. Because the preservation of the body was so crucial to their belief system, the ancient Egyptians developed a complicated process known as mummification. Although the ancient Egyptians were not the first or the only people to mummify their dead, they were among the most prominent of ancient peoples to develop such an extensive and complicated process for it.

Originally reserved only for the royalty, mummification was an exceptionally costly and time-consuming process. However, the mummies that resulted are so well preserved that many remain in exceptional condition even today, millennia after their creation.

In the period of the Old Kingdom (2686–2134 BCE), only pharaohs were accorded the rite of mummification. Their mummies were interred in elaborate tombs known as *mastabas* (despite common misconceptions, no mummies were ever found buried inside the three Great Pyramids at Giza). The Pharaohs were buried with every conceivable item that they might need in the Afterlife: chariots, beds, jewelry, weapons—even games to pass the time. They were also given servants to help them in the otherworld. These took the form of *ushabti*, little statues, each with its own name. Each of these statues represented a spiritual being that the dead Pharaoh could call upon to help him with any chores he might be asked to do once he crossed over into the realm of the gods.

It was believed that the passage from this world to the next was a difficult one, often fraught with danger, and so the walls of the Pharaoh's tomb were elaborately painted and carved with prayers, scenes and passages from myth, and even maps to help him find his way. These funerary writings, which offered spells for warding off harm in the Afterlife as well as advice on what paths to seek in the otherworld, are collectively known as the "Pyramid Texts," and they were the first written version of what is now called the "Egyptian Book of the Dead."

By about the Middle Kingdom (2040–1640 BCE), mummification became more widespread. In addition to Pharaoh and members of his immediate family, various government officials and even certain wealthy citizens could afford to be mummified. This took the cult of the dead to a whole new level, and the Pyramid Texts, once scribed only on the walls of the Pharaoh's tomb, began to be written directly inside the coffin for the dead man to see them. This was a little more manageable than paying dozens of scribes and artisans to incise the prayers, letter by letter, into the stone walls of a tomb. Eventually, the spells came to be written on amulets and bits of papyrus that were wrapped right in with the bandages of the mummy. These make up the final portion of what has come down to us as the Egyptian Book of the Dead.

The Flesh and the Spirit

An entire priesthood was dedicated to the process of mummification, and a veritable zoo of animal-headed gods oversaw various steps and tools used in the process. The most memorable of these is the jackal-headed god Anubis, a guide and guardian of the dead. Anubis was the mortician of the gods, and he is frequently depicted bending over a mummy and applying its wrappings. Since jackals are scavengers who eat the dead, their association with corpses makes them perfect animals for Anubis.

In addition to Anubis, countless other gods and goddesses were associated at some level with the cult of the dead. Wepwaret, another

Funerary image depicting Isis and the frog-headed goddess Heket ministering to the body of the deceased.

complex species of soul

Akh: This was the transcendent, immortal soul, represented by a type of bird similar to the Benu bird, or phoenix. The Akhu were the blessed dead who had ascended after death.

Ba: Depicted as a bird with a human head or, less frequently, as a bird with a ram's head, this was the migratory aspect of the soul that flew forth at death.

Ka: Represented with a pair of upraised arms, the Ka was thought to linger in the tomb after death. It was the spirit-double of the deceased, and it received the funerary offerings of the priests.

Kha: This was the physical corpse itself. The hieroglyph for this word included the symbol for a particularly stinky type of fish because the physical body was prone to decay.

Ren: This was a person's name, and it represented both their personality and their essence of self. Names had power, and if the ancient Egyptians wanted to destroy someone after death, they would strike out all instances of that person's name in written texts.

jackal god, was the guardian to the gates of the Underworld. The goddess Neith was said to be the weaver of the mummy's linen wrappings. The scorpion goddess Serket watched over certain parts of the dead man's body. The sister-wife of Seth, Nephthys, was a goddess of the Underworld, and the dying-and-rising god Osiris was lord of the realm of the Afterlife.

In a country as hot as Egypt, preserving a corpse for even a few weeks is a daunting task, let alone for a couple thousand years. But the preservation of the body was crucial to the Egyptian view of the Afterlife. Not only was the mummy considered the vessel of the *Ka*, or body-soul, which remained in the tomb and fed upon the energy of offerings from priests and family members, but the condition of the physical body reflected upon the immortal spirit-body that the deceased achieved in the afterlife. Unless the physical body was safe and whole, a spirit could not be healthy and whole in the otherworld. Even the *Ba*, that portion of the soul that the Egyptians believed flew forth from the corpse in the shape of a bird, was thought to return to the physical body once in a while.

Since corpse preservation was so integral to their religious beliefs, the process the ancient Egyptians hit upon was naturally considered sacred, and each step was a ritual in its own right carried out by special mortician-priests. The steps of mummification, as well as the prayers and rituals that accompanied it, were elaborate and very strict, and they could not be deviated from if the venture was to be a success.

It took seventy days to completely mummify a body. This included packing the corpse with natron and allowing this salt-like substance to naturally dehydrate the body over a period of forty days. After the body had dried out, the natron was removed, and the limbs were packed with clay or sand. The body itself was stuffed with resin-soaked linen and a number of expensive aromatic agents, including cinnamon and myrrh. The body was further treated with perfumes and ointments. Beeswax was liberally used. The Coptic word for wax was *mum* and this may have inspired the term *mummy*.

After all of these preparations, the treated corpse was wrapped in finely woven linen strips. Each finger and toe was wrapped individually, then each limb, then the whole body was bound tightly together. In all, no fewer than 1,000 square yards of linen strips were used to wrap a mummy. There was magickal significance to the direction in which the wrappings were wound, so the mortician-priests had to be very careful as they bound the mummy for its trip into the Afterlife.

Because the soft tissues decay rapidly and these will quickly spoil a corpse, the internal organs had to be removed. The lungs, liver, and other viscera were all preserved separately from the body. Each organ had its own guardian deity and there were prayers and rites to attend the preservation of each. For the main organs, there were four Canopic jars, each topped with the head of a different guardian deity. These jars were usually stored in a small shrine close to the body, and four goddesses stood around this shrine, further ensuring the protection of the vital organs.

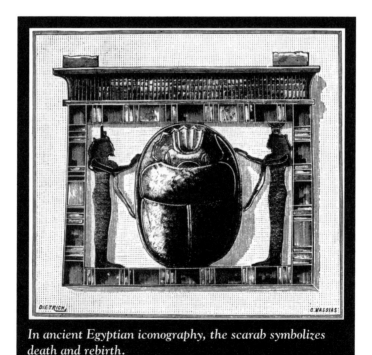

In ancient Egyptian iconography, the scarab symbolizes death and rebirth.

The heart of the mummy was very important, for it was the heart that measured a man's worthiness in the Afterlife. Once a person had made the transition to the otherworld, he would come to a hall of judges. A set of scales stood in this hall, and usually Anubis stood by this, along with Thoth, the scribe of the gods. Here, the deceased performed a litany of negation, reciting a list of sins and asserting that he had not committed such wrongs. Once this was done, Anubis and Thoth would weigh the person's heart against an ostrich feather, which symbolized truth. If the heart was heavier than the ostrich feather, the dead man was deemed unworthy, and his soul was fed to Ammit the Devourer.

To help ensure that the dead man would pass this test, his own heart was often removed and preserved separately, and an amulet, known as a heart scarab, was put in its place. The heart scarab was inscribed with prayers that declared the man's innocence and worthiness of a special place in the Afterlife. When he got to the hall of judgment and the gods asked him for his heart, he would simply hand them this amulet in its place. Even if he had not lived a perfect life, with the help of the heart scarab, he would be judged worthy.

While the ancient Egyptians placed high value upon the heart, the brain of the mummy was viewed as disposable. Usually as the first step in the process of mummification, the brain was removed in pieces with the help of a long-handled, spoon-shaped instrument that was inserted through the nostrils and forced up past the nasal cavities. The skull had to remain intact, as did the face, because the face was very important to the dead man. The face was his identity, and in addition to preserving it as well as possible on his physical body, an ornate representation of the face was usually crafted from precious metals in the form of a funerary mask. Perhaps the most famous Egyptian funerary mask is the mask found with the boy-king Tutankhamen, a beautiful work crafted from precious gold.

Amulets and fetishes of all kinds were placed on and within the body, and certain ones had to be inserted in the mummy's wrappings at various points in the proceedings. Prayers were said over the corpse during the entire process, and these prayers and ceremonies continued right up until the mummy's interment in its tomb, culminating in the Opening of the Mouth ceremony, which symbolically enabled the mummy to eat and breathe in the Afterlife.

The House of Eternity

After the Opening of the Mouth ceremony, the mummy was placed in the tomb with all the possessions the person had prized in life. In ancient Egypt, tombs were known as the "Houses of Eternity," and it was believed that the dead person carried on a kind of shadow-life once sealed in the tomb.

The aforementioned Ka, or body-soul, was believed to live on in its House of Eternity, and regular offerings had to be made in order to keep the Ka fed. If it was not properly sustained with offerings, there was a chance that the Ka might leave the tomb and, vampire-like, seek sustenance among the living. The feasts offered up to the Ka were sumptuous and costly. The "Liturgy of Funerary Offerings" gives extensive lists of proper offerings, including bread and beer, meat and other delicacies.

While numerous priests were employed specifically to make offerings to the dead, the family of the deceased was also expected to make regular offerings. However, the places of burial were located far away from human habitation, usually in the desert hills of the west. Making the trip down to the tomb could be time-consuming, not to mention dangerous. Despite its high order of civilization, ancient Egypt was surrounded by wild country. Travel along the Nile held risks of attacks from crocodiles and hippopotami, while the desert lands on the outskirts of human civilizations were the hunting grounds of fierce lions, leopards, and other wild beasts.

In order that the family of the deceased did not have to make the perilous journey out to the tomb more than once or twice a year, a compromise was achieved. The deceased was represented in the family home with a memorial stela and offerings were made directly to it. The memorial stela was a rectangular slab of stone, rounded on top just like our traditional tombstone. Carved with images of the gods, the stela showed the dead man being accepted among the company of the gods. Beneath the picture, the stela was incised with offertory prayers for the deceased. Over all of this was a winged solar disc, the symbol of the Egyptian sun god, Ra.

For the Egyptians, the sun in its many guises represented the concept of death and rebirth. By placing the sun disc on their memorials for the dead, the Egyptians were expressing their hope that the soul of their departed loved one would, like the sun, be eternally renewed. This was the goal of the entire funerary process: rebirth and renewal as an ever-living being.

Meditation: Tomb of the Pharaoh

To prepare for this exercise, look through books, magazines, or online for a suitable image of ancient Egyptian iconography. You may also consider purchasing a small statue or figurine, perhaps an image of Anubis or a scarab. Prepare as you ordinarily do for work at your altar. Approach your threshold space with this Egyptian item in hand. Burn sweet incense and light the candles of death and life. Look deeply into your eyes through the veil over the mirror and summon the mindset you have come to associate with this kind of spiritual work. When you feel you are connected and in the right space, place the item or image in the middle of your altar. Move the other items around if necessary to make a small amount of room. Sit or kneel in front of your altar and contemplate the image of ancient Egyptian art you have chosen. If you do not have a physical image, close your eyes and call one to mind.

Take a few deep breaths to help yourself relax, then think of what you have learned about the ancient Egyptians and their beliefs about the Afterlife. Consider the time and expense that went into preparing the honored Egyptian dead for their journey into the Afterlife. Call to mind all the many images of Egyptian tombs and sarcophagi that you have seen through books, television, or the Internet. Consider that all the rich gravegoods that have survived the journey of the years in Egyptian graves are only a small portion of offerings originally made.

Once you have impressed upon yourself the intricacy and grandeur of ancient Egyptian funerary practices, imagine that you yourself once lived in that time. You have died, and the time has come to prepare your body for its journey through eternity. Because the funeral rites are not complete, the many aspects of your spirit linger close to your mortal flesh, and you can observe each stage of the mortuary proceedings. Your body is carefully washed and cleansed, then set in natron and other spices to dry. You grow lighter and lighter as the natron does its work, leeching the fluid from your tissues to prevent decay. After days upon days, the priests carefully lift you up, rubbing further unguents and ointments into your body. Then come the carefully woven bandages, yards upon yards of fresh linen strips that are wrapped around your arms and legs and each individual digit. As the priests wrap your body, other priests recite prayers from the various funerary texts. Still others prepare amulets and talismans carved of precious stones. Each of these has a specific place upon your body, wrapped safe within the bandages that cover you from head to toe.

When all of the bandages are firmly in place, you are fitted with an ornate funeral mask. In gold and shining gems, this amazing piece of art seeks to reproduce an ideal version of your face in life. Your kohl-lined eyes are open wide, eager to face eternity.

Eventually, your family and the priests transport your body to the tomb that has been waiting for many, many years. All of your most prized possessions, together with images of the gods and little ushabti statues—servants who will work for you in the Afterlife—are arranged within the secure stone walls. The walls themselves are works of art, passages of the various holy texts having been painted upon them by the best scribes and artisans that your family's money could procure. Even the ceiling of the tomb is painted, and it depicts the vault of Heaven, an image that you will be able to enjoy once the sarcophagus is closed, for it is also painted on the interior of your coffin.

Before you are placed in the tomb, the Setem priest performs the Opening of the Mouth Ceremony, a ritual that symbolically breathes life back into your corpse and gives you the power to feed on the offerings left at the tomb. Finally, you are placed in your house of the dead, with golden statues of goddesses standing guard at all four corners. The scent of rich cooking lingers even in your desiccated nostrils as the meat of bulls, goats, and ducks is offered up to you, together with offerings of bread, wine, and beer. With such a feast, you are sent off to spend eternity in the tomb, while portions of your spirit fly forth to join the gods in the fields of the blessed or to roost among the stars.

As you complete the visualization, consider how it must feel to wait in the tomb for eternity. Do you take comfort in all the riches that surround you? Can you feel the nourishing energy of the offerings made periodically by your family's priests? What happens when the priests no longer come? Sleeping in your sarcophagus, perfectly preserved for the journey through time, you have outlasted your children and your children's children. Even the oldest of your descendants has long turned to dust, and yet you remain . . .

Open your eyes and allow yourself to return to this life and this body. Stand and feel the floor beneath your feet. Take a moment to reflect upon your experiences at your altar, thanking any powers that you called upon to attend your sacred space and asking them to depart. When you are ready, blow out the candles, and close the sacred space. Do what you need to in order to ground back to ordinary reality, then write about your experience in your personal Book of the Dead.

JOURNAL EXERCISE: THE EVERLIVING DEAD

1. When you performed the visualization, how did it make you feel to be treated with such grandeur? What sort of sentiments do you think inspired the ancient Egyptians to go to such lengths to preserve their dead?

2. When you were left to linger forever in the tomb, what emotions did this inspire? Were you happy to be surrounded by such luxury, or were you saddened by the fact that your family members were no longer near? If a portion of the spirit truly remained, tied to the preserved body, how happy do you think it would be, living in its House of Eternity? Explain.

continued on page 118

DEATH AS A THRESHOLD

As we continue to explore our expansive city of the dead, we come across this evocative monument. Somewhat secluded, it stands at the door of a remote mausoleum. Stepping into the shadowed entrance, we see an elegant figure poised upon a threshold, her whole body pressed against the door. She has turned her back on the world of the living, and she waits for the portal to open so she may cross into the realm of the dead.

She is naked, except for a simple drapery, and this can be seen as an expression of both innocence and vulnerability. Her body is a perfectly sculpted, idealized form, already unburdened by the imperfections of earthly existence. She steadies herself upon the casing of the door, and although she hangs her head in sorrow, it also seems as if she is working up the courage to take that final step. In many ways, her unearthly beauty invites us to take that step along with her, and to explore the mysteries that wait on the Otherside.

As you gaze upon this image, consider your own attitudes toward life and death. If you found yourself suddenly standing before that door, would you be ready to cross to the Otherside? What parts of your life would you mourn the most if you had to suddenly leave them behind? What emotions might you experience in those moments right before you crossed over to an entirely different realm of existence?

As a final part of this meditation, imagine yourself opening the door and looking beyond. Allow yourself to experience this vision to its completion, then record the results of this meditation in your journal.

continued from page 115

3. If you were to plan your funeral now, how elaborate an affair would you want it to be? How would you feel if your family went ahead anyway with a funeral of great expense? Do you think costly funeral arrangements are fair to the living?

4. What purpose do you think these complicated funeral preparations really serve, beyond the practical aspect of preventing decay before burial? Who do you think benefits the most from an elaborate funeral: the dead person or the family? Explain your answer.

5. Imagine that you know you are going to die soon, and you have the opportunity to plan every aspect of your funeral. Describe what you would want done. Explain your reasoning for these choices.

6. Imagine that someone you love is going to die soon, and you are the person they have chosen to plan the funeral and all the arrangements. Describe what you would want done. Explain your reasoning for these choices. If your funeral plans for a loved one are different from your funeral plans for yourself, explain why. What does this say about the real purpose of funerals?

9.

DISPOSING
OF BODIES

In our modern, Western world, corpse
preservation is not nearly as ritualized as
it was in ancient Egypt, although it is almost
as involved in some respects. Certainly, we
in the Western world go to great lengths
to preserve the bodies of our dead, even
though most of us do not share the ancient
Egyptians' belief that the soul of the dead
person somehow requires that physical body
once they are in the next world. Nevertheless, our corpses are treated to a number of
intricate procedures intended to give them
a façade of life. In several cases this is a
façade indeed, for it all revolves around the
display of the body in the coffin. Like the
ancient Egyptians, we typically remove the
soft tissue of the brain which is so vulnerable to rapid decay, but unlike them, we do
this through a sizeable hole in the back of

the head. The vast majority of mourners remain ignorant of this gaping wound in their beloved's cranium, as the corpse lies on its back when in the coffin.

In modern embalming practices, the soft internal organs are also removed. Again, this is mainly because they are so prone to rapid decay. Our internal organs are donated or discarded, and the empty body cavity is stuffed with sawdust or some other filler to replace the lost mass. Instead of soaking a corpse in natron or wrapping it in resin-soaked bandages, we Westerners use an intriguing contraption to flush out any blood remaining in the circulatory system, replacing it with embalming fluid. This soup of largely toxic chemicals can maintain the integrity of a corpse for many years even after it has been interred, although the main goal is to have the deceased appear peaceful and lifelike for the duration of the wake and funeral.

The jaw, which grows lax in death and often falls open (hence the signature kerchief sported by Marley's ghost in Dickens' *Christmas Carol*), is wired shut. The eyes were covered with coins in ancient times. Later, we adopted the practice of sewing them shut with tiny, near-invisible sutures. These days, however, it is the miracle of powerful adhesives that keeps the eyes of our departed loved ones from staring blankly at us from within the coffin. The same glue is applied to the lips to keep the mouth firmly shut.

A liberal amount of make-up is applied to the corpse to remove its deathly pallor, and wax or putty may be applied to reconstruct portions of the face in cases where death was brought about by some terrible physical trauma. All of this, of course, comes after the dead person has been washed, shaved, given a manicure and a haircut and dressed in their Sunday finest. However, it's a good thing the suit is going into the ground, because, true to the façade that is Western mortuary practice, the clothing is usually slit up the back and artfully lain over the corpse.

After it's been put on display for friends and family members to mourn over, we Westerners almost universally bury dead bodies. This type of burial practice is known as inhumation. It is something that has been practiced since the Stone Age, where some of our earliest ancestors buried their dead in the fetal position and spread red ochre on top of them. Burying the dead is typically seen as returning the deceased to the womb of the earth, and the ancient Stone Age practices clearly illustrate this. The fetal position obviously recalls the infant in the womb, and some archaeologists believe that the red ochre was intended to symbolize birthing-blood.

There is a certain beautiful simplicity inherent in allowing a body to go back to the earth that sustained it during life, even though with all our embalming and other treatments, we Westerners do not let our corpses go gently into the arms of Mother Earth.

Here Lies the Body

Pretty much every culture that has practiced inhumation has set up some kind of marker to memorialize the place of burial. The simplest of this kind of gravemarker is nothing more than a pile of stones heaped up in a vague conical shape on top of the grave. This is known as a cairn and, in part, it was implemented to prevent scavengers from digging up the corpse and tearing it apart. (Dogs were so well known for eating dead bodies that this is believed to be the reason they often were depicted as guardians to the threshold of the realm of death. To return to the shamanic way of thinking, a being that devours the dead actually facilitates their transition to the Otherside.)

Later Christian burials were usually surmounted by a cross, sometimes inscribed with the person's name. As the years wore on, gravemarkers grew more elaborate and more permanent. Large and ornate markers became signs of power and wealth, and it was not long before the skilled works of sculptors and other artisans were employed in the construction of memorials.

Mausoleums, essentially houses for the dead, were often constructed for noble or wealthy families to inter the honored dead of their entire family line. Mausoleums also, it should be noted, are a very useful way of "burying" the dead when physically putting them into the ground isn't an option. This is especially true in places where the soil is just too swampy or prone to flooding. The famous cemeteries of New Orleans, for example, are made more striking by their profusion of artfully crafted mausoleums. These exist because the region is so prone to flooding that it was not uncommon for entire graveyards full of coffins to be brought to the surface and scattered about during times of heavy rains.

The Victorian era was perhaps the height of Western funerary art, and from this time period we have such glorious necropolises as London's Highgate Cemetery and Cleveland's own spectacular Lakeview. Gravemarkers from this era can take the form of weeping angels, covered funerary urns, grand Egyptian obelisks, or even classical columns that look like they've come from some Greek ruin.

These days, cemetery stones can take any number of shapes, though these are often stark and simplistic compared to those found on Victorian graves. A number of modern stones are built flush to the ground. These are simple and unadorned and also very unremarkable. However, cemeteries with these stones just don't look like cemeteries. The typical gravestone that is envisioned in the popular imagination is the archetypal tombstone.

Mausoleum row at Woodlawn Cemetery, located in the Bronx, New York.

Everyone here in the West knows what a tombstone looks like; many of us spent at least a part of our childhood cutting them out of gray construction paper for Halloween when we were in school. A very simple marker, the tombstone is a rectangular slab of marble or granite, inscribed on one side with a memorial, and rounded at the top. The oldest examples of these tombstones in America typically have a winged death's head inscribed in the curve at the top. These traditional stones can be found in a number of old Puritan cemeteries in the New England states, but the archetypal form of the tombstone is far older than even the Puritans probably knew. Our traditional tombstones were directly inspired by the funerary stela of the ancient Egyptians, with the often winged death's head ultimately replacing the winged disc of Ra.

The Purifying Flame

In addition to inhumation, there are a number of other methods for disposing of the dead, many of which may seem bizarre and macabre to those who've grown up in the West. Nearly all the methods of disposing of a body rely upon some natural element to facilitate the body's dissolution from flesh. Burial, of course, commits the body to the arms of the earth, allowing the process of decomposition to take place out of sight and out of mind. Cremation is a more immediate method that harnesses fire for the disposal of the body.

Second to inhumation, cremation is probably the most popular method of disposing of the dead. Cremation has an ambivalent reception in the West, however, in part because of our attachment to the

The Art of
The Epitaph

On the tomb of Irish poet and occultist W. B. Yeats:

> Cast a cold eye on life, on death
> Horsemen, pass by!

On the grave of Carl Jung, psychologist:

> Vocatus atque non vocatus deus aderit
> (Bidden or unbidden, God is present)

On the grave of author Virginia Woolf:

> Against you I will fling myself,
> Unvanquished and unyielding, o death!

On the grave of English poet John Keats:

> Here lies one whose name was writ in water.

On the grave of statesman Winston Churchill:

> I am ready to meet my Maker.
> Whether my Maker is prepared for the great ordeal of
> meeting me is another matter.

From the first century CE memorial of the Greek Seikilos:

> Shine, as long as you live; do not be sad.
> Beause life is surely too short,
> and time demands its toll.

appearance of the body, but also because both Christian and Jewish beliefs prohibit the burning of the dead. Among the Christians, this prohibition is tied to the notion of Judgment Day, when the angel Gabriel will blow his trumpet and all the dead will rise for their final assessment by God. Christianity and Judaism hold that destroying the body with cremation denies the person resurrection (what happens to those who happen to die in violent ways isn't clear). The Catholic Church, in particular, opposed the perceived destruction of God's creation. More religions have begun to accept cremation in recent times, however

Those in the West who do opt for cremation often choose it as a more economic method of disposal. Others choose it in direct reaction to our culture's often obsessive need to beautify the dead and maintain the façade of life.

A small portion of the deceased's ashes are kept in an urn, though sometimes the remains are split up among several and kept by a number of different family members. Some individuals who are cremated ask for their ashes to be scattered over a favorite piece of land or deposited in the ocean (a method that combines burial by fire and water). Sometimes a person is cremated for space considerations, and the resulting ashes are stored in an urn and buried in the same plot as a spouse or parent, resting in the dirt above this loved one's coffin.

Despite the scarcity of wood on the Indian subcontinent, the cremation of the dead is as fundamental to Hindu religious beliefs as it is antithetical to most Christian and Jewish sects. The Hindus believe in reincarnation, and they feel that a person's soul can get tied to its body unless that body is reduced to ash. Cremation grounds line the banks of the Ganges River, and the remaining ashes and bits of bone are gathered up and tossed into the sacred river. Only the most holy among them are given bodily to the Ganges without the purifying benefit of going through the fire. Such holy ones are believed to have passed beyond the Wheel of Death and Rebirth, and so will not be tied in spirit to their fleshly bodies.

Burning a body is not as easy as it might seem. The human body is about 80 percent water, and so a very hot fire is required to burn this away and ultimately reduce the body to ash. Even with sufficient fuel for the pyre, there are still some interesting quirks about cremating a body. For one, it's nearly impossible to reduce the entire body to ash. Teeth and bits of bones almost inevitably remain, and there's always quite a bit more ash than one might expect. Many years ago, a friend's mother passed away, and as she lacked sufficient funds for much of anything else, he had her cremated. When he went to the crematorium to pick up the remains, he was given a little brass urn with some ashes in it. Thinking that this was all that was left, he turned to go but was stopped by the attendant. She then handed him a large, square black box. Inside was all the rest of the ash—thick, cloying gray stuff shot through with whitened bits of bone.

There was quite a lot of it, and the weight of the box was appreciable. Later, when we scattered her ashes as per her request, it seemed to take forever to dump the contents of the box out. We also learned another valuable lesson about cremation that night: human ash is very light and easily caught by the wind. A particularly strong gust blew up when my friend upturned the box, and many of those in attendance wore a good deal of his mother home.

Another interesting thing about cremation is that not all of the internal organs burn completely. In many other forms of burial, the internal organs are the first to decompose because their tissue is so soft and wet. Yet these self-same qualities make the internal organs very resistant to fire. The heart, especially, has a tendency to resist flame. Partly because of the density of its muscle mass, this fleshy organ often remains relatively intact even when all else has been reduced to ash. Englishman Edward Trelawny, in his autobiographical account of the last days of poets Byron and Shelley, tells of the seaside cremation of Percy Bysshe Shelley, who had drowned off the coast of Italy in a storm. Shelley's body had washed up onshore and Byron, along with Shelley's widow Mary (author of the famous novel *Frankenstein*), set about creating a fire to burn the body where it lay. They gathered driftwood and stood by the pyre until the body was reduced to ash. Nothing but the heart remained. Then, Lord Byron, who was given to such macabre acts as having a chalice crafted from a human skull, reportedly plucked the heart out of the ash to keep as a memento of his friend.

The Arms of the Ocean

Had Percy's corpse remained within the depths of the ocean, he would have enjoyed an unintentional burial at sea. While countless are the sailors who have gone to a watery grave due to shipwreck and drowning, quite a number of corpses have intentionally been committed to the arms of the ocean. In days gone by, it was a tradition among seagoing men to dispose of their dead in the water, in part because it was simply impractical to keep a corpse on ship until the next port was reached (it also was considered exceptionally unlucky).

There was a romantic element to this kind of sea burial as well. Many sailors from bygone eras viewed the sea as a living, almost sentient entity, and their career upon the waves was in part a love affair with that inscrutable, protean goddess. By committing their flesh to the depths of her embrace in death, they were symbolically giving themselves over to their truest and greatest love for the rest of eternity.

For a burial by water, a corpse must be weighted down (hence the "cement overshoes" made infamous by the old mob). While a recently dead body will initially sink in water, once decomposition begins in earnest, the gases produced by this process tend to buoy the corpse to the surface again. Burials by sea that have been thus rejected are not at all pretty to behold. The water does not work quite so lovingly as the "sea change" described in *The Tempest* by playwright William Shakespeare. Dead flesh becomes horribly bloated and water-logged after even a small amount of time spent in a watery grave. Water rapidly speeds decomposition to the point where the body becomes quickly discolored and distorted and most distinguishing features become unrecognizable. If Mother Ocean is kind, she keeps her dead, but if she yields them back to drier shores, her briny kiss produces some of the ugliest corpses one can know.

On the Wings of Death

Perhaps the most outlandish method of burial (at least to those of us native to the obsessively sanitized world of the West) is the practice of excarnation. Sometimes known as "sky burial," excarnation relies upon carrion birds, such as vultures, to dispose of the dead. This unusual method of corpse disposal was practiced by the ancient Persians, by Tibetan Buddhists, and by a number of Native American Indian tribes. Modern Zoroastrians still place their dead in so-called "towers of silence," tall ziggurat-style structures surmounted by an open area to expose the newly dead to carrion birds. In the floors below, rows of ossuaries store the denuded bones.

The cult of the vulture goes back a long, long way. In the Middle East, the ancient city of Çatal Huyuk, estimated to have been founded around 8000 BCE, features paintings on the walls that seem to depict instances of sky burial. The vulture, often reviled in the West, was clearly held in high regard by this ancient people, for countless bones from the wings of various species of vulture have been found in areas associated with the culture. Vulture skulls are inserted in one cult statue so that the beaks poke out of a set of woman's breasts in place of nipples. This strange image calls to mind the fact that in ancient Egypt the symbol for "vulture" was synonymous with the word for "mother."

If equating a carrion-eating bird with motherhood seems strange in this day and age, simply consider the recurring shamanic theme of devouring giving way to rebirth. Like the carrion-eating jackals that inspired the concept behind the Egyptian god Anubis, the cult of the vulture draws upon the notion that the animal that relieves

The vulture, a reviled carrion bird in modern times, was depicted as a motherly, protective goddess in ancient Egypt.

the deceased of his out-worn flesh is the self-same animal that conducts the spirit of that dead person to its place in the afterlife. The same can be said for the crow, an animal who serves a similar function in both Native American and Celtic cultures due to its penchant for eating carrion. Many of the totem animals associated with death destroy the physical body, but enable the soul to achieve new life through that destruction.

Whether the corpse is buried, cremated, devoured, or preserved, this sense of preparation for rebirth lies at the heart of virtually all funerary practices in all places and all times.

JOURNAL EXERCISE: PLANNING YOUR OWN FUNERAL

1. Have you attended a funeral? If so, how many of them have involved inhumation (burial in the earth)? Has anyone in your family ever been cremated or buried at sea?

2. What are the traditional burial practices of your birth religion? What reasons does this religion give for adhering to these practices?

3. Of the four methods of corpse disposal, which seems most appealing to you? Why do you prefer this method over any of the others?

4. Is there a method of corpse disposal that you feel uncomfortable with? Why do you think this method makes you feel uncomfortable?

5. Take a few pages to plan your own funeral. How would you like your body to be handled when you die? Explain your wishes and your reasons for each step, from the initial cleansing of the body to the final interment.

6. What kind of memorial would you want erected in your name? Explain your reasons for this selection. If you are feeling artistic, draw this memorial, or find an image that reminds you of the picture in your head.

7. Write up an epitaph that you would like to appear on your memorial, something that is no more than four lines in length. This can be a few lines of verse you have composed yourself, or it can be something drawn from another person's work. Get creative and try to capture the essence of who you feel you are with these few words. Additionally, see if you can capture your relationship with both life and death. If you are exceptionally pleased with how this exercise turns out, consider scribing this verse just inside the cover of your personal Book of the Dead or printing it out on a tablet or scroll to keep on your altar.

Back to Life

In this chapter, we have considered all the many ways in which humans have traditionally disposed of their dead. The methods are many and varied, but the purpose in almost all cases remains the same. Funerary practices exist partially for sanitation, but the main reason for the ritual is that the living need closure when it comes to the dead.

In planning your own funeral, you have cast an eye toward the (hopefully) distant future, considering the type of memorial you would like to have left behind so that friends and family members can honor your memory. Anyone you have touched with your life will be impacted by your death and will, like anyone else, need a sense of closure. But why wait for a funeral or wake to celebrate the good things in your life? Plan a party for yourself, or, if you're not inclined toward boisterous events, plan a quiet dinner. Invite those people who you think would be most likely to attend your funeral and need closure because of your death. Use this event as a celebration of your life while you are still living it—a living wake, as it were. You may not want to frame the event as a living wake to your friends and family, as this might cause them to worry unnecessarily about your emotional state. Instead, simply invite them to celebrate life with you in whatever way seems most appropriate.

10.

RETURN TO THE
ELEMENTS

The following rituals build upon the
concepts of burial addressed in the
previous chapter. Each rite addresses the
revelation of another element and how
that element interacts with the body of the
dead, returning its physical components to
the physical world. The order of the elements continues to reflect the elemental
order of physical dissolution presented in
the Bardo tradition of Tibet. These rites
should take place over a series of at least
four nights. You may want to space them
out even further, giving yourself a couple of
days between each rite to contemplate and
recover from your experience.

To prepare for these exercises, gather
items representative of each of the four
elements. Retain the basic elemental symbols that your altar already contains, but

for each night, give particular emphasis to one element by adding other items to your ritual space. For earth, you can gather more cemetery dirt, bits of stone such as marble, granite, or basalt, and perhaps some cuttings of plants like cypress, willow, or yew. For water, consider sea shells, vessels of water, small pieces of fishing net, and beads or tumbled stones of blue and green. For fire, pick out anything that has been kissed by the flames. This can include forged metal, blown glass, ash, or charred wood from a fire. You can also include a number of small candles as well as stones or glass beads that remind you of the color of dancing flames. For air, gather items that are the color of storm clouds or a clear sky in the afternoon. You can include dandelion seeds, feathers, and butterfly wings as well as airy veils and scarves that range in color from white to sky blue to gray. Little flags or even pinwheels can work as well.

In addition to these elemental items, you will also need a small pillow for your head and a funeral shroud. The shroud can be obtained at any fabric store. Depending on your height, you will need at least 2 to 2 ½ yards of fabric. If you want something very drapey, err on the side of caution and get an even 3 yards. This may be a little long, but there is a certain magickal potency in the formula of three times three. Magickal correspondences aside, the shroud needs to be long and wide enough to cover you completely from head to toe when laid upon your body.

You want something light and sheer, like a veil. Alternately, you can look for natural muslin, linen, or even a very loosely woven cotton. Be certain that the cloth is thin enough to comfortably breathe through; you will be laying it over your face for the majority of each exercise. You want a solid color, either white, natural, black, or deep purple. When you have chosen your funeral shroud, bring it home and wash it once on a cold setting. Do not put laundry detergent into the water. Instead, pour about a dram of perfume oil into the washing machine. You want a funereal scent, so anything with myrrh, cypress, or other earthy scents will do. Hang the scented shroud up to dry rather than placing it into a dryer; the dryer will destroy the scent and, depending upon the type of material you have chosen, it can also shrink the cloth.

As you go through the process of gathering these items, keep the ones you have already procured somewhere on or near your altar, allowing them to charge in the days leading up to the rituals themselves. You may also consider anointing these items with an appropriate ritual oil to further attune them to your work.

When you are ready to begin the first exercise, remove all of the other elemental tokens you have gathered for this rite from your altar space and set them aside. Collect the tokens you have gathered to represent earth and put them in a large bowl or other vessel. Place this either directly on your altar, assuming you have the space, or on the floor near the foot of your altar. Neatly fold the funeral shroud. Place this on the pillow and set both of these on the floor near your altar.

Once you have set up the altar and related tools, you may want to prepare yourself for the rite with a ritual bath. The first element you will be working with is the element of earth. Instead of adding cinnamon to the blend of myrrh and sea salt in your bath sachet, add one of the following: patchouli, vetivert, cypress, horehound, or mugwort. If you do not have time for a ritual bath, consider anointing yourself with an oil scented with one of these herbs in order to cleanse and attune yourself to the desired energy of the rite.

Earth Burial

Approach the altar, prepared and attuned for entrance into the sacred space. Stand between the candle of life and the candle of death. Light these, raise your hands, and meet the eyes of your reflection beyond the veil. Address the spirits thus:

> RITUALIST: Spirits! Guardians! All you immortal beings who walk the shadows between darkness and light! I call to you and ask that you attend me, here in the twilight. I stand on the threshold between the living and the dead, and I open myself to the secrets you have to share.

Light incense as an offering. Gently waft the smoke. First, guide it toward your own body, inhaling the mingled scent of precious resins and herbs. Then waft the smoke toward the candles of life and death in turn, and, finally, waft it toward your veiled reflection in the mirror. Listen inwardly for the response of the spirits. When you feel their presence crowding around you, dip your finger in the water on your altar and anoint your forehead, lips, and heart, opening each to a better perception of the threshold state. Say:

> RITUALIST: I open my mind. I open my lips. I open my heart. Gather round, ye spirits, and witness me in my rite. Tonight I commit my body to the earth, so the earth may receive me and wear away the bonds that tie my spirit to my flesh. Gather round and lend me power as I call to the element of earth.

Hold in both hands the bowl or other vessel of elemental tokens you have gathered and raise it before the mirror in blessing. Once you have focused your power and intent into this collection of items, set the bowl on the floor. Kneel before your altar and remove the tokens from the bowl. Arrange these items in a U shape at the foot of your altar. The U shape should point out from your altar and contain enough space within the U for you to lie down comfortably without disturbing any of the items. Eventually, you are going to lie down at the foot of your altar, and this collection of items will curve around your head and shoulders. Depending on how many items you have collected and how distantly you space them, the items may run down along your torso as well. Once you have outlined the space where your body will lie, place the small pillow, together with the scented funeral shroud, in the center of the U. Still kneeling before this, cross your arms upon your chest and say:

> RITUALIST: Although I have not passed beyond the veil of life, I ask that you receive me as one dead. I commit my flesh to earth, that the earth may accept me and return my body to the dust from which it came.

Lie down amidst the tokens of the element of earth. Stretch out fully on the floor with your head lying on the pillow at the very foot of your altar. Unfold the funeral shroud, then lay it across your body, covering everything from your feet to your head. Fold your hands on your stomach or cross them upon your chest and close your eyes. Lie there, breathing slowly and evenly, holding yourself as one who is dead.

Imagine that you lie beside an open grave. Family and friends gather round you. It is a simpler time, so there is no coffin and no embalming has taken place. You are simply a body, washed and wrapped in a funeral shroud. The scent of the newly turned earth is strong in your nostrils. You can smell the grass beneath you and the open air above. You feel yourself lifted and placed upon another length of strong cloth. Those who have gathered at the graveside use this to lower your body into the ground. Gently, gently you are eased into the arms of the earth.

The walls of the grave rise around you, and everything is thick with the loamy scent of earth. Then you feel the first few spadefuls of earth falling onto you like hard clumps of rain. The scent of the earth grows ever thicker as the loose soil is returned to the open grave. It descends upon you, blocking out all other scents or sensations. But rather than feeling smothered or crushed, the weight of the earth upon you is like an embrace, the firm arms of a mother holding you tight against her breast.

Around you, the tomb is dark and moist, and, like an infant in the womb, it takes you days, weeks, months to change and develop, trading your flesh for naked bones. Other life gathers round you—insects, moles, mice, and worms. Each of these does its work upon your body, helping the earth to reclaim you as her own. And yet, this is not a taking, but a giving. Bit by bit, your flesh is gathered up and becomes part of something more. The earthly part of your body returns to the earth; eventually, even the bones of your skeleton degrade, becoming one with the soil of your tomb.

Feel the weight of the earth and the gentle insistence of this cycle: your physical flesh will remain a part of the physical world, even after your spirit has flown. Let the simplicity of this truth be a comfort as you lie stretched out at the foot of your altar, the funeral shroud soft across your face.

When you feel replete with the knowledge of your relationship with earth, draw the funeral shroud away from your face and sit up. Uncross your arms, and gather some vital energy into your cupped hands. Turn and present this energy in the direction of your altar as an offering to the element of earth.

> RITUALIST: Hail to thee, Mother Earth! You are the dark of the grave and the mystery of the tomb. You take our flesh back into yourself, holding us as infants in your womb. May I not forget this lesson when it is my time to surrender up this precious flesh.

Continue to kneel for a few moments and reflect upon the revelation of earth. Then stand and ask the spirits to depart.

> RITUALIST: Spirits of the threshold! All you beings who walk between the darkness and the light! I thank you for attending to bear witness to this rite. As you have gathered, may you freely depart.

Anoint your forehead, lips, and heart.

> RITUALIST: I close myself as I close this space. I stand upon the threshold, but for now I walk away, passing from death back into life.

Snuff the candles. Facing the mirror, cross your arms upon your chest and bow your head, then depart. Once you have come down fully from the ritual mindset, go back to your altar and gather up the tokens of earth. If this is a rite you want to perform again, store the tokens in some safe place. Otherwise, find time to cleanse them and use them for something else.

Water Burial

As you prepare for the revelation of water, you should cleanse yourself with a ritual bath. When you put together your bath sachet, blend myrrh and sea salt with one of the following: willow, spikenard, trillium, dulse, or another variety of seaweed. Alternately, anoint yourself with an oil scented with one of the same. In a bowl or other large vessel, gather together all of the tokens you have selected to represent the element of water. The pillow and funeral shroud should already be set out at the foot of your altar.

Approach the altar, prepared and attuned for entrance into the sacred space. Stand between the candle of life and the candle of death. Light these, raise your hands, and meet the eyes of your reflection beyond the veil. Address the spirits as before:

> RITUALIST: Spirits! Guardians! All you immortal beings who walk the shadows between darkness and light! I call to you and ask that you attend me, here in the twilight. I stand on the threshold between the living and the dead, and I open myself to the secrets you have to share.

Light incense as an offering. Waft the smoke toward yourself, toward each of the two candles, and finally toward your veiled reflection in the mirror. Give the spirits a few moments to gather round you, then anoint your forehead, lips, and heart with the water kept on your altar.

> RITUALIST: I open my mind. I open my lips. I open my heart. Gather round, ye spirits, and witness me in my rite. Tonight I commit my body to the ocean, so the water may receive me and wear away the bonds that tie my spirit to my flesh. Gather round and lend me power as I call to the element of water.

Hold in both hands the bowl or other vessel of elemental tokens you have gathered and raise it before the mirror in blessing. Once you have focused your power and intent into this collection of items, set the bowl back down on the floor. Kneel before your altar and take the tokens from the bowl. Arrange these items in the same U shape at the foot of your altar. Once you have outlined the space where your body will lie, arrange the pillow and shroud in the center of the U (assuming they are not already there). Cross your arms upon your chest and say:

> RITUALIST: Although I have not passed beyond the veil of life, I ask that you receive me as one dead. I commit my flesh to the ocean, so that the water may accept me and return my body to the elements from which it came.

Lie down and cover yourself with the funeral shroud. With the elemental tokens of water arranged around you, fold your hands upon your chest and breathe slowly and evenly. Hold your body still in the repose of a corpse.

As you lie with your eyes closed, imagine that you are lying on the deck of a ship. You are wrapped in the stiff canvas of a sail. It covers you from head to toe, and rope binds the canvas tighter around your shoulders, your waist, your knees, and your ankles. You can hear family and friends gathered around you, each saying their final farewells. The murmur of their words mingles with the murmur of the ocean as gentle waves lap the side of the ship. Then you feel yourself gathered up in strong arms and lifted from the deck. There is a giddy moment as you are thrown off the side of the ship, then, with a splash, you enter the water.

Weights have been tied to your ankles and around your chest, so the water quickly closes around you. Your nose and mouth are filled with the scent of brine. The ship and the light of the sky above both grow distant as you drift down, down, forever down into the darkness of the sea. Eventually, your body comes to rest against something, but the current of the ocean plucks at you, rocking you gently as a mother rocks her child. You are surrounded by a pressing silence and the constant ebb and flow of the waves. Water permeates everything, and you feel as if the boundaries between your flesh and the water are growing indistinct. You are flowing, flowing out, the water washing deeper and deeper into your flesh until you can feel it flowing in and out of your naked bones. Fish and tiny crustaceans pick at you, swimming in the empty spaces between your ribs. Others cling tightly, making your naked skeleton their home. And everywhere around you there is the hushed whispering of the waves, like the voice of a mother soothing her child. You are washed, over and over again, cleansed until there is nothing left. Your hair, like streaming seaweed, your flesh, your bones, all have become a part of the ocean, at one with the dance of life and death in the deep. And even when there is nothing left of your physical remains but a few grains of sand, you can still feel the water rocking you, like a mother rocking her sleeping child.

When you feel replete with the knowledge of your relationship with water, draw the funeral shroud away from your face and sit up. Uncross your arms, and gather some vital energy into your cupped hands. Turn and present this energy in the direction of your altar as an offering to the element of water.

> RITUALIST: Hail to thee, Mother Ocean! You are keeper of the deep places where mysteries we can barely comprehend are hidden beneath your waves. In our blood, we carry a memory of your waters, and when we pass, our water returns to you again. May I hold close this lesson when it is my time to surrender up this precious flesh.

Continue to kneel for a few moments and reflect upon the revelation of water. Then stand and ask the spirits to depart.

> RITUALIST: Spirits of the threshold! All you beings who walk between the darkness and the light! I thank you for attending to bear witness to this rite. As you have gathered, may you freely depart.

Anoint your forehead, lips, and heart.

> RITUALIST: I close myself as I close this space. I stand upon the threshold, but for now I walk away, passing from death back into life.

Snuff the candles. Facing the mirror, cross your arms upon your chest and bow your head, then depart.

The Ceremony of Fire

Allow a night or two to pass between your experience with water and the ceremony of fire. When you are ready to approach the revelation of fire, prepare yourself, as before, with a ritual bath. This time your bath sachet should contain sea salt, myrrh, and one of the following: amber, cinnamon, ginger, or dragon's blood. A perfume oil scented with one of these fiery herbs can also be used to cleanse and attune your energy to the rite. Gather together all of the tokens you have selected to represent the element of fire and place these near your altar, along with the pillow and funeral shroud.

Approach the altar, lighting both the candle of life and the candle of death. Meet the eyes of your reflection beyond the veil and, raising power to your outstretched hands, call the spirits.

> RITUALIST: Spirits! Guardians! All you immortal beings who walk the shadows between darkness and light! I call to you and ask that you attend me, here in the twilight. I stand on the threshold between the living and the dead, and I open myself to the secrets you have to share.

Light an offering of incense and waft the smoke, first to yourself, then to each of the two candles, then to your veiled reflection in the mirror. Be silent as you feel the spirits gather. Then anoint your forehead, lips, and heart.

> RITUALIST: I open my mind. I open my lips. I open my heart. Gather round, ye spirits, and witness me in my rite. Tonight I commit my body to the flames, so the fire may receive me and burn away the bonds that tie my spirit to my flesh. Gather round and lend me power as I call to the element of fire.

Bless the tokens of the element of fire, then arrange these items in the same U shape you have used before at the foot of your altar. While it is perfectly acceptable to use tealights or small votive candles to represent the element of fire in this rite, you should be certain to place these far enough away from where you will be lying so there is no chance you will knock them over or be burned. Also consider that you will be draping yourself with the funeral shroud, which could catch fire if it gets too close to any open flame. Arranging a number of burning candles around you has a very dramatic effect for this rite, but if you do this, you must take every precaution with your safety. (Also keep in mind that nearly every college dormitory has rules against the use of candles in its rooms.) Once you have used the tokens to outline the space where your body will lie, arrange the pillow and shroud in the center of the U. Cross your arms upon your chest and say:

> RITUALIST: Although I have not passed beyond the veil of life, I ask that you receive me as one dead. I commit my flesh to the flames, so that the fire may accept me and return my body to the elements from which it came.

Lie down and cover yourself with the funeral shroud. Once again, if you are using open flame, please be very, very careful in your placement of the shroud. Once the shroud is in place and you are *safely* surrounded by the elemental tokens of fire, fold your hands upon your chest. Breathe slowly and evenly, holding your body in the pose of a corpse.

You are in a far distant land, where it is the tradition for the dead to be burned to help their spirits move beyond their mortal flesh. You have been wrapped in a shroud and carried to the burning grounds, where the cloying, sweet scent of human ash hangs thick in the air. There are other fires burning, and they carry a sharp scent—the burning scent of fingernails and hair. The heat of the flames combined with the heat of the day makes this place almost stifling.

When it is time, you feel yourself lifted and placed upon the pyre. The priests light sacred incense, and the scented smoke drifts lazily over your head. You hear prayers being recited, and then you hear the distant crackle of the flames. There is no heat at first, just sound, a whisper that crescendos into a roar.

And then you feel your flesh kissed by dancing flames. There is no pain, only sensation. The shroud catches quickly and is lifted from your flesh and scattered to the wind. The heat of the fire causes an updraft that urges every stray bit of ash toward the sky. The fire on your skin feels like a thousand tiny insects crawling everywhere, all at once. It prickles, just on the edge of tickling. This sensation swarms over you, more intense than even your awareness of heat—although the heat is there. It dries you out. At first, your hair is lifted in its updraft, and then it merely blows away as ash. You feel every part of your body shrinking, pulling into itself and, once it can shrink no more, it shrivels away to ash. Your skin sears away to reveal charring bone, held together by shriveled ligaments and musculature. The heat of the pyre is so intense that even this begins to char, burning to ashes behind a dancing veil of flame.

The fire grows more and more intense, lifting layer upon layer of your mortal flesh away and casting it upward, as ash, to the sky. At first, you are reluctant, for the fire makes your face and form unrecognizable. As the skin shrivels and chars, it quickly becomes impossible to identify your age, your sex, your race. But then, it seems that the roar of the flames contains a whispering—a deep, crackling voice that tells you that this is the way of things. You are not the face you see daily in the mirror. You are not your age, your weight, your ethnic background. You simply *are*, as free and dancing as the flames. You'll know this truth if you just let go and allow the rest to scatter in the wind.

As your ashes scatter across the burning ground, you feel yourself growing lighter. You feel as light and free as the ashes, as wild and unrestrained as the flames. Then you feel yourself rising up and up, no longer burdened by the weight of mortal flesh.

When you feel that you have grasped the nature of your relationship with fire, draw the funeral shroud away from your face and sit up. Uncross your arms, and gather some vital energy into your cupped hands. Turn and present this energy in the direction of your altar as an offering to the element of fire.

RITUALIST: Hail to thee, Lord of the Flames! You are the wild one who dances in the midst of destruction. When you embrace us, you reduce us to carbon, the very source of life. May I hold close this lesson when it is my time to surrender up this precious flesh.

Kneel for a few moments, contemplating the revelation of fire. Then stand and ask the spirits to depart.

> RITUALIST: Spirits of the threshold! All you beings who walk between the darkness and the light! I thank you for attending to bear witness to this rite. As you have gathered, may you freely depart.

Anoint your forehead, lips, and heart.

> RITUALIST: I close myself as I close this space. I stand upon the threshold, but for now I walk away, passing from death back into life.

Snuff the candles. As you face the veiled mirror, cross your arms upon your chest and bow your head, then depart.

Sky Burial

As you prepare for the revelation of air, you should cleanse yourself with a ritual bath. When you put together your bath sachet, blend myrrh and sea salt with one of the following: lavender, lemongrass, anise, or acacia. Alternately, anoint yourself with an oil scented with one of the same. In a bowl or other large vessel, gather together all of the tokens you have selected to represent the element of air. The pillow and funeral shroud should already be set out at the foot of your altar.

Approach the altar, prepared and attuned for entrance into the sacred space. Stand between the candle of life and the candle of death. Light these, raise your hands, and meet the eyes of your reflection beyond the veil. Address the spirits as before:

> RITUALIST: Spirits! Guardians! All you immortal beings who walk the shadows between darkness and light! I call to you and ask that you attend me, here in the twilight. I stand on the threshold between the living and the dead, and I open myself to the secrets you have to share.

Light incense as an offering. Waft the smoke toward yourself, toward each of the two candles, and finally toward your veiled reflection in the mirror. Give the spirits a few moments to gather round you, then anoint your forehead, lips, and heart with the water kept on your altar.

> RITUALIST: I open my mind. I open my lips. I open my heart. Gather round, ye spirits, and witness me in my rite. Tonight I commit my body to the winds, so the air may receive me and scatter my flesh like so much dust. Gather round and lend me power as I call to the element of air.

Hold in both hands the bowl or other vessel of elemental tokens you have gathered and raise it before the mirror in blessing. Once you have focused your power and intent into this collection of items, set the bowl on the floor. Kneel before your altar and take the tokens from the bowl. Arrange these items in the same U shape at the foot of your altar. Once you have outlined the space where your body will lie, arrange the pillow and shroud in the center of the U (assuming they are not already there). Cross your arms upon your chest and say:

> RITUALIST: Although I have not passed beyond the veil of life, I ask that you receive me as one dead. I commit my flesh to the winds, so that the air may accept me and return my body to the elements from which it came.

Lie down and cover yourself with the funeral shroud. With the elemental tokens of air arranged around you, fold your hands upon your chest and breathe slowly and evenly. Hold your body still in the repose of a corpse.

As you close your eyes, you find yourself at the base of an ancient tower. Men and women have gathered around you. They are clothed in dark robes, and their faces and heads are covered. They wash you and anoint your body with sweet oil. Then, together, they lift you and bear you upon their shoulders. They enter the looming tower that stands before you. Inside this imposing edifice, all is hushed and the shadows hang thick upon the air.

The first floor of the tower reveals walls that are lined with bones. Denuded skulls peer down at you from empty sockets. The mourners barely stop here. Instead, they head for stairs that run along one side of the tower. Silently, reverently, you are borne upon the shoulders of the mourners. Staircase after staircase, they carry you up, higher and higher. Finally, they emerge with you onto the uppermost platform of the tower of silence. All you can see is sky, a vault of perfect blue. Powerful winds blow around you, plucking at the mourners' robes. They put their heads down and move against the wind, carrying you to a raised platform. As one, they lift you onto this, raising you even closer to the azure arch of the sky.

You lie facing the heavens, gusts of wind whipping your hair across your face. The mourners step silently away, disappearing into the belly of the tower. You are alone on the wind-swept roof. There is only blue above you and around you—and then dark spots seem to swirl into being high above you. Lazily they circle, closer and closer, spiraling down until you can see the huge expanse of dark wings. The vultures glide easily on the updrafts, allowing the wind to do the work for them. They almost never flap their wings. You watch with a detached sensation, amazed at the power of these birds, the way their wings hug the winds. And then they are upon you, feasting. There is no pain, only a silent offering. Sharp beaks make quick work of your eyes, your face, and your skin.

As the vultures do their work on you, the soft rustling of their wings in the wind begins to sound like voices. The whisper of their feathers, the ceaseless moan of the wind, all converge until you know that they are speaking. They explain to you why they must consume your body. They will convey your soul with them to the skies, but they must have payment first. You pay by giving nourishment, yielding your flesh to living creatures so your soul may fly free.

When they are finished with their meal, the vultures carry your spirit up and up, spreading their wings. They leave nothing but a memory of form in the shape of clean and naked bones.

When you feel replete with the knowledge of your relationship with air, draw the funeral shroud away from your face and sit up. Uncross your arms, and gather some vital energy into your cupped hands. Turn and present this energy in the direction of your altar as an offering to the element of air.

RITUALIST: Hail to thee, Father Sky! From the vault of the heavens, you pour forth the winds, which gust and blow and scour the land. With every breath, we take you into ourselves, and with our last breaths, our spirits fly forth to travel your airy void.

Continue to kneel for a few moments and reflect upon the revelation of air. Then stand and ask the spirits to depart.

RITUALIST: Spirits of the threshold! All you beings who walk between the darkness and the light! I thank you for attending to bear witness to this rite. As you have gathered, may you freely depart.

Anoint your forehead, lips, and heart.

RITUALIST: I close myself as I close this space. I stand upon the threshold, but for now I walk away, passing from death back into life.

Snuff the candles. Facing the mirror, cross your arms upon your chest and bow your head, then depart.

JOURNAL EXERCISE: ELEMENTAL AFFILIATIONS

1. Before you undertook these exercises, did you feel a particular affinity for any of the four elements? After you performed these rites, did that affinity change? Explain.

2. Was there an element that you never really resonated with? Once you did these rites, did your relationship with that element change at all? Describe your experience.

3. How did these four exercises help to continue the work begun in Chapter 6, Accepting Impermanence? Do you feel that you have a better grasp on your relation to both spirit and matter now?

4. When you surrendered yourself up to the elements, were there any particular images or messages that seemed to come through? If you feel that you experienced some deeper level

of communication from any of the elements, record that communication to the best of your ability.

5. What meaning does this message hold for you as you proceed along the Twilight Path?

Back to Life

In this chapter, we used ritual and guided visualization to gain a greater appreciation for the role each of the elements play in the dissolution of the physical body. We have reached out to each of the elements and connected with them, seeking the lessons of impermanence that they can convey. But the elements are not strictly the tools of death. Each of the four elements worked with in this chapter helps sustain life as well. To help remember the balance that is fundamental to this path, you should take some time to acquaint yourself with the living aspects of the elements as well. Think of places in your local area where you can connect with earth, water, fire, and air. Plan an outing and focus on each of the elements in turn, calling out to the element in its aspect of life-giver and life-builder. Meditate on how this particular element supports and nurtures all living things.

If going out to connect with the elements is not feasible, take some time at home to meditate on a symbol of each of the elements in turn. Imagine that you are out in the wide world, sitting in the center of some wild place where this element holds sway. Connect to the element internally, and visualize all the ways in which this element sustains and builds life. When you are finished, compare and contrast the nature of the element in the two aspects which you have now explored: death-bringer and life-giver. Record your thoughts and observations in your journal.

11.

GIVING UP THE GHOST

We have seen the physical side of death and what happens to the body *after* the spirit has departed, and we have communed with the elements responsible for returning dust to dust. But what about the internal experience of death itself? What does it feel like to actually have the body die around you as your immortal spirit lives on?

Few cultures have had the strength, courage, and wisdom to address this question directly. But the monks and lamas of Buddhist Tibet have applied themselves to the question for hundreds of years. Their impartial, dispassionate, and largely scientific approach to the experience of death has resulted in a body of teachings that is perhaps the most complete in existence on the science of dying and what comes after. Known in the West as the Tibetan Book of the Dead, the *Bardo Thodol* not only explains all the stages one can expect to experience through the process of death, but it also addresses in fine detail the subtle world of experience that the deceased enters when existing between lives.

The Process of Death

According to the Tibetan tradition, the body contains five main *rlungs*, or "winds." *Rlung* (pronounced lyoong) is comparable to the Sanskrit concept of *prana* and can also be translated as "vital-air," "vital-force," or "psychic-force" (Evans-Wentz, 90). In the Tibetan system, each of these five winds are tied to an element, a chakra, and a physical sense. When death is imminent, these winds, their elements, and their corresponding energy centers begin to disintegrate and dissolve from the body. The stages through which these winds dissolve follow a set sequence, and the symptoms experienced at each stage allow one to judge the progression of the death process.

The first stage of death begins with the destruction of the navel chakra and is known to the Tibetans as "earth sinking into water." At this stage in the death process, the body becomes heavy. The dying person feels as if he or she is being pressed down by a great weight. As the earth element dissipates, this gives way to a shaky, watery feeling in all the limbs. He or she can no longer digest solid food but can only take in liquids. The warmth of the body retreats from the limbs and remains only in the center, near the heart.

The outward signs of this stage that are visible to observers include a growing pallor that makes the skin take on a pasty or moldy appearance. The face becomes shrunken and hollow. The eyes, which once were bright, become lackluster. The eyes may tear and the nose runs uncontrollably. As the dying person experiences the inner signs of this stage of the death process, he or she begins to feel mentally heavy and sluggish. The body loses strength, so the dying person can no longer hold things or stand on his or her own. The voice changes and talking becomes difficult. The sight begins to blur so that images become indistinct, and it seems as if one is gazing through water. The arrival of this water-like mirage is the secret sign that tells the skilled practitioner that this stage of the death process has begun.

The second stage of the death process is known as "water sinking into fire." At this point, the dying person first feels clammy. Then the cold, damp sensation gives way to an overpowering sensation of fevered heat. Everything in the body begins to feel dried out. The mouth and tongue become dry; it becomes hard to swallow, as there is almost no spittle. The lips become pale, white, and shrunken. The sensation of hearing becomes dim, so the dying person cannot perceive sounds or speech distinctly.

The inner signs at this stage involve a loss of mental clarity. The dying person becomes confused and bewildered. He or she hallucinates and may be lucid one moment, then recognize nothing of his or her surroundings in the next. The dying person also becomes anxious and fretful. As the ties to the body have begun to slip away, the body begins to grow unresponsive and numb.

The secret sign is one of smoke, and the dying person perceives that he or she is enveloped by it. The dissolution here is concerned with the heart center, which in the Tibetan system is a merger of the heart and solar plexus chakras, situated about midway between these two. As the water energy is released and consumed by the fire, this center begins to dissolve.

As fire gives way to wind, there is a sensation of lightness and rising, "as though the body were being blown to atoms" (Evans-Wentz, 93). This is the dissolution of the "downward-moving wind" tied to the sacral center (Rinpoche, 89). The dying person loses control over the bowels and bladder. He or she also loses the sense of smell. The feverish heat that beset the dying person in the previous stage is all burned away and the dying person begins to feel cold. Internally, the dying person finds it difficult to think, to hold on to any thought at all. If he or she is capable of perceiving the secret sign, it will seem to the dying person that he or she is surrounded by rising sparks, or fireflies.

The upward-moving wind, tied to the throat, then dissipates. This is the stage known as "wind to void." Breathing becomes difficult. Exhalations are long and rattling, while inhalations are short and come only with much strain. The dying person can no longer swallow either food or drink. Eventually, the breathing becomes very irregular and shallow, so the dying person takes short breaths in wheezing gasps. The sensation of taste is lost, as is the sense of the body. At this point, the dying person will feel as if he or she is at the center of a dying candle flame, which is about to go out.

After the dissipation of wind, the dying person may be, for all intents and purposes, clinically dead. But experiences continue, nevertheless. Although the physical breath has stopped, the internal circulation of energy continues. This pranic "breath" continues within the central nervous system for a span of time, during which the dying person experiences the rising of the white, the red, and the black.

The experiences of white, red, and black require a little background explanation. The white and the red elements are *bindu*, or spiritual seeds, given to a child by its male and female parents at the moment of conception. The female element is connected to the moon, luminosity, and whiteness. It is stored in the brain center and is associated with the quality of desire. The male element is connected to the sun, radiance, and redness. It is stored in the sacral center and is associated with the quality of aggression.

After the dissipation of the wind, the white essence descends from the brain to the heart center. At this point, the dying person internally perceives a glow like luminous moonlight in an expansively dark sky. After the descent of the white, the red essence ascends from the sacral center to the heart. At this point, the dying person experiences another glow, like the radiance of the setting sun. When the two drops merge at the heart center, there is the experience of utter darkness, or what Thurman describes as a "sky full of bright darklight" (Thurman, 43). This is the experience of the black. At this point, the dying person loses consciousness.

After the darkness descends within, the dying person, if he or she is attentive, may then experience one final stage of dying. This is the stage of imminence to transcendence. The consciousness expands to a pure, non-dualistic state, and the dying person perceives the pure light of transparency. In the West, this stage has been associated with the "light at the end of the tunnel" that is such a hallmark of near-death experiences. The Tibetans believe that at this point, the individual soul experiences itself as it truly is: immortal and undifferentiated from the totality of the universe. If the dying person can hold on to this state of super-consciousness through the death process, he or she can attain Buddhahood and gain both release and conscious control over the process of incarnation.

This experience of the pure light of transparency lasts for but a moment, and then what the Tibetans call the "sixfold knot of the heart," the lynchpin of the subtle and central nervous systems, unravels, and the dead person is propelled completely from his or her body. It is at this point that the physical death process is complete, and the deceased is now in the *Bardo*, or between-life state.

Tripping the Bardo

The whole point of the Tibetan Book of the Dead, which is read aloud during and after the process of death, is to help the dead person navigate the Bardo state and achieve as positive a rebirth as possible. Although the Tibetan Buddhists believe it is ideal for the dead person to merge with the pure light of transparency, it is acknowledged that only very skilled practitioners are likely to be able to do this, especially upon the very first moment wherein this light presents itself.

The gateway to liberation from a passive experience of the rebirth process presents itself several more times to the deceased over the course of the next forty-nine days, and so the instructions are read throughout the funerary process in the hopes that the deceased will at some point recognize his or her route out of the world of karmic suffering and into the pure light of ultimate reality.

In the Tibetan system, much ink has been spilled to develop instructions that will enable a faithful practitioner to harness the death state and move beyond the cycle of death and rebirth. For our purposes, however, the point of interest is the process of death itself and the meditations that allow living individuals to achieve a foretaste of that process. The art of practicing dying is a potent tool for retaining, at the moment of death, the awareness necessary for propelling the soul beyond this cycle of existence, but it also can be applied to understanding near-death experience without the risk of physical death itself. By learning how to reproduce the energetic steps that physical bodies undergo just prior to the release of the spirit, we can actively put ourselves in a state that straddles the very threshold between life and death.

Exercise: The Practice of Dying

The Tibetans believed that the self-same process of five-fold release that occurred when one descended into the state of death was at work when one also descended into the state of sleep. Falling asleep and awakening to dreams was seen as concurrent with relinquishing this life and awakening to the next. Obviously, falling asleep is not quite as permanent as dying, and so the exercise of the five winds could be practiced safely as one bridged the threshold between the waking mind and the dreaming mind. I have found that this exercise is especially helpful for learning how to consciously experience and harness what scientists call the hypnagogic state—the borderline state between waking and sleeping that many use as a launching point for out-of-body travel. This borderline state is explored more completely in works by astral projector Robert Monroe, as well as in my own book, *Psychic Dreamwalking*, but suffice it to say that there is power in any state of consciousness that exists between different states of being, and the connection between the slumbering world and the world of spirits becomes immediately apparent once one learns to harness this borderline state.

Practicing the dispersion of the five winds is best done in your bed, as you are preparing to go to sleep for the night. The exercise can be used as a potent relaxation technique, and because it launches your consciousness into that borderline state, it can also be used as a tool to promote lucid dreaming, trance states, and out-of-body experience. Once you are lying down and comfortable, mentally rehearse the five stages of release.

The first few times you do this exercise, it is very likely that you will fall asleep. Don't struggle against this. Allow it to happen natu-

HALLMARKS OF AN OUT-OF-BODY EXPERIENCE

Out-of-body experiences, or OBEs, have often been reported in conjunction with near-death experiences. Sometimes harnessed consciously through the practice of astral projection, the following characteristics are typical of most OBEs:

- Your body begins to tingle or vibrate
- You feel as if you are sinking into your bed or, alternately, rising off of it
- Your physical body may become paralyzed, unable to move
- You feel as if a point of consciousness projects outside your physical body
- You are able to perceive your own physical body from an outside perspective
- Your new form is non-material, behaving much like a spirit
- You are able to fly, float, or levitate
- You are able to pass through solid objects, such as walls
- You are able to cross great distances with a thought alone
- You are largely invisible to those around you

rally, and try to make a point of remembering the dreams this opens up in you (if you make a regular practice of keeping a dream journal, it can help during dream recall). You may also find yourself slipping into either a visionary state or an out-of-body experience. Either of these is fine, and you should not panic. Simply allow the experience to go where it wants to go, and try to retain enough conscious awareness so you can recall the images and record them later.

This visualization becomes especially potent when paired with internal energy work. As you go through the process of visualizing the release of the five winds, associate each wind or element with a specific chakra. Imagine that the center of the chakra contains a knot of energy, like the knots that are released as part of the Tibetan understanding of the process of dying. As you imagine the dispersion of the wind associated with that chakra, also imagine that you're untying the knot and releasing the energy of this chakra.

Although the Tibetan placement of the five winds does not correspond directly to the traditional Western model of the chakras, I have nevertheless found the following correspondences to work best:

- Earth dissolving into Water: Root Chakra
- Water dissolving into Fire: Navel Chakra
- Fire dissolving into Wind: Heart/Solar Plexus Chakra
- Wind dissolving into Void: Throat Chakra
- Void expanding into Dark-Light: Third Eye Chakra

Dispersion of the Five Winds

Lying in your bed, preparing for sleep, you say, "My flesh is earth." Your body grows heavy and you feel as if you are sinking further and further into the depths of your bed. Your limbs stiffen, and they become so heavy you can no longer move. This does not panic you, for you know that this is simply one step among many in the process of letting go. Your mind remains detached from the experience of your body, feeling and experiencing, but not trapped or crushed by the experience.

You say, "Earth dissolving into water," and you are being drawn down, as if sinking into the depths of the sea. All of your flesh feels weighted down. Now, not only are you so heavy that you cannot move, but the very thought of movement seems strange to you. There is a growing sense of disconnectedness with this heavy, weighted flesh. Your mind remains distinct, but your body is drawn down, and further down. And then it is as if the water closes over your head and you feel yourself sinking even more, yet the heaviness begins to subside. You are dissolving into the water, the heaviness of your flesh dispersing so that everything feels watery, flowing, spreading out and draining away. Water now flows through your unmoving limbs, and whatever strength remained in your muscles and in your bones flows away with it. You feel lighter, but undefined, flowing out in every direction. The sense of detachment grows stronger still, and your mind retreats a further step away, merely observing the sensations of your body.

You say, "Water dissolving into fire." You grow cold as the rushing water leeches the strength and heat from your veins, but then, even as the last of your body's warmth seems to flow away, you feel the water begin to recede. It has flowed through you, flowed away, and now you are dry, dry as the desert, dry as brittle sticks set near a fire. You feel a fire kindling within you, and this races through your distant flesh, consuming yet another level of your connection to the physical world. The fire consumes but does not burn—there is no sense of searing, or of pain. It is a dry heat, running through you, making your flesh feel lighter than ashes. You can see the fire dancing behind your eyes, bright against the shadows.

You say, "Fire dissolving into wind." The fire increases in intensity until its all-consuming light is all that you can see. Everything is like sparks rising in your consciousness. Your mind, distant until now, a detached observer, is awash in reddish light and the dancing of the flames. For a moment, fire is all your consciousness knows, and then you feel as if a strong wind has scoured a desert plain. The wind rises up, blowing away the fire. There is smoke, and then you feel like the last vestiges of your body are merely ashes, and these are dispersed and carried upon the wind. The wind blows through you with a hollow sound, and you realize that there is no further sense of your physical form. Your mind remains, but it is awash in smoke and shadow, and that hollow wind rings through every remaining sense.

You say, "Wind dissolving into void." There is nothing but ash and less than ash, now. All that you felt weighing you down before, everything that connected you to the fleshly world has been scattered upon this wind, and then even the wind itself begins to disperse, the tiny motes of ash swirling up and up as if into the deepest vault of a midnight sky. There are not even stars, just the vast expanse of space, and the last few specks that remain of you scatter everywhere throughout this vastness, spreading out and out so that you yourself become the vastness of space. There is no light. There are no physical sensations. Even your mind, detached observer, feels drawn out and expanded beyond all recognition, simply a memory of thought in this echoing vault of empty space.

You say, "Void expanding into Dark-Light." You are suspended in the void. You are the void itself, until it seems that you will lose all sense of who or what you ever were. And then the void itself seems to expand and disperse, and the darkness is suffused with light. Ruddy at first, it is like the fiery light of sunset. Then it shifts to the watery light that suffuses the sky just before dawn. And then this, too, changes, until the darkness around you itself becomes luminous. It is like the light that exists at the furthest edge of reality, a light that makes darkness itself visible. Enrapt in this luminous darkness, you exist beyond your body, beyond even your sense of mind. There is just this luminous sense of being, and you release yourself to the experience, awash in a feeling of peace.

At the end of this exercise, you should at least be deeply relaxed, if not drifting off to sleep. It is very natural to want to cross over into the dreamstate after completing this exercise, so do not fight it. Allow your mind's surrender to sleep to be the final act of slipping away, a sort of little death that frees your spirit to roam the pathways of dream. Perform this exercise prior to sleep for several nights running and pay attention to how you feel upon waking the next morning. Also pay attention to the impact this practice has upon your dreams. Record anything that stands out to you in your journal.

JOURNAL EXERCISE: THE ART OF CROSSING OVER

1. What was your first experience with the Dispersion of the Five Winds? How did you feel as you progressed through each stage of the exercise?

2. Were you happy with your results the first time that you performed this exercise? What could you have done differently? Make a list of ways you think you can improve your experience.

3. How successful did you feel you were at performing the energy work at each chakra? Do you feel confident working with your own energy this way? What do you think you could do to improve?

4. Perform the Dispersion exercise every night for at least a week and keep your journal on a nightstand or somewhere else close to your bed. When you wake up in the morning, take a few minutes to think back through your dreams. Before you get out of bed to prepare for the rest of your day, record what you remember of your dreams in your journal. At the end of the week, examine what you have recorded. Do you think that the exercise has had an impact upon the content of your dreams? What about their frequency or their intensity? What are your thoughts on this?

5. Pay attention to how you feel the day after performing the Dispersion exercise. Do you notice any difference in your energy? Does the exercise seem to have any noticeable impact on your health? What about your psychic sensitivities? How do you feel about these changes?

6. Perform the Dispersion exercise at your altar, inviting the spirits to attend and reach out to you. Is there a point where you feel closer or more in touch with the spirits? If

you feel that the exercise facilitates communication, record your experiences. What kind of perceptions has this exercise allowed you to achieve?

Back to Life

In this chapter, we looked at the Tibetan understanding of how the spirit detaches from the body during the process of death. Through meditation, we have walked through this process, getting ourselves

The gates of death loom ominously, but they open to change, not an end.

comfortable with the process of letting go. Continuing in the Tibetan tradition, we have applied the Dispersion of the Five Winds exercise to the process of going to sleep, for the Tibetans view the realm of dreams as a state of existence very similar to the realm of the dead. Practicing the Dispersion of the Five Winds prior to going to sleep can result in very profound dreams as well as out-of-body experience. However, it can also leave you feeling very detached and ungrounded in the physical world.

As a way to help balance this work, consider performing the dispersion exercise in reverse, just after waking up. This is called the Descent of the Five Winds. Instead of lying down, stand up and pull the energy of your spirit back down into your body with your hands as you recite the five stages from dark-light to void, void to air, and onward down to earth. You will end with your hands cupped over your root chakra. Then take three deep, cleansing breaths and touch the ground beneath your feet. Use the exercise to bring yourself out of the realm of dreams and more firmly into the realm of ordinary consciousness, grounding your perceptions firmly in the physical world for the day that lies ahead.

DEATH AS TRANSCENDENCE

Walking through the cemetery, we come upon a stone that commemorates the life of one who died quite young. Upon this stone, lofty and silent, stands an angel. The angel, expertly crafted in bronze, has been weathered through the years to a rich green patina, and streaks of black brindle her wings.

This otherworldly being lifts her face heavenward, wings and hands outspread in a gesture that is both inviting and exultant. Worn and weathered by the passage of the years, there is still no mistaking the expression of ecstatic serenity that transfigures the statue's features. Running your hands along the statue, you caress the expertly sculpted folds of the angel's robe. The angel is smooth and cool to the touch, and the weathered bronze, warmed as it is by the sun, almost has the feel of living skin. An ineffable silence surrounds the grave of this long-dead child. There is a hush, and it seems as if the world around you is holding its breath. You can feel it, the promise of something trembling just on the edge of reality. Solemnly, thoughtfully, you place a single rose at the foot of the grave. Then, like the angel, you raise your face in solemn expectation to the cloudless skies above.

Take a few moments to hold on to the emotions inspired by this meditation. Then bring out your journal and reflect upon your thoughts and feelings. Imagine that the angel can speak. Record the message you feel it would have to impart to you about the transcendent aspects of death.

PART THREE

*The Bridge
Between
Worlds*

"O soft embalmer of the still midnight . . .
Turn the key deftly in the oilèd wards
And seal the hushèd casket of my soul."
—*John Keats, "To Sleep"*

12.

A FINE AND PRIVATE PLACE

As you progress on the Twilight Path, your next task is to find a cemetery. This cemetery will become the stage for several important encounters with death. Where your altar represents a threshold that stands between the realms of the living and the realms of the dead, the cemetery will allow you to travel into the realm of the dead. Think about what a cemetery really is. One of the older terms for a cemetery is *necropolis*, which is a Greek word that literally means "city of the dead." A cemetery is a place in our ordinary reality that we have set aside as the realm of the dead. There is nothing in a cemetery that properly belongs to the living. The living may walk there, but it is not their space.

Although we Westerners profess to have grown away from the "superstitious" behavior of ancient peoples such as the Egyptians, we nevertheless retain many of their beliefs and practices concerning the dead. We simply observe these practices in an unofficial capacity. Remember how ancient Egyptian priests would make elaborate offerings at the tomb to provide nourishment for the deceased in the next life? Some ancient Egyptians even wrote letters to their departed loved ones, addressing them as they led their new life in the tomb, asking for favors, or, in at least one case, asking for the permission to marry another woman. The vast majority of modern Westerners would laugh at such behavior, and yet how many people have done exactly the same things at a cemetery? When people want to "visit" their dead relatives, they go to the cemetery where that person has been interred. Many individuals will talk directly to the gravestone as if it were a one-way speakerphone between the living and the dead. In the northern United States, Memorial Day is a time for parades, but in much of the South, it is known instead as Remembrance Day, and families go down to the graveyard to clean the plots of the deceased and share a meal among the graves.

Signpost for Fern Avenue, one of the many small roads that wind through Woodlawn Cemetery in the Bronx, New York.

Even though we are hardly a Pagan culture, offerings are left regularly to our departed loved ones, just as in cultures that have a strongly established tradition of ancestor-worship. The offerings most often take the form of flowers, but I've seen people leave photographs, food, small polished stones, and even teddy bears, dolls, and balloons. These offerings are brought directly to the cemetery and placed on or around the grave. This shows that on some unconscious level, mourners feel that their connection to their beloved dead is the grave itself, that place where the earthly remains are at rest.

Cemeteries are cities of the dead, and yet they occupy physical space in the realm of the living. As such, they serve as the perfect bridge into the other realm, a place where a living person can walk among the dead. As a bridge to the Otherside, you are going to find a cemetery that speaks to you. Then you will reach out to the slumbering dead until at least one of them deigns to answer.

A Simple Plot of Land

What should you be looking for in your personal city of the dead? Ideally, you want a cemetery with character. When you walk onto the grounds, the place should speak to you. You should be able to feel the lingering energies of the dead as well as the energies left behind by those who come to mourn them. You should also feel as if you are walking into a sacred space. Cemeteries are hallowed ground, and the land most cemeteries occupy has been blessed in accordance with the rites of its main religion. However, some cemeteries simply don't feel as sanctified as others. You will know what I'm talking about once you walk onto the grounds of a burial site and feel an immediate hush fall over the world. A cemetery that inspires that kind of reaction is exactly what you are looking for. A place like that has spirit, and you are far more likely to be able to contact real spirits when on its grounds.

The ideal cemetery for this kind of work should be relatively old, with a lot of history buried beneath its grass. New, modern cemeteries are so sanitized, it's next to impossible to get an impression from any of the graves. Also, there's something awe-inspiring about really old tombstones. They don't make gravemarkers like they used to. These days, a marker is often little more than a simple stone slab sunk into the ground and that's it. A hundred years ago, artists from all over the world were commissioned to sculpt ornate angels, Grecian columns, and veiled urns. Even the simple stone slabs that were used a hundred years ago had more character to them than the ones that are produced with high-tech machinery from a slab of granite. There was always an effort at embellishment, and if no pictures were carved on the stone, then extra care was put into the lettering. The fact that this was done by hand made even the simplest gravestone a work of art, imbuing it with the energy and emotion of the artist.

It may take you a while to find just the right cemetery for you. Do a little research and see what cemeteries are located in your immediate area. Then plan an afternoon outing to visit them all. Give yourself a little time for each graveyard, so you can casually walk the grounds and get a good feel for the place. Take your journal with you and record your thoughts and observances for each of these graveyards. Don't feel as if you have to make your decision right away. Take some time to consider and compare how each of these cities of the dead makes you feel.

As you try to decide which place is right for you, ask yourself the following questions:

1. Is the cemetery secluded enough that I will not be disturbed in my meditations?

2. Does the cemetery have the kind of energy I am looking for?

3. Does the cemetery appeal to me visually and symbolically?

4. Is the cemetery close enough to my home that I can get there easily? (If you don't have a car, this might be a big consideration.)

5. Also, is the cemetery a safe place for me to be wandering around in alone?

This last consideration is a fairly important one. Some cemeteries in big cities are ideal for finding graves with character—but they are located in such bad neighborhoods that you might be risking too much just visiting them. Some of the more isolated country graveyards may leave you open to attacks from wild animals and wandering dogs. Don't laugh. There is an absolutely wonderful cemetery only a few miles away from my home, but I refuse to go there alone or at night because the people in the neighborhood tend to let their dogs run loose. It's a rural area, so there aren't many police patrols and there really isn't anyone within earshot who'll come to my aid if Rover decides to take a chunk out of my thigh. So, unless I go with friends, that one's off the list.

Always keep safety in mind during your exercises. After all, if you can't guarantee your physical well-being, how can you even begin to work on your spiritual self?

Supplies for Your First Visit

Once you have found a cemetery that you want to work with, set aside a day to pay a formal visit to this city of the dead. Although you have likely visited this cemetery at least once before, this is going to be your official introduction to the cemetery and any spirits that reside within its walls. There are several things you will need to take with you for this formal introduction. First, you should have a camera in order to capture images of several of the most appealing graves. You will eventually keep at least one of these photos on your altar. You should also take an offering to leave at the cemetery to demonstrate both your gratitude and your respect. Because you will be working with the cemetery itself as an entity as well as with several individual graves, you should probably consider bringing a number of small items to leave as offerings. Flowers will do, as will polished stones, coins, or food.

Your offerings do not have to possess inherent monetary value. Their value will exist in the energy you invest into them. To this end, it is possible to also simply make an offering of energy to each of the graves you will be working with, but I have found that it helps on both a symbolic and a psychological level to have a physical item to give along with the offering of energy.

In addition to taking pictures, you may also want to do rubbings of the tombstones. A rubbing makes a copy of the text and images that have been scribed into the stone, and many taphophiles (cemetery lovers) collect them. A rubbing is relatively easy to make, and it

OFFERINGS TO THE DEAD

Candles: A light in the darkness and also a living flame that represents the life force. There are many traditions that involve lighting a single candle in remembrance of the dead.

Coins: The ancient Greeks believed that the dead required coins to pay for passage from the ferryman Charon, who rowed the dead across the River Styx.

Flags: In the West, national flags are typically placed upon the graves of war veterans. In the East, prayer flags may be strung near tombs to convey a blessing to the dead.

Flowers: Flowers are symbols of life and they also contain vital energy that can be harnessed by spirits. Different flowers have different traditional meanings. Lilies, for example, represent resurrection.

Food: From elaborate feasts to a simple offering of bread, cultures the world over have made food offerings to their dead.

Libations: In many folk traditions, alcoholic spirits are poured out as offerings to the dead.

Prayers: This can be something as simple as a short blessing written out on a little slip of paper. Roll it up and leave it at the tomb, or tie it with a ribbon to a nearby tree.

Further offerings, as well as recipes, appear in Appendix III.

often has more character than a simple photograph. All you need is a sheet of paper large enough to cover the area you wish to copy and a piece of artist's charcoal. If you have trouble finding artist's charcoal, you can use a crayon in a pinch. The paper ideally should be thin, like tracing paper or even onionskin. The thinner the paper, the better the impression you will get with the charcoal. You can then keep your rubbings rolled up like ancient scrolls and store them somewhere on or near your altar. A particularly attractive rubbing may become something you will want to frame and put on display.

If you are the ghost-hunting type, you may also consider bringing along a hand-held tape recorder or a little digital voice recorder. Either of these can be used to capture EVP—electronic voice phenomena. Many thinkers, from Thomas Edison onward, have suggested the possibility of recording spirit voices with modern gadgetry. Thanks to shows like SciFi's *Ghost Hunters*, a number of very convincing EVPs have been played on national television, increasing awareness of and interest in this phenomenon. Not everyone is good at getting EVPs, and it can be frustrating to listen to hours of empty background noise in order to catch the one or two words that are a legitimate EVP. But the notion that spirits can talk to us by harnessing the energy of technological devices is a compelling one. To this end, when you are taking your photographs of the cemetery, be on the look out for orbs, flares, or strange mists that weren't visible when you took the picture. While there are often perfectly ordinary explanations for photographic abnormalities, every once in a while, something is captured that no one can explain.

Working from the perspective of the Twilight Path, we are hardly hunting ghosts in search of scientific proof that they exist. We feel and hear them, and that level of personal experience is often worth more than a hundred EVPs. However, it can still be fun and spine-tingling to hear the voice of one of your spirit contacts crackling out of a recorder, or see an orb hanging in the air exactly where you felt the presence of a spirit. If this is an area that you would like to explore further, look into books like Richard Southall's *How to Be a*

Ghost Hunter as well as Loyd Auerbach's *Hauntings and Poltergeists: A Ghost-Hunter's Guide*.

Ritual Preparations

Once you have gathered all the necessary items for your visit to the cemetery, you should prepare yourself for ritual. Your formal introduction to your personal city of the dead should begin in the threshold space that you have established at your altar. As you prepare for this rite, keep in mind that you are going to leave your altar and go directly to the cemetery. To this end, carefully consider what you are going to wear. You may have very elaborate ritual attire, including a mask to help put you in the proper frame of mind. Wearing this to the cemetery may not be practical, as the cemetery is a public space. For the next few exercises, you may have to develop modified ritual attire, simply so you do not attract unwanted attention as you pursue your work in the cemetery. Even though you know that you are not intending anything illegal or destructive during your visits to the cemetery, it is important to understand that others observing you may not understand this. Always be discrete when you go to the cemetery so you do not have to engage in an uncomfortable explanation with local authorities.

When you have settled on your ritual attire, prepare yourself and approach your altar. The ritual of introduction will build upon the opening meditation that you have been performing daily, making you as receptive as possible to the energies that reside at your chosen cemetery.

Rite of Introduction

Approach the altar and cross your arms upon your chest. Light the candles of life and death and take a moment to gaze through the veil into the mirror. Dip your fingers into the chalice of water and touch them to your forehead, then your lips, and then your chest over your heart. As you do this, say the following:

> RITUALIST: I anoint my forehead, that I may open my mind to the thoughts of the dead. I anoint my lips, that I may loosen

my tongue to communicate with the dead. I anoint my chest, that I may open my heart to the needs of the dead.

Spread your arms wide and will the gate to open around you. Silently reach out to the spirits and invite them to gather. Once you feel power building and you can sense the presence of spirits as they answer your call, say:

> RITUALIST: I stand here on the threshold between darkness and light, and I open myself to the mysteries of death and transformation. Gather round, ye spirits, and let me hear you speak the sacred names. This day, I travel to the city of the dead. I ask all of you to gather round me. Become my escort as I traverse your realm.

Say the name of your chosen cemetery three times, slowly and with reverence.

> RITUALIST: This is my chosen city of the dead. In this place, I will go seeking a partner on the Otherside. All you who gather round me! Guide my choices so that I may find one who is willing to reach across the Veil and teach me the mysteries I have yet to learn.

Take a moment of silence to reflect on the qualities you seek in a guide. When you are ready, snuff the candles of life and death, then touch water to your forehead, lips, and heart once again.

> RITUALIST: I close this space, for I must depart, but I myself remain open. Spirits, attend me as I go forth! Escort me to the gates of mystery.

Leave your ritual space. Collect whatever items you have chosen to take with you, and head to the cemetery. Make certain that some token offering is among these things. Ideally, you should have one main offering for the cemetery itself and at least five smaller things, which you can leave at specific tombs.

Whether you drive or walk, it makes no difference. Try to maintain the heightened state of mind that you achieve when standing in ritual space, but do not allow yourself to be so detached from the ordinary world that this poses any danger, especially if you are driving. If you can feel the spirits hovering around you as they follow you to the cemetery gates, consider speaking casually to them, as if they were old friends. You may also want to make the entire process of travel something that is formal and ritualized, like an ancient, sacred procession or a hero's journey into the Underworld. Do what feels best so you do not lose the energy and power you felt in your private ritual space.

In your previous visit to your personal city of the dead, you explored the grounds and made note of certain areas and tombs that stood out to you. For this ritual of introduction, you are going to expand upon that, entering the cemetery and walking its grounds in a heightened and spiritually open state. When you first enter the cemetery, greet it by name, as you would an old friend. If you drove, find a convenient place to park, and then get out and walk the cemetery. If you traveled in a car, take only your main offering for the initial part of this rite. Leave everything else, including your journal, in the car. Then walk the cemetery, continuing to open yourself to your perceptions of the spirit world. It may help to hold your arms outspread as you walk slowly among the graves, visualizing tendrils of your energy extending from your arms, hands, and fingers and sweeping down into the earth. Expand your inner vision so that you see not only the graves that lie atop the ground, but also the caskets and bones that huddle in the earth below. Pause in your explorations to close your eyes and feel this deeply: the impressions both above and below in this sacred city of the dead.

Cover as much of the cemetery on foot as possible. As you explore, your ultimate goal is to locate the heart of the cemetery. This is the very center of the sacred space, a sort of well of energy from which everything else extends. The heart of the cemetery may be immediately identifiable. Some cemeteries have a central area with a prominent statue or mausoleum situated more or less over their heart. Others have centers that are harder to identify. All of this will depend upon the nature and layout of your particular cemetery.

Once you have found the heart of the cemetery, bow your head and take a moment of silence to reach out as completely as you are able to the presence—sentient or otherwise—that resides within this heart. If you are having trouble sensing or connecting, try whispering the name of the cemetery over and over again, under your breath. When you feel that some sort of contact has been established, take out the offering you have prepared and hold it up along with a gift of your energy to the cemetery.

> RITUALIST: I greet you, [name of the cemetery]. I have come to these grounds seeking revelation and wisdom. I ask that you open yourself to me, that I might speak with the dead while safe within your arms.

Hold the offering in your hands, and hold your hands close to your chest, just above your center. Gather energy and channel this into the offering. Call to mind the emotions of love and respect as well as your desire to learn the lessons this place is willing to teach you. Pass these emotions into the energy as you are charging the offering. When you are satisfied with the offering, set it down, either at the foot of the central monument, or some other safe place, such as at the foot of a shrub or tree.

> RITUALIST: I offer my reverence, my dedication, and my desire to learn. Please accept this gift and welcome me into your city of the dead. May your pathways be known to me, that I might find the places of power that you protect. May your spirits reach out to me, that I might discover a guide willing to lead me safely through the realm of the dead.

Kneel before the offering, opening yourself to the whispers of the spirits. Cross your arms upon your chest and close your eyes for a few moments, listening intently with all your subtle senses until you feel that your offering has been accepted. When you feel that sense of acceptance, be certain to voice your gratitude.

> RITUALIST: I thank you for accepting my offering. Please continue to watch over me as I explore the mysteries waiting here.

Rise from the ground and return to your car for your other things if you drove. Do not drop out of the ritual frame of mind, but allow yourself to be a little more grounded. Continue your exploration of the cemetery, but now expand your search beyond just the cemetery's heart. You are seeking graves that call to you. You may have encountered some of these in your very first visit to the cemetery. If you must, consult your journal as to their locations, then seek out these spirited graves. From the potently open and receptive frame of mind generated by the ritual, extend your perceptions to these special graves. As you made contact with the spirit of the cemetery, try to make contact with the spirits of the individual graves themselves. Read the names on their headstones. Whisper them or speak them out loud if that seems to help. Explain to them your intentions and invite them to convey any messages of their own. Finally, make note of any graves that seem especially responsive. If you feel a strong connection to one or more of these graves, leave a small offering at the foot of the headstone, imbuing the offering with a portion of your vital energy as you do so.

As you explore, take notes in your journal. Write down the names and locations of at least five graves that really stand out to you. Take photos or do rubbings, so you can take a little something of these graves home with you. For this stage of exploration, all you are doing is allowing the cemetery and its inhabitants to speak to you. Immerse yourself in the energies of this city of the dead and try to discover the best way of making yourself receptive to those energies.

When you feel that you are finished, return to the central location where you made your initial offering. If you have dropped a little too far out of sacred space internally, take a few moments to re-center yourself and regain your ritual frame of mind. Cup your hands over your center and gather energy, then approach the place of offering with your arms outstretched, energy trailing from your hands. Once again, address the cemetery itself as an entity, imagining it as both a person and a place. After all of your explorations, you probably now have a much clearer image of its personality and character.

The Manifesta-
tion of Spirits

Spirits manifest themselves to us in many ways, most of them so subtle that they are easily overlooked. Below are a few signs to look for that may indicate an attempt at spirit communication.

- An inexplicable drop in temperature
- A sudden, eerie silence
- A draft, wind, or breeze that suddenly kicks up, seeming to come from nowhere
- An unexplained buzzing in your ears
- The sense of whispered voices in the back of your mind
- A sudden flash of images that seem separate and distinct from your own thoughts
- The sensation of a ghostly touch
- Tingling or vibrating in your arms, hands, face, or limbs
- A shimmering gray spot that appears in your vision or just out of the corner of your eye
- Electrical disturbances, equipment failures, or a sudden drain in batteries
- Knockings, rappings, or other noises from an indeterminate source
- One or more small objects seeming to move by themselves

RITUALIST: [Name of the cemetery], I thank you. You have opened your arms to me and guided me toward revelation. I offer you my gratitude. I must depart now, but I ask that you allow me to return to you so I may explore your mysteries once again.

Cup your hands and gather energy to make another offering. Allow this additional offering to flow like water into the item you first placed on the ground. Now address the spirits—not just those that you have discovered through your exploration of the cemetery, but also those that followed you from your threshold space to this city of the dead.

RITUALIST: Spirits, companions, all you who linger on the Otherside! I thank you for your patience in attending me. Your guidance has been appreciated. I must depart now, and leave the city of the dead for the realm of the living. As I leave, you are welcome to attend me, but I will understand if you must remain here among your kind. Until we meet again.

Bow or incline your head to the spirits. Then once again touch your forehead, lips, and heart.

RITUALIST: The door is closed, but I carry it within. If a lesson presents itself to me, may it open again, so I may see, and, seeing, learn.

Gather your things about you and depart. Complete the circle created by this ritual introduction by driving (or walking) home and sitting down for a few moments in front of your altar. As you sit at your altar, contemplate your experiences at the cemetery. You may even wish to read back over the notes you took in your journal. When you are finished, cross your arms upon your chest and bow to your image in the veiled mirror. Then you should remove yourself from the ritual frame of mind and return to your ordinary routine.

JOURNAL EXERCISE: CEMETERY THOUGHTS

1. What led you to choose this particular cemetery? What aspect of the cemetery appeals to you the most?

2. Do you have any favorite graves in the cemetery? Take a moment to record your impressions of at least five graves, noting the names and birth and death dates here. Why do these stand out to you? Do you think you're attracted by something other than aesthetic appeal? What is your reasoning for this?

3. If you were encountered by another person while you worked in your cemetery, what would you do? If they asked you to explain your activities, what would you say? How do you think the average person would respond to your words? What does this teach you about the need for discretion?

4. When you did your first walk-through of the cemetery, were you surprised by any of the impressions you got? Were you expecting something different? What led to these expectations?

5. Think about how your cemetery looks and feels to you. What does it inspire in you? Now take a moment to write at least twenty words that can be used to describe your cemetery. Once you are finished, look back over these words. What descriptors stand out to you as especially important? Is there an overall theme to the words you have chosen? What does this say about you and your relation to your cemetery?

6. Try to visualize the spirit of your cemetery. What are your perceptions of this spirit? What is its personality like? Does it seem male or female—or is it gender-neutral? How do you think you can expect this spirit to behave? Take some time to describe in detail your impressions of the spirit of your cemetery.

7. How could you best relate to the spirit of your cemetery? If you were able to meet with this spirit at a coffeehouse and have an ordinary conversation, what would you say? What do you think the spirit would have to say to you? Do you think you would be friends after several such conversations? Consider conversing casually with the cemetery every time you visit it, even if you do not clearly perceive a response. How does this change the way the cemetery feels to you?

continued on page 184

DEATH AS STRUGGLE

We return to our personal city of the dead. A scrim of snow and ice covers the ground, crackling underfoot. A severe wind sweeps down from the north, driving speckles of ice against every portion of exposed flesh. The cold of the wind bites to the bone. Undaunted, we plunge forward until we come to a striking monument. Larger than life, this masterwork in marble crouches upon a family tomb, wrapped in draperies that completely obscure its intended sex.

The weathering of this sculpture has lent portions of it an almost fractured appearance, like the crackleur effect on certain paintings. This crackled effect only serves to heighten the inherent tension of the sculpture. The figure, whose ambiguous features could belong to a woman just as easily as to a man, leans forward, clutching its head in profound thought. Its neck seems bent beneath the weight of the entire world.

In this statue, we encounter a figure who seems deeply troubled. Anxiety, not sorrow, is the most significant emotion carved into its features or the lines of its limbs. Here we see death as a struggle—possibly for the deceased him- or herself, but certainly for the friends and family left behind. The process of dying is hard on everyone, especially if death is the result of a long illness or extensive old age. This statue eloquently captures the struggle one must endure, the nagging questions that plague us as the end approaches. Is life really worth all the heartache and pain? Do the joys and accomplishments balance out against this kind of suffering? Why are we born if it is our ultimate destiny to die?

Consider the problems that seem to weigh on the heart of this figure. Do any of these questions carry a similar weight for you? Knowing all that you have learned through your work thus far, is the struggle of life and death worth it in the end? Record your thoughts in your journal and prepare to move on.

continued from page 181

8. If you had the ability to set up an altar in your cemetery, where would you choose to do so? Why would you choose this particular portion of the cemetery for your personal sacred space? How would you change or decorate this area to make it more appealing and/or inspiring to you? How do you think the spirit of the cemetery would react to these changes?

Back to Life

The purpose of this chapter is to establish a rapport with a particular cemetery. The cemetery will become an external embodiment of the threshold state you have been cultivating in your life through the meditations and rituals performed at your home altar. Your home altar integrates the threshold state into your personal space, but it may become so familiar that the sense of traveling from one realm of being to the next is lost or blurred. Your visits to the cemetery, because they involve physical travel, can also help to remind you that you are undertaking a journey to the land of the dead.

But what about the land of the living? We live in this world every day, and again, because of familiarity, the significance of our environment can become lost. After you have finished the cemetery work in this chapter, take a few moments to consider locations that you have access to which, to you, embody the realm of the living. Where can you go to immerse yourself in humanity and watch adults conversing or children at play? Pick a location where you know you will be surrounded by living people just as, in the cemetery, you are surrounded by the dead. This may be a shopping mall, a coffeehouse, or a public park. Take an afternoon to visit this location and people-watch. Observe the living and try to connect a little bit to their lives. What do they talk about? What makes them happy or sad? What things can you learn about them as you observe this tiny fragment of their lives? Record your experience in your journal, and focus especially on the contrast in the energy you feel immersed in this place of the living, as opposed to the energy of your city of the dead.

13.

A NECROMANTIC
MEDICINE BAG

While you are at the cemetery immersing yourself in the energies of death,
it may be very tempting to bring home a
souvenir. As much as you may want this,
you should never take anything from the
memorials themselves. Not only would you
be stealing valuable items intended to honor
the memory of the dead, but you would also
be committing an act of supreme disrespect
for the departed spirits. Still, it is very helpful to have some physical object that resonates with the energy of your particular
cemetery. Being able to carry such an object
on your person allows you to connect to
those energies even when you are far from
the cemetery itself.

In the Native American culture, individuals in some tribes would collect objects

of power and store these in a personal medicine pouch. A person could spend years collecting items to add to the pouch, and each item held special significance for the person to whom the pouch belonged. In addition to the symbolism inherent in many of the items, there was power in the act of gathering the items themselves, and sometimes the gathering process was approached as a spiritual quest. The seeker would put a prayer out to the world when he or she was seeking an object of power to add to the pouch. Objects found under unusual circumstances were often interpreted as gifts from the spirit-world given in response to such prayers. In Native American cultures, the objects collected in a medicine bag were symbolic of the beliefs of each particular individual as well as each tribe. For our necromantic medicine pouch, we are going to draw upon a rich cross-cultural history of items and images, all of which will allow us to connect more completely with the energies of death.

Crafting the Token

Start with a small cloth or leather pouch. You can purchase something appropriate or, if you are feeling exceptionally crafty, you can sew the pouch yourself. The pouch does not have to be large—something that is two or three inches in width and length will suffice. The pouch should have a cord or a place to attach a cord so you can wear it around your neck. It can be any color that most appeals to you, but you will probably achieve the best results if the color is in some way representative of the energies you seek to invoke. Given traditional Western associations with the color, black is then a good choice for the color of this pouch. If your associations are more Asian, the traditional color of death is white. While for many the color green is a symbol of life and growth, green is strongly connected to death and the otherworldly in portions of the British Isles. You may also choose brown, to represent the earth to which we all return, or red, the color associated with blood.

Once you have chosen or crafted your pouch, you are ready to consecrate it. Place the new pouch upon your altar overnight. Before you place the token upon your altar, hold it in your hands and contemplate your purpose. Think about what you want to achieve with the pouch, and imbue this intent into the material. If you are working with a deity or with a guiding spirit, you should ask this being to help you charge the pouch with the appropriate energy.

When you are ready, pay a visit to your cemetery. Take your pouch along. You may also want to bring a small pocket knife or other tool along to help you extract a small portion of dirt from the ground. Hold the empty pouch in your hand as you walk among the stones. Reach out and feel the energy of the cemetery as it stretches all around you. Allow your sense of this energy to guide you to the proper spot. This may be a grave, or it may simply be an area near the foot of the tree.

Now, take out the pouch or small velvet bag. With the pocket knife, or even just with your fingers, dig up a small portion of dirt. You do not need much, and you should be careful not to deface the grass in the cemetery in any significant way. If you have been drawn to a tombstone, you may be able to gather a few shards of stone that have crumbled away at the base. A smooth stone or pebble caught in the roots of the grass will suffice as well. Place anything that you gather immediately into the little pouch. Make an offering of vital energy in exchange for this gift. You may find it tempting to take more than just a token amount of soil, but please try to exercise restraint. You do not want to deface the grave by leaving bare spots in the grass, and groundskeepers may see extensive digging as vandalism. Exercise common sense in how you gather this token amount, and if you have to lift up a small patch of grass, be certain to do so carefully, and to pat it back down when you're done.

The cemetery has more than just graveyard dust to be gathered as part of this token. Most cemeteries have huge, stately trees planted over burial plots as a symbol of new life growing out of death. These trees get their nourishment from the earth of the cemetery but also from the corpses that rest within that earth. Every twig, branch, and leaf is therefore imbued with the energies of death. By taking a leaf from such a tree, you can carry some of that potent energy with you. Consider also the many plants that are growing in your cemetery.

Often, groundskeepers plant flowers that have a special significance in relation to death. Sometimes, flowers are simply planted for their aesthetic appeal. Take a little time to study the things growing in your cemetery. Gather a small portion, like a petal or a leaf, from one or two plants that really stand out to you. You may want to dry these out on your altar before adding them to your medicine bag.

When you have collected some power items from your cemetery, take a moment to thank the cemetery and everything that resides there for sharing some of its power with you. When you go home, place the partially full medicine pouch on your altar again. You may not feel content with just dirt and stones and twigs, so you may wish to add other items that represent the energies of death. From ancient Greek times until fairly recently, it was customary to place two coins upon the eyes of the deceased. From a practical perspective, the coins served the purpose of weighting down the eyelids so mourners did not have to face the cold stare of their departed loved one. On a more mythic note, the ancient Greeks believed that these coins would later be used to pay the toll of the eternal ferryman, Charon.

You can evoke the sentiments of this ancient practice by adding a penny to your medicine pouch. Pennies are the best American coin for this purpose because they are made at least partly of copper (a good conductor of energy), and their color is reminiscent of blood. In addition, in Great Britain, large copper halfpence were often the coins of choice for covering the eyes, and pennies are the closest American equivalent to these coins. Ideally, you want a penny that was minted before you were born, both to evoke the power of antiquity and to remind yourself of the brevity of your life.

If you find yourself drawn to Egyptian iconography, you may wish to consider placing a small scarab in your medicine pouch. The ancient Egyptians associated scarab beetles with the process of death and rebirth, identifying the scarab with Khepra, one of the forms of the sun god. Large, elaborate scarabs were often buried with the ancient Egyptian dead, wrapped up among the many layers of linen bandages that encase the mummy. Scarabs often had prayers inscribed upon them, and, as we saw in an earlier chapter, the large heart scarab could be used by the deceased in the hall of judgment in place of his or her own heart. Smaller scarabs, scribed with prayers and coated a vivid blue, were thrown after the corpse in blessing as it was led into the tomb. Reproductions of the smaller, blue scarabs can be found in many New Age shops or even beading stores.

If you're planning on looking through a beading store in search of scarabs, you may also want to keep an eye out for other appropriate beads. There is a type of Hindu rosary that is traditionally crafted of bone. It has 106 beads, each carved into the shape of a human skull. Each of them represents one of the 106 names of God. Much like scarabs, these beads are often imported into the West, and they can be found in jewelry, occult, and even craft stores.

Many stores will also have small images cast in pewter or carved in stone. Occasionally, these images include skulls, crosses, or even coffins. All are appropriate for your personal medicine bag. Gemstones or herbs are another fine addition. For herbs, cypress, yew, and willow are all associated with graveyards or death. A small, polished

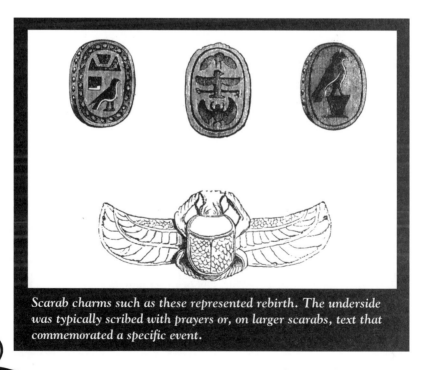

Scarab charms such as these represented rebirth. The underside was typically scribed with prayers or, on larger scarabs, text that commemorated a specific event.

garnet could be used to represent a drop of blood, while any black stone, such as onyx or obsidian, could be used to represent the dark mystery of death.

Make your medicine pouch personal by collecting the items that seem most right and most powerful to you. When everything is finished, set the pouch on your altar overnight again. As night falls the next day, consecrate the pouch as your personal token of the cemetery and the energies it represents. You can use the following ritual as an example or create a ritual of your own.

Consecration of the Token

The altar is set with the representations of the elements. The incense should be burning before the start of the ritual. The two candles of life and death, one black and one white, stand on either side of the altar. These are unlit, but matches or a lighter should be nearby. The mirror is veiled, and the medicine pouch or token occupies a central position on the altar. The Ritualist may be naked or clothed. This ritual can be performed alone or with others as witnesses.

> RITUALIST: I stand before my altar as night settles upon the world. Now is the time of thresholds as darkness swallows the light. I invoke that threshold, where the many realms converge. May my sacred space hang between the living and the dead, and may I walk now balanced between the darkness and the light.

Light the candle of life and the candle of death as a sign of establishing sacred space.

> RITUALIST: I stand here on the threshold, and I call upon the power that hovers between the darkness and the light. Spirits, I call thee! Gather round this sacred altar and bear witness to my rite!

Cup the token in both hands and gather energy, directing it into the token.

> RITUALIST: I invoke the sacred energy of [cemetery name], my personal city of the dead. Day and night I walk its paths,

seeking the mystery that lies beyond life. I seek now to carry some of that mystery with me, so I may ever be connected to both life and death.

Hold up the token and present it to your reflection in the veiled mirror. Speak the name of your cemetery three times.

RITUALIST: Across the Veil I call to you. My words resound for both the living and the dead. We have stood, spirit to spirit, flesh to flesh, in the space beyond, between, within. You are my gateway to the Underworld journey. You are my door to the realms of the dead. May this token remind me of that threshold, representing the bridge between the living and the dead.

Sprinkle a pinch of the element of earth over the token, thus consecrating it to earth.

RITUALIST: With the element of earth, the ashes to which we all return, I do consecrate thee.

Dip your fingers into the chalice of water and sprinkle some of this over the token, thus consecrating it to water.

RITUALIST: With the element of water, my blood and my tears, I do consecrate thee.

Pass the token through the flames of first the candle of life and then the candle of death. Allow the flames to gently kiss the item, but do not allow the token to burn.

RITUALIST: With the element of fire, which has the power to shine and to consume, I do consecrate thee.

Pass the token through the smoke of the incense, thus consecrating it to air.

RITUALIST: With the element of air, the breath of my lungs, I do consecrate thee.

Now cup the token once more in both hands and focus energy into the item. Bring the token up to your heart, filling it with an offering of life energy.

> RITUALIST: And with the element of spirit, my very life itself, I pass life into death and I do consecrate thee.

Take a moment of silence to focus all of these energies and blessings into the token. Then kiss the item and place it around your neck. Gaze once more into the veiled mirror and address both your shadow-self and the spirits who have gathered to attend this rite.

> RITUALIST: I wear this token as a bridge between the living and the dead. In every place that I walk, may I walk in both worlds at once. I ask you spirits to bear witness. Thus do I consecrate our bond and commit myself to this path!

Bow your head and take a moment of silence, thanking the spirits and other powers for witnessing your rite. Then begin the process of closing the sacred space.

> RITUALIST: I pass now from the threshold, to walk again in life. I thank you, spirits, for attending. You are welcome to remain or to depart. For now, I close this sacred space, but carry it forever in my heart.

Blow out the candles as the final sign that the ritual has ended. Gaze one last time into the veiled mirror, then return to your ordinary affairs.

Try to wear the token at all times after this, and be certain that you wear it when you visit the cemetery, so you can periodically refresh the charge. When you are not wearing the token, keep it on your altar with your other consecrated tools.

A Shade Beyond Real

When you do your daily meditation, add a new step. Immediately after opening yourself, clench your hand around the medicine bag and focus power into this token that bridges you constantly with the realm of the dead. Speak the name of the cemetery that this token represents. If you do not like the name of the cemetery, or if you feel as if its name simply does not adequately reflect its essential being, give it a new name. Ask the spirit of the cemetery itself what it wants to be called, or formulate a name that speaks deeply to you of everything that place represents.

Begin to think of your city of the dead as both a real place and as a place that exists on a different level, in visions and in dreams. Make the cemetery real in your sacred space so that you can close your eyes and walk its grassy paths regardless of where you actually are. Whenever you stand at your home altar doing deathwork, touch the token and call to mind a clear image of the cemetery. Project that image of the cemetery onto the threshold space between the candles of life and death. Integrate these two thresholds so that, even at your home altar, their energies are intertwined. Practice holding this connection in your mind, so that when you stand before your altar, you can also clearly call to mind all of the feelings and impressions that you experience when you walk through your city of the dead. Make the circle complete by also calling to mind your altar space whenever you stand at the heart of the cemetery. Whenever you choose to walk its paths in waking reality, maintain a mental connection with the threshold in your home. They both represent the same door, and that door it not limited to just one physical place.

Allow this integrative work to extend into dreams, so that this threshold space gains an even greater reality for you. Place the token beneath your pillow while you sleep, and try to walk the pathways of the cemetery in dreams. Invite the spirits that have made contact with you to join you in this space, and record what you remember of your nightly interactions with these denizens of the Otherside.

JOURNAL EXERCISE: THE POWER INSIDE

1. In addition to dirt from your cemetery, what did you choose to put inside the medicine bag? Make a list of these objects and explain your reasoning for each.

continued on page 196

the
personification
of death

We return to our cemetery, this time as dusk settles over the land. The trees are stripped bare, and even the wind lies hushed. As we let our feet lead us through the solemn stones, we become aware of an overshadowing figure. We look up and see this angel. By his trump, we know it to be Gabriel, who calls the dead home. The carven statue is poised high atop an obelisk, distant and alone. With the fading light of day behind him, he is mostly a silhouette, his features obscured in shadow. We can barely make out the sculpted folds of his robe.

Gabriel, as the angel of the Last Trump, is an angel of death. In Christian myth, it is his responsibility to wake the dead and bring them to their final judgment. Although other angels are attributed with the power and responsibility for claiming human lives, Gabriel is the angel that all the dead will eventually see. Here in this statue, backlit with restless clouds, he appears as Death personified.

Beautiful and terrible, the angel is a being beyond mere mortal understanding. He takes no pleasure in his work, but neither does he regret it. He is the inexorable servant of powers greater than himself. As you stare into the distance, searching for the eyes of this towering statue, consider the possibility of Death given form. If Death had a shape, what would he—or she—look like? How would such a being act and feel?

Imagine that you are standing in front of the personification of Death. Study the form this being takes for you. Talk to Death. Ask it (or him, or her, or them) what you need to know. Record your experiences in your journal, and prepare to continue along the Twilight Path.

continued from page 193

2. What material did you ultimately use to hold this collection of objects? When you first considered crafting this bag, was color, texture, or shape important to you? Explain why you chose the container that you did.

3. As you charged the medicine bag at your altar, did you have any unusual perceptions? When you hold the bag in your hand now, does it feel different from the way it felt when you first crafted it? Can you explain this difference?

4. As you continue to wear the medicine bag and work with it in your daily exercises, have you noticed any change in its energy? What impact do you think your daily work is having upon the bag and its contents?

5. If you have a friend who is psychic or who practices some type of magick, ask this friend for his or her impressions of the object you have crafted. Do not immediately tell this friend what you have crafted the item for. Wait to hear what he or she picks up from the object itself. Ask your friend how strong the impressions are. If your friend cannot pick up anything useful from the item, explain why you think this may be. What could you do differently to increase the potency of the energy imbued into this object?

6. As you wear the medicine bag throughout your day, are there times when you become more aware of its presence than others? What is going on around you at these times? How does your awareness of the item manifest itself? When you go to visit your cemetery or approach your altar for deathwork, do you feel any change in the energy of this item? Explain what you feel and offer some ideas as to why these changes do or do not occur.

7. If you sense a growing power from this item, where do you think the power is coming from? Is the strength coming from the dirt and other items collected within the bag, or is the strength coming from you? Explain your answer.

14.

LIFE AMONG
THE DEAD

You have made an initial introduction to your cemetery and you have crafted a token that helps tie you to this space, bridging the gap between your home altar and your personal city of the dead. You have continued work at your home altar, integrating the growing connection you have with the city of the dead and all the spirits that reside there with the threshold space erected in earlier chapters. Now it is time to make more direct contact with the individual spirits of your cemetery, inviting them to communicate and to join you in your continuing explorations of the Twilight Path.

Around the beginning of April, the Chinese celebrate the Qingming Festival. This is known variously as the Pure Brightness Festival or as Tomb Sweeping Day. According to legend, this holiday was founded by a feudal lord from the Spring and Autumn Period (770–476 BCE) to commemorate the sacrifices of a loyal subject, Jie Zitui. The festival combines the solemn remembrance of the dead with whimsical, happy pursuits such as flying kites or riding on swings. In the past, people also wore willow branches on their heads as, in the legend, willows were found growing where Jie Zitui had died.

For Qingming, families take spring outings and go to the graves of relatives. They sweep away last year's leaves and enjoy a pleasant meal at the graveside. To most Westerners, the idea of remembering the dead with such frivolous activities as flying kites might seem strange, but Qingming is about both sorrow and joy, reminding us that, even in the face of death, life must go on.

Tomb Sweeping Day

To build a better rapport with your cemetery, you should take an afternoon out of your schedule to go visit your favorite graves. These are the graves that stood out to you in the previous exercise, the ones that seemed to make contact when you attempted to communicate.

Plan to be at your cemetery for at least two hours. In reality, this visit will probably last longer, so be certain that you know when the cemetery closes. You don't want your visit to be unexpectedly cut short.

In the tradition of Qingming, make this a pleasant outing. Pack a light picnic lunch for yourself. Bring an extra plate and a little more of each food than you think you will eat. You may also want to bring a small broom or cloth to help in the task of cleaning off the graves.

Consider bringing a book to read as you lounge on the cemetery grass. There is a great deal of poetry that contemplates the beauty of life and its relationship with death, and many of these poems can help induce a thoughtful, mystical, and receptive frame of mind. Music would also be nice. Because you will be visiting your favorite graves and sweeping them clean, you may also consider bringing enough small tokens—such as polished stones, flowers, or coins—to leave at the base of each of the graves.

ΤΗΕ GRΑVEYARD POETS

Both the brevity and beauty of life have been subjects explored by poets throughout the ages. Many poets also have had a marked fascination with death. Here is just a short list of poets whose work explores the passage of life into the next world.

Percy Bysshe Shelley:
"Music, When Soft Voices Die," 1824
(published posthumously)

Edgar Allan Poe: "Annabel Lee," 1849
(last complete poem by Poe before his death)

Lord Byron: "Darkness," 1816

Dylan Thomas:
"Do Not Go Gentle into that Good Night," 1951,
"Death Shall Have No Dominion," 1936

William Cullen Bryant: "Thanatopsis," 1817

Thomas Gray:
"Elegy Written in a Country Churchyard," 1751

Sylvia Plath: "November Graveyard," 1956,
"The Ghost's Leavetaking," 1958

Charles Baudelaire: "The Death of Lovers," 1857

Rainer Maria Rilke: "Duino Elegies," 1912–1922,
"Sonnets to Orpheus," 1922

Algernon Charles Swinburne:
"A Forsaken Garden," 1878

Although you should approach the cemetery with reverence, try to also maintain a casual sense during this outing. Greet and speak with the spirit of the cemetery. Talk with the residents of your favorite graves. Visit each grave in turn, greeting the resident by name. As an offering, clean off these graves, sweeping away any leaves or grass cuttings or washing away stray bird droppings. Leave a further offering of energy, focusing this into a small stone, coin, or other item you have brought along.

Spend some time just walking around the cemetery before you settle down to your meal. Make a point of enjoying this walk and exploring all the sights your cemetery has to offer. What kind of trees are in your cemetery? Do the groundskeepers plant flowers every year? What offerings have been left recently by family members at the newer graves? Approach your walk through the cemetery as you would a walk through a beautiful park, but remember to pay attention to your deeper insights as well. If you feel pulled to a certain place, then go there. If you feel as if someone is trying to communicate with

View of graves from Woodlawn Cemetery in the Bronx, New York.

you, take a moment to listen. Make note of these experiences and record them later in your journal.

When you have visited all of your favorite graves and spent a little time with each of them individually, find a nice, scenic spot in the cemetery for your picnic lunch. Spread out a cloth or just sit down in the lush grass and enjoy the meal you brought with you. Set a small portion of each type of food aside on the extra plate you brought. Set this on the grass across from you as if you were waiting for a friend to join you at this meal. This is your food offering to the dead as well as to the cemetery itself.

When you are finished with your meal, take this food offering and place it neatly at the base of a shrub or tree. Ideally, this should be somewhere near where you made your first offering to the cemetery at the very heart of the place's energy. Be certain to pack up any wrappers or other trash created by this meal. It would be supremely disrespectful to litter in your cemetery.

When you are finished, take a moment to walk to the heart of the cemetery and greet the spirit of your city of the dead. Thank the cemetery and bid it goodbye with the following words:

> RITUALIST: [Name of the cemetery], I thank you. You have opened your arms to me and guided me toward revelation. I offer you my gratitude. I must depart now, but I ask that you allow me to return to you so I may explore your mysteries once again.

Return home and record your impressions about this experience.

The Echoes of Lives

Allow a few days to pass between your visits to the cemetery. In the interim, continue your daily meditations at your home altar. When time and the weather permit, plan another outing to your cemetery. This time, you are going to focus expressly on the graves that stood out to you in the last few exercises. You will need to bring a camera or materials to perform a rubbing as well as several small items to leave as offerings.

For this exercise, you are going to take a few moments to speak to the residents of these graves, asking them to rouse from their slumber and forge a bond with you. As a general rule, most spirits do not linger around the remains of their bodies, but this does not mean that they have no connection to those bodies at all. Cemeteries can be haunted places simply because they are where the living go to commune with the dead. Consider all of the energy that is put into a memorial, all of the emotion—both sorrow and love—left by family members who visit a grave. These things build up, drawing a spirit back to his or her grave. Given that spirits are not bound to their earthly remains, the cemetery is hardly the only place a spirit will walk. But they can be called here, and if there is even a lingering echo of the person who occupies a particular tomb, you can summon that energy and get a sense of who they were and what they meant to the people who came to mourn them.

The following is a short rite intended to pull a spirit's attention back to the place of his or her interment. If any of the graves in your personal city of the dead have stood out to you, chances are they contain some lingering energy that ultimately connects to the person who is buried there. With this rite, you are connecting with that energy and following it, allowing it to lead you to the intelligence that is the source of that energy. You are not binding these spirits, nor are you strictly summoning them. Rather, you are inviting them to pay attention, and you are seeking to initiate a relationship you can build upon in the future. Once you have whispered to them and made your offering, they may remain to hover round you, but they are also free to go.

Wake the Dead

Approach the grave with reverence. Cross your arms upon your chest and kneel down at the base of the headstone. Close your eyes and gather energy internally, bringing yourself into that heightened, ritual frame of mind. When you feel power gathered at your center, cup your hands over your heart and make an offering of vital energy. Present this to the stone. As you do so, speak the name as it appears on

GRAVEYARDS AND HAUNTINGS

Graveyards may be devoted to the dead, but that does not mean that every person buried there lingers near their grave as a spirit. Many ghost-hunters will insist that ghosts are more likely to be found near the places and people that were dear to them in life. They argue that the spirits are not so concerned about their mortal remains that they perpetually hover around their bodies. Nevertheless, some cemeteries are quite haunted. Sometimes the dead are attached to their bodies

In the ancient Greek and Roman worlds, a great deal of importance was placed upon the proper burial of the dead. If someone died and their corpse did not receive proper burial, that person then became a restless spirit. The spirit would haunt the place where the forgotten bones resided, importuning travelers to find the body and give it a proper burial. If a corpse were mutilated after death (instead of being accorded proper respect), this would also result in a haunting. Several ancient peoples, including the Greeks, believed that the spirit of the deceased would exhibit the same injuries done to the body in the afterlife. This is why the Trojans were horrified when Achilles dragged the body of their hero Hector behind his chariot in Homer's *Illiad*, and why Agamemnon's death at the hands of his wife, Clytemnestra, was such a terrible tragedy. Clytemnestra, in her rage, was said to have cut off Agamemnon's nose and ears in order to mutilate the Mycenaean king in the afterlife.

the stone three times. Speak with authority, but do not attempt to command the spirit of the grave. Your goal is not to issue orders or demands but to offer a friendly invitation. After speaking the name out loud three times, whisper the following in a compelling voice:

> RITUALIST: [Name], born [date on stone], died [date on stone], I call to you! Though your flesh has fallen since to dust, though your soul has crossed to better things, return to this world you left behind.

Stretch your hand out and touch the stone. Using the stone as a focus, feel the energy that lingers at this grave. Close your eyes and reach out along this energy, following it as if it were a pathway leading you to the person here interred. Will yourself to reach this person and make contact.

> RITUALIST: [Name], awaken and attend! I offer companionship and care, and I offer a portion of my own vital force. [Name], hear me and awaken! Come to me. Come to me. Come to me.

Cross your hands once more upon your chest. Bow your head, close your eyes, and listen. Spirits rarely communicate as obviously as they do in the movies, and each person's perception of spirit communication manifests in different ways. At this point in your studies, you should be aware of the subtle signs indicating that a spirit has answered your call. Focus all of your attention on listening with every psychic sense you possess for the presence of this spirit and any message it may have to convey.

Not every spirit will answer. This is fine. Your goal is not to compel, but to invite a willing participant to join you in your exploration of the boundaries between life and death. Give the spirit some time to respond. Even if you feel no response whatsoever, take a moment to thank the resident of the grave before getting up and moving on. If you have brought a token of remembrance, take this opportunity to leave it at the base of the grave, along with a small offering of vital energy.

You will repeat this process at each of the graves you have selected. It is a good idea to pause between graves, and you can take this opportunity to record your impressions in your journal. List the name and dates of each grave that you visit during the ritual, and make note of the spirits that seem coherent and eager to respond. Put a star next to the entries where you feel the response was the strongest.

Once you have visited all of the graves on your list, take a few moments to go over your notes. As you look back over the list of graves you called to awaken, briefly answer each of the following questions:

1. Which of the graves seemed to respond to your call to awaken?
2. What were your impressions of the spirits that responded to your call?
3. What emotions did your contact with these spirits inspire?
4. Did one of the graves feel more "right" than the others?
5. Weigh your impressions and reactions to the spirits that you called to awaken. Now choose one of these spirits to become your Companion on the Otherside.

When you have made your decision, prepare yourself to return to that grave. As you approach the grave, greet the resident, speaking his or her name out loud. Kneel before the headstone and thank the resident for his or her response to your call. Close your eyes and gather power at your center, summoning a ritual frame of mind. Then lie down atop the grave, placing your head at the base of the headstone and stretching out so that your body mirrors the body of the person lying six feet beneath the ground. Fold your hands upon your chest in the aspect of the dead and close your eyes. You may wish to place coins over your eyes to further heighten your identification with a corpse. This will have the added effect of helping to block the sun from your eyes, should you be sensitive to the light.

As you lie atop the grave, open yourself up to the psychic impressions of the world around you. Feel the grass beneath you, and the cool earth beneath the grass. Extend your perceptions into the earth, reaching down and down until you can feel the coffin six feet below. Reach out and feel the bones of your companion slumbering deep within the grave. Connect with these physical remains as completely as possible, all the while lying like a corpse yourself upon the grave. Whisper, think, or speak aloud the following lines:

RITUALIST: I lie here, full-length upon the grave, mirroring your bones with my living flesh. I call to you, [name of deceased], I reach out across the Veil. Become my Companion on the Otherside. Complete this bond, spirit to spirit, flesh to flesh.

Continue to reach down with your subtle senses, connecting mentally, emotionally, and spiritually with the resident of the grave. Allow every aspect of your own body to grow still and open yourself to this bond across the Veil. You may experience a series of images as you do this. The connection may also manifest in a sudden rush of complex emotions or even an internal sense of music or words. Allow these things to come and immerse yourself in the experience.

In your mind, imagine that you stand before the resident of the grave. Your Companion across the Veil is nothing but naked bones. You are a being of flesh. You are surrounded by swirling darkness, and you each stand on one side of a gate. This is another version of the gate you have erected in your ritual space. As one, you and your Companion reach out across the gate, joining hands to bridge the gap between the world of the living and that of the dead. See this image clearly in your mind as you stretch atop the grave, and make the event real within your internal world.

Once contact has been made, release your Companion to return to his or her side of the Veil, whispering your thanks. Take a few moments to come back to yourself, and then slowly begin to stretch life back into your arms and legs. Remove the coins from your eyes and sit up, then turn to the gravestone. Run your fingers over the etched letters of your Companion's name. Whisper the name once more, holding it close to your heart.

Finally, if you have brought a camera, take a picture of the headstone. Alternately, you can make a rubbing of the stone. If neither of these options is open to you, carefully copy all of the writing that appears on the stone into your journal, if you haven't already done so.

When you are finished at your Companion's grave, walk to the heart of the cemetery and thank all the spirits there for accepting you and helping you along your journey. Then pack up your things and head home.

Bridging Back Home

If you took a photo of your Companion's grave, place a copy of this on your altar as soon as you can. If you do not have a visual representation of your Companion's grave, such as a rubbing or a photo, craft a representation. On a slip of parchment or a piece of cardstock, write out your Companion's name. Beneath the name, write out the

Morning mist in Woodlawn Cemetery, the Bronx, New York.

dates of birth and death. Include any other material from the actual grave that you feel is relevant, such as the person's epitaph. Make this miniature representation of the tombstone aesthetically pleasing, taking care in how you form the letters of each word. You may want to cut this paper into the shape of a tombstone, or you may want to burn the edges a little so it looks old and mysterious. When you have created something to your liking, place the item somewhere on your altar, to serve as a visual reminder of the connection you have forged. From now on, when you perform your daily meditation or other rituals, call your Companion by name when you invite spirits to attend.

JOURNAL EXERCISE: COMPANIONS ON THE OTHERSIDE

1. Go over the list of graves that you sought to awaken. What attracted you to these graves in the first place? How did interacting with them make you feel?

2. Look at the birth and death dates for each of the residents in these graves. Calculate how old these people were when they died. How close are they to your own age? Which ones are older than you? Which ones are younger? Did you pick up different impressions at the graves of those who died young? What about the impressions at the graves of the elderly?

3. How recently did these people pass on? Did you notice a different feel in those graves that are older as opposed to more recent ones? Was the impression of the resident stronger or fainter? Why do you think this is?

4. If you took photos at the cemetery or did rubbings of the graves, take these out and spend some time looking over them. If you look at these items, can you feel a connection with the graves they depict? How strong or faint is this connection? What emotions do you experience as you look over these images? What state of mind do they inspire in you?

5. From among the list of the deceased, select one who died younger than you are right now, one who died older, and one

who died at around your same age. Take a few moments to put yourself in these people's places. For the one who died younger, think back to your own life and what you were doing, or planning to do, around that age. How would it have affected you to have all your plans cut short? If you had died at that age, would you have felt fulfilled in your life? What emotions would that inspire if you had remained aware of the world even after your death?

6. Now think about the person who died much older than you. Put yourself in this person's place and try to think of where your life will be when you reach this person's age. Will you have lived a full life by then? Will you be reluctant or eager to die? Think of all the things you want to accomplish with your own life. Do you think that by this age, you will have done these things? If you remained aware of the world after your death at this age, how would you feel?

7. Consider the person who died right around your age now. Consider where you are now in your life. What have you accomplished in your time upon the earth? What things would go undone should you pass away tomorrow? Do you think that the person who slumbers in this grave expected to die at this age? What does this tell you about living life to its fullest, without fear?

Back to Life

Much of our work in the cemetery has been dedicated to reaching out to the spirits of the dead and attempting to establish some form of communication. By immersing yourself in the energies of death, you not only embrace the potential of change in your life, but you also open yourself up to all the things that linger on the Otherside. Communication with spirits is both enlightening and alluring, but it is possible to become so immersed in the realm of spirit that you lose touch with the living.

After you have completed the cemetery exercises in this chapter, set aside a day to communicate with the living people in your life. You may want to make a list of your family and close friends and consider when last you took the time to really talk to them. It is especially important to remember to reach out to elderly friends and relatives more frequently, because the time you have to spend with them is limited. Although, given the uncertainty of life, it never hurts to say what needs to be said to anyone you cherish, just in case tomorrow steals them—or you—away.

Many spirits linger as the restless dead simply out of regret that they did not say goodbye. They feel continued attachment to their loved ones, and they are reluctant to let them go. Use this exercise to connect with the people in your life right now so that, should something happen, there will be no regrets. Call relatives that live at a distance. Visit someone you know who is in a nursing home. Spend the day with your best friend, just appreciating what this person brings to your life. And remind yourself how precious communication is when you are still alive together in the realm of living flesh.

15.

PREPARING THE WAY

Having been born into a culture that has lost touch with the positive, transformational power of death, we have had to reacquaint ourselves with that power. We have been taught to shrink from the reality of death. As a result, the essence of death, which is *change*, has been obscured by anxiety and fear.

Much of our work has been devoted to accepting impermanence, overcoming fear and revulsion, and coming to terms with death as a natural part of life. Each step along this lengthy journey has brought us closer to the realm of spirits, closer to a more complete experience of the worlds of both the living and the dead. The culmination of this path is a shamanic death and rebirth, a ceremony that allows us to open the door within ourselves and fearlessly walk through to the other side. The things that each person sees there will be unique, but the wisdom gained through the visionary journey will help lay the foundation for all future work.

The death and rebirth ceremony is the real start of your journey on the Twilight Path, and we are almost ready to take that step. But that final step is one that should be approached with caution. This chapter contains a brief interlude of visualizations to help set the stage for your final, most crucial step. While it is possible to skip these exercises and still complete the self-initiation, both can provide helpful insights into the final process of crossing over.

The visualizations in this chapter can be performed either at your home altar or at the cemetery. Performing these exercises at the cemetery allows you to carry them out while lying atop a grave, preferably the grave of your Companion. However, performing the work at home affords a good deal more privacy, and it also places no time constraints on when you carry out the exercises. One of the downsides of working in the cemetery is the fact that it is a public place, and, as such, you do not have absolute control over its hours. Although it would be ideal to perform all of your cemetery exercises at night, this is simply not a workable option. Nearly all cemeteries close before dusk, and breaking into cemetery grounds after hours is illegal. Especially because of the overtly dark nature of this path, you should avoid illegal activity at all costs. Even though the Twilight Path is neither malevolent nor harmful, you cannot expect mundane authorities to understand. Their very fear of death will be projected onto you, making them quicker to judge your activities and assume that you are up to no good.

One of the reasons you crafted the medicine bag to forge a tie between yourself, your private ritual space, and the cemetery, was to circumvent the troubles created by issues of trespassing and limited cemetery hours. By building the cemetery up as a space that exists beyond its physical boundaries, you allow yourself to draw upon its threshold energies regardless of where you actually perform your work.

Keep this in mind as you determine where precisely you wish to carry out these visualizations. In the end, the location is far less important than your ability to immerse yourself and connect with the threshold state.

With both of the visualizations below, you may want to record the visualization ahead of time so you can play it back on your computer, CD player, or MP3 player. Performing a ritual bath prior to the visualization will help put you in the proper frame of mind, as will burning incense or anointing yourself with scented oil. It is helpful to perform these in the dark, with just a candle or two for light, but you may also consider placing two coins over your eyes as you stretch out, lying in the aspect of one who has died.

If you are at the cemetery, stretch out on the grave of your Companion, placing your head just at the base of the gravestone. If you are at home, lie down in front of your altar, with your feet pointing away from the threshold space. As a final touch, you may also want to cover yourself with the funeral shroud you used in the elemental rituals. For both of these visualizations, call your Companion by name and ask him or her to serve as your guide, participating in the visions.

Dancing with Death

You are lying in the cemetery on the grave of your Companion. The tombstone stretches just above your head. You can hear the wind rustling through the grass. The wind gets stronger, and you can feel it moving over your entire body, caressing your clothes and your flesh. Above the sound of the wind you hear another sound. It is brittle, like dead leaves. It whispers, rising and falling, just out of your range of perception.

You feel the ground move slightly beneath you. It moves again, swelling against your back. You move away, rolling to the side just as a skeleton rises from the ground at your side. The skeleton is covered with a thin layer of flesh. Tatters of hair cling to its withered scalp. Scraps of clothing hang wetly against the sunken flesh. Dirt and wet things cling to it all over. Its eye sockets are empty, but even so, it turns and looks at you. Its bare teeth are permanently fixed in a wild grin. Its nose has collapsed, leaving a hole in the center of its face.

It continues to gaze at you. You look quickly around, and realize that there are skeletons and shriveled bodies emerging everywhere. The rustling noise you heard earlier was the sound of their flesh whispering as they moved. You look back to the one nearest you. It has extended its hand toward you. You realize that all the other skeletons are moving toward the center of the cemetery. You can just see them over the swell of the earth, gathering in a great, shambling group. This one has remained behind, waiting for you.

Uncertainly, you extend your hand. Bony fingers clasp around yours. The flesh that looked so shriveled is not dry but clammy and moist. It squishes a little as you tighten your grip. The skeleton beside you smiles wider, and together you begin to walk toward the others.

As you approach, you realize the skeletons are dancing. At first, there is no music, and you can hear their limbs creak as they move. That whispery, rustling sound of their desiccated skin fills your ears. The skeleton who has led you here takes your other hand and draws you closer. You get a close-up view of that decayed skull, the withered flesh, the dirt and moss clinging between the teeth. You feel the arms close around you in a bony embrace, and then your grisly dance partner whirls you away into the throng.

Your first partner bends as if to give you a kiss, and then whirls you away into another skeleton's arms. You dance and sway, caught up in the strange rhythm that moves these dead bones, and are passed from partner to partner in a grisly progression that leaves your head spinning.

Somehow, you find yourself in the very middle of the group. The skeletons ring you about on all sides, still caught up in their songless dance. Now you become aware of another presence. You turn, and a woman is standing close to you. Her skin is completely black, not black like human skin, but the black of a midnight sky that is void of stars. Her lips are red and dripping with blood. She smiles at you and darts out her tongue. It is as crimson as her lips and its pointed tip laps at the blood. Her teeth are white and very, very sharp.

She is naked, but around her neck is a garland of skulls. It hangs heavily upon the swell of her breasts. Around her waist is a skirt of long bones. Flesh still clings to most of them, and you realize they are human arms. Partly decayed hands dangle at the ends like grisly tassels.

She gazes at you, and you meet her eyes. Her eyes are blacker than her body, huge drowning pools. Her tongue is still out, her lips parted. With a sensual gesture, she snakes the tip of her tongue along her upper teeth and smiles.

The grisly dancing continues on around you, but you hardly take notice of it now. This woman, standing before you, takes up your entire world. She reaches out her hand and touches your face. Her touch is warm and slick. Her fingers are covered in blood. She leans close to you, never taking her eyes from yours, and she whispers in your ear.

You feel that message to your core. She leans in close again and brushes lips against your forehead. Again, you feel the oily slickness of blood. Then she reaches out and touches you, smiling. Her hand goes straight through your chest to your heart. As she squeezes you, you can feel your body dying around you. It is painless, like a sigh.

You look down and see the flesh sink against your bones and then fall away entirely. You feel your lips stretch against your teeth and then disappear. Your hair falls away in clumps. You look around you. You are now no different from any of the corpses moving in her dance. And now, with no ears left to speak of, you can hear the music. The music is her voice, low and sultry, chanting a beat. With her hand still gripping your too-still heart, she sways with you. Partners in this grisly dance, you move against one another, turning, swaying, sighing. You feel her body press against yours, full, lush flesh moving heavily against old, dry bones. Yet you cannot resist the urge to move to the rhythm of her voice, to dance with her in this haunted graveyard.

She pulls you close against her in a tight embrace. You smell the scent of her dark-skinned flesh: sex and blood. There is a pulse to her deeper than even the rhythm of the dance that you can feel reverberating through you. Time is drawn out, and she holds you close, life cleaving to death. Then she lets you go. You feel life creep back into your body, slowly. She starts walking away. The skeletons part in front of her. They, too, begin walking away. You feel the ground moving beneath you as it swallows them up, one by one. The lady turns once more to regard you. You meet her eyes without fear. Then she, too, is gone, melted away like a shadow. You feel your heart beating once more in your chest. But distantly, you still hear that music.

Returning to Life

When you are finished with the visualization, give yourself some time to come back to the waking world. Focus on your breathing and feel the floor beneath your shoulders and back. Take a few deep, cleansing breaths and stretch, allowing feeling to return to all your limbs. Draw the shroud away and sit up. When you are ready, find your journal. Record the visionary journey as it appeared to you and any impressions that still linger in your mind. Describe your reactions to the Black Lady, whom other cultures know as Kali, fierce dancer of death. Think back to how the dancing made you feel. Record the message that she whispered in your ear, and reflect upon the meaning it holds for you.

A Leap into Darkness

Once again, you lie upon the grave, feeling the grass beneath you. The chill of the earth is damp against your shoulders and the backs of your legs. You can hear the whispering wind as it moves stealthily through the cemetery. It rustles the grass and teases a few stray strands of your hair.

You turn your vision inward and reach down to the earth beneath you. You are lying on the grave of your Companion, and you are seeking to feel the bones that slumber six feet beneath you in the earth. You reach down and down with your internal senses, imagining the shape of the coffin directly below. You feel yourself begin to make a connection. You can feel the thoughts of your Companion reaching out to you. Beneath you, the ground seems to shift and the grave opens up. You find yourself pulled into the earth. You are spinning, drawn deeper and deeper, until you see the coffin directly below. You have turned so that now you face the coffin as it lies in the earth. The earth around you is insubstantial. You can move through it like a thick liquid. Before you, the lid of the coffin opens up, but from your perspective, it appears to be more like a door. You just barely catch a glimpse of another figure inside that doorway. It is your Companion. You are beckoned in.

You step into the coffin that has become a threshold. There are rough stone steps beyond its door. These stairs lead down and down, deep into darkness. You can barely hear your Companion descending ahead of you, whispering, *Come*.

As you descend further and further, you eventually find yourself standing in a rough stone hallway, deep underground. It is dark, lit only with a few guttering torches. The shadows are thick in this hallway, making it seem unnaturally tall and long. You look down the hallway as it stretches away from you, and dimly you can see the shape of a great wooden door.

As you examine the hallway, trying to determine what to do next, you feel a presence behind you. You turn, but you see only darkness. Then the darkness begins to coalesce, and you can almost make out a face and a form. Insubstantial as a shadow, your Companion stands beside you. You greet one another, but you cannot touch: here, as in the waking world, the spirit is only energy, and you are solid flesh.

Your spirit Companion gestures down toward the doorway at the end of the hall. There is something foreboding about that doorway. It is the only door you can see anywhere in this place. The stairs behind you seem to have disappeared magically. The ominous doorway is now the only way out.

Your spirit Companion asks you, with the voice of a thousand whispers:

Are you ready to cross the threshold? Are you ready to let go?

You pause and take a few moments to think about this. For a little while, you stand, unmoving, and regard the door. As you watch, the

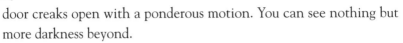

door creaks open with a ponderous motion. You can see nothing but more darkness beyond.

Again, your spirit Companion whispers:

Are you ready to cross the threshold?

You almost feel a hand, like the memory of a touch, upon your shoulder. The cold lingers on your skin. Your spirit Companion begins easing you forward, guiding you with a chill, ethereal hand.

The hallway is longer than you expected, or it grows with each forward step you take. As you draw closer and closer to the ominous door, the walls stretch up into blackness, and the candles lighting the hall behind you begin to waver and go out. Darkness descends upon everything until the only thing you can see is the indistinct shape of the door frame. The door is wide open now, gaping into nothing.

Your spirit Companion has brought you to the very edge. You stand before the threshold, and you can see nothing at all of what lies beyond. There is a chill draft coming from the doorway, and it seems to be wafting up from a very great depth. You consider moving forward, but it feels like you are standing at the edge of a bottomless pit. If you step forward, there is no way of knowing how far you might fall.

Your spirit Companion nudges you forward, saying in a barely audible whisper:

You cannot be afraid of falling. You cannot be afraid to let go.

As you stand there debating, the last of the candles gutters in the wind and goes out. Darkness descends completely. You know only by instinct that the doorway stands before you, and now you are certain that your next step forward will plunge you to a depth you can barely comprehend.

Your spirit Companion urgently whispers:

Jump, and be free.

Fighting past the knot in your stomach, you take a deep breath and step into the doorway . . .

Your immediate sensation is one of falling, falling, rapidly falling, but you cannot tell whether it is up or down. Darkness surrounds you, a darkness so palpable it seems to caress your flesh as you fall. And then the sensation of falling is replaced with a feeling of floating. You grow lighter and lighter until you are suspended in nothingness, surrounded by darkness, silence, and void.

You are no longer falling. Instead, something within you is falling away. You grow lighter and lighter, until the darkness no longer seems as impenetrable. There is still no light, but now you can see. And you realize that the palpable shadows you felt moving past you are other people, spirits, like your Companion, moving this way and that in the expanse of the void. You look down at yourself in this not-light and see that you, too, are a shadow, a being made of whispers instead of flesh. You retain the sense and memory of your form, but there is nothing solid about you. You are as insubstantial as the darkness billowing in the void.

You feel a ripple, like movement underwater, and something touches your arm. The grip feels real, if a little cold. You turn in the darkness and see your Companion, features clear and distinct for the very first time.

Let me show you my world, the spirit says, and you realize that you hear this voice not with your ears but with all of your being. The sense of the words echoes through everything you are.

The spirit begins moving forward—if there is a forward in this place that seems bereft of up and down. But you hesitate, uncertain how to move in a substance that seems part air, part water, and part whirling shadow.

The spirit turns back to you: *Will it, and you will move.*

Without the familiar motion of muscles levering bones, you glide after your Companion, directing your progress with only a thought.

Follow me, the spirit says, and follow you do. The other spirits in this place part around you. Others do not move aside, but pass right through you as if you occupied different parts of a double exposure. Your Companion leads the way, and you follow, seeing all that you need to see of this realm. Seek things out and explore, taking all the time you need.

continued on page 222

Death as Initiation

As we near the end of our walk through the cemetery, we see Gabriel again, only this time he appears in his role of psychopomp, the Guide of the Dead. He is here as both guide and guardian, conducting the soul of the deceased to the next world. His manner is gentle and protective, his outspread wings shielding her from harm.

The deceased holds her shroud about her, and her expression is both vulnerable and trusting. She has given herself entirely into his care, and although her features belie some trepidation for what lies ahead, she nevertheless yields to her guardian's care.

In this particular monument, we are reminded that death is not an end, but a transition. However, it is not a transition everyone is capable of making on their own. There are pitfalls and dangers for one who is not accustomed to the journey. Fortunately, guides often present themselves, but the question remains: can you give yourself over to trust? When the moment comes to take the leap and descend beyond all that you have known, are you willing to believe that somehow, gentle hands will be there, waiting at the bottom to catch you?

Consider the experiences you have had with your Companion. If you are still plagued with issues of trust, write your concerns in your journal. If you have no fears, explain your reasons. You may wish to communicate with your Companion about your thoughts and feelings on this particular icon. When you feel ready, continue on.

continued from page 219

When you are ready to return to the world of the living, reach out for your Companion's hand. Ask to be returned to your body, led back up to the world of light. As you return, draw the funeral shroud from your face and take several deep cleansing breaths. Come back to your body and stretch, rolling your ankles and flexing your muscles. Work feeling back into your fingers and other limbs and, when you feel ready, sit up. Speak the name of your Companion and offer your thanks. Record your experience in your journal.

Woodlawn Cemetery, the Bronx.

16.

THE GATES OF LIFE AND DEATH

In shamanism, an individual undergoes a ritual death and rebirth in order to become a walker-between-worlds. By crossing into the realm of the dead and then returning to the world of the living, the shaman becomes a mediator between the two realms, someone who stands with a foot in each. The word *shaman* originates from a Tungus Siberian word, and yet the elements of shamanism can be found in religious and mystical practices around the world. Tibetan Buddhism retains elements of shamanism from the indigenous Bon culture that existed long before Buddhism made its way to the Tibetan plateau, and many of these lingering elements have influenced the *Bardo Thodol*. Ancient Greek and Roman necromancy developed out of the older shamanic practices of the *goês*, specially trained magicians who were skilled in dealing with the spirits of the dead. The necromancy practiced in medieval Europe, although deeply corrupted, retained a few traces of this much earlier tradition.

A shaman is a spirit-speaker and a psychopomp, someone who can contact the spirits of the dead and help them navigate the pathways of the Otherworld. The shamans themselves know how to cross over, for they have done it before as part of their initiation. Through these journeys, the shaman gains power from spirit guides and guardians. This power comes mostly in the form of knowledge, although it can also manifest in healing. The main role the shaman plays in his or her community is to help facilitate healing and communication when the worlds of the living and the dead collide.

Our Western image of the shaman has gotten all tangled up with romanticized notions of Native American spirituality. However, the shaman is essentially a necromancer, someone who has a special tie to the spirits of the dead because he or she has tasted death.

The death and rebirth ritual that is integral to shamanic initiation is perhaps one of the most striking qualities of shamanism. In many cases, the death suffered by the initiate is not so symbolic. There are reports the world round of shamans whose initiation involved actual, physical death, usually after a long illness. In such cases, the shaman-to-be awakens in the middle of the funeral preparations, much to the surprise of his mourning relatives. In his book *Dreamtime and Inner Space*, ethnopsychologist Holger Kalweit cites numerous accounts from around the world where a shaman's death and rebirth were more than just metaphorical.

The shaman's initiation goes much deeper than mere physical death. The death and rebirth ritual is about the death of who one used to be and crossing over into a new existence. It is about coming to understand the process of dying through direct, personal experience. And it is about learning to walk between two worlds for a more complete understanding of both. These are the same goals of the Twilight Path. At its core, the path you have learned throughout this book is about achieving a deeper experience of both life and death, then learning how to mediate between the two in order to facilitate personal empowerment and transformation.

A Visionary Journey

Everything you have learned until now has been preparation for this final step: a death and rebirth self-initiation. Performing this ritual does not draw your studies in the Twilight Path to a close, however. On the contrary, this rite is really the first time you will step through the door.

The goal of this ritual is to allow you to achieve your own personal taste of death. It is a demanding ritual, and it should not be undertaken lightly. It combines a number of the rites and exercises that have gone before, but it is designed to take the threshold state further than you have yet experienced. Combining the vision of an Underworld journey with the Dispersion of the Five Winds, the rite will allow you to unwind the knots of energy tying you to your flesh.

The death that you experience once all these knots are untied is primarily symbolic. However, you may find yourself pulled so completely into the ritual that you enter the ecstatic state of the shaman. In this state, your spirit is free to roam while your physical body may appear, for all intents, dead. The ritual has to be particularly intense for you to achieve this state, but there remains a possibility for it to happen. The key to getting through such an experience and turning it into something both empowering and revelatory is not to panic.

You may feel everything slowing down within your body, so that your breathing and your pulse both become very minimal. You may feel your limbs grow heavy and cold, and you may find it difficult to move. You may also feel a tingling or vibrating throughout your body, a sensation that has been reported by a number of out-of-body experiencers, including author Robert Monroe. If you overcome the urge to be afraid, you can harness this disconnected state to achieve an out-of-body experience of your own, moving through your ritual space and beyond in the form of a spirit.

Forging a Lifeline

It is not easy to return to your body once you have entered the liberated state of death and rebirth. The hardest part, at least in my experience, is *wanting* to come back. Once your spirit breaks free of your physical body, it can seem almost painful to surrender all that freedom in order to sink bank into the heavy world of flesh. But it's not a death and rebirth rite unless you come back from your journey to the Otherside.

To make it easier, before we undertake the final journey, we are going to craft a token. This token will be your anchor to this life as well as to the physical world. In Chapter 8, I briefly mentioned the use of heart scarabs. These finely crafted items were often wrapped with the mummy as a replacement for the dead person's own heart. Armed with such a charm, the deceased could stand in the Hall of Judgment without fear of being found wanting, for the heart scarab would be weighed on the scales in the place of the real heart.

We are going to take a page from the ancient Egyptians and craft a charm to keep you safe as you journey through the Underworld. However, rather than trying to cheat the scales, this charm will serve as a lifeline, leading you back to your living self. The charm does not have to be in the shape of a scarab. In fact, it does not have to be anything more than a simple piece of paper. The shape of the charm is not important; it is the content of this charm that is going to count. For the purpose of this ritual, your heart scarab needs to be something that represents who you are, in this moment, now.

Take a little time to think about your current sense of self. You may want to break out your journal and think out loud on this for a little bit. Write down a list of words that describe who you are. Write down a list of names that you go by, including your real name, your magickal name(s), and any nicknames you might use (don't forget handles that you use online!). Write out titles you hold or words that describe your relationship with others around you. Do you work nights at a convenient store? Then "cashier" is one of the terms you should write down. Are you currently taking classes toward a degree? Then include "student" in your list. Brother, sister, friend, child, neighbor—try to cover everything that others call you, or how they might perceive you.

Once you have a good long list, go back over all the different names and terms and titles and circle those that you feel really name you. Compile these into a shorter list. Now try to come up with some image or symbol that encapsulates all these things. If you cannot design a symbol that is complex enough to contain the real you, simply write all the most important terms out on a piece of paper. Consider decorating this paper with colors or images that appeal to you. If you're not the artistic type, rubber stamps or even stickers can be wonderful tools. Words or even images might not do it for you, so consider putting an actual piece of yourself into this token. Try a lock of hair, a fingerprint, or even a drop of blood.

Work your heart and soul into this item. After all, you want it to contain a little slice of you. When you are finished making your heart scarab, find a piece of red cloth. Silk is best. Wrap this around your heart scarab, then place it on your altar.

Now the real fun begins.

Preparing to Descend

You should set aside at least one full day to perform the death and rebirth rite. Ideally, you should give yourself two days: one day to perform the ritual, and one day to recover and integrate the experience. In the past, initiates prepared for weeks and even months before performing a ritual like this. In this modern age, we cannot take weeks off from work to undergo rigorous hours of fasting and meditating. We simply do not have the luxury of that much free time. Some of the potency of our rituals suffers because of this truncated time of preparation, but there are very few options save to adapt.

Purchase a bottle of pomegranate juice for this rite. Pomegranates are deeply symbolic of death and rebirth. When the goddess Persephone was held captive by Hades in the Underworld, she resisted eating any of the food of the dead. Eventually, she gave in and ate six seeds from a pomegranate. When her mother Demeter finally convinced the gods of Olympus to have her daughter released, these seeds ensured that Persephone would spend half of every year with Hades in the Underworld. Each seed represented one month that she was tied to the land of the dead.

If you cannot find pomegranate juice (and you happen to be of legal drinking age in your country) buy a special bottle of red wine. I've always had a fondness for Ravenswood merlot, although admittedly that's just because I like the design of triple ravens on the bottle. If you purchase wine, put some thought into your choice, and make the bottle something attractive that adds to the symbolism of the rite. Be certain that you also have a wine key to open the bottle.

The juice or wine will not be poured into a goblet. Instead, you need to procure an offering bowl that is eight or more inches in diameter. This bowl can be of any material, although it must be something that is safe to drink from. Consecrate this bowl as you have all of your other ritual tools. When you are preparing your altar space for the rite, set the bowl as close to the center of the altar as possible. You may have to shift things around a little, but for this rite, the offering bowl is central.

You should also select a ritual dagger or knife. This can be your regular athame, or it can be something you have purchased especially for this rite. As with all your other ritual tools, make certain this object appeals to you both symbolically and aesthetically. It does not have to be functional or even sharp. This is a ritual blade, and its purpose will be to symbolically cut your life away. To ensure that the knife is able to cut energy, consecrate it ahead of time, anointing it with oil and imbuing it with both energy and intent. Make it real in the realms of both spirit and flesh.

You will start your ritual preparations at least twenty-four hours before the actual rite itself. Plan to begin the ritual at night, either a few hours after sunset or right on the stroke of midnight. The timing should be significant to you, and it should be fully dark outside when you being the rite.

Around dusk of the day before the ritual, take a cleansing shower or bath. Wash yourself from head to foot and anoint your skin with myrrh-scented oil. As you cleanse yourself, reflect upon what you want to accomplish with this rite. Once you have performed this first cleansing, you will start your fast. For the next twenty-four hours, allow yourself to eat only bread and to drink only water. (If you happen to have a wheat allergy, limit yourself instead to water and rice. People with medical conditions such as diabetes should adapt the fast so that it does not endanger their health.) Eat as little food as possible, and cut yourself off of food completely at least four hours before you begin the rite. Try to sleep no fewer than four and no more than seven hours the night before the rite.

Two hours before you plan to begin the rite, prepare your altar space. Double-check all of your ritual tools. Fume the space with incense. Make certain that you have several candles on hand as well as a method to light them. Clear any clutter that might have built up in, near, or around the ritual space. Retrieve your heart scarab, offering bowl, and ritual dagger from wherever they are stored. Place the offering bowl in a central location of the altar. Put the heart scarab off to one side. Place the dagger on the edge of the altar, in front of the bowl.

Find a pillow (you probably still have the one you used in the elemental rites) and place this at the base of your altar. You may also wish to spread a blanket on the floor in front of your altar. If you do, set the pillow on top of this, as you will be lying on this blanket for most of the rite.

If you bought a bottle of wine for this rite, open the bottle now so you do not have to struggle with it after the rite. This also allows the wine to breathe a little, something which improves the taste of most red wines. Stand the bottle next to the offering bowl on the altar.

Check the temperature in the room and make certain that you find the atmosphere comfortable. Turn off electronics that are in the immediate vicinity, including computers and cell phones. If you have a landline, turn the ringer off. If you live with people, or if people frequently stop over to visit you, make certain that they know not to disturb you during this time. If you have pets, make sure that they also will not disturb you during this time.

An hour prior to beginning the ritual, draw a ritual bath. The water should be tepid: not cold, but only slightly warm. Scent the water with myrrh and sea salt. Light a few candles in the bathroom, and turn off the electric lights. As you wait for the bath to fill up, go around and turn off all the electric lights. If there is a streetlight or other outside light shining into any of your windows, this window should be blocked. From this point forward, you should only work by candlelight.

Do not leave candles burning at your altar while you take your bath. Instead, carry a candle with you to light your way as you go from room to room.

Set fresh clothes out for yourself in the bathroom. This can be a ritual robe or some other set of clothing appropriate for the rite. Everything should be fresh and clean. Place your necromantic medicine bag with your clothes. When the bath is ready, strip in silence. Look at yourself in the mirror as you remove your clothes. Reflect upon your clothing. Reflect upon the image that your clothing choice projects. See the process of disrobing as an act of stripping away your public face—any façade you may maintain in the mundane world. Strip yourself down to the truth, then stand naked for a few moments and regard that truth in the mirror. Do not look away from the imperfections you perceive in your body or in your face. Look at yourself with brutal honesty, and accept yourself for what you are. Fold your discarded clothes neatly, then step into the tub.

Take time to wash your body thoroughly in the ritual bath. Splash water over your face and concentrate on washing away all distractions. Run a sponge or washcloth down first one arm and then the other. As you run the cloth down your arm, focus on your energy as well, wiping away any stagnant or chaotic energy from your aura. Perform the same kind of sweeping motion down your torso and hips, working from the center outward. Continue to your legs, wiping down first the front, then the sides, then the backs. Concentrate on cleansing both flesh and energy all the while that you do this. Let the water wash away everything that does not belong. Finally, cup water into your hands for a final ablution, and splash this over the top of your head. Let the water trickle down your face, your neck, and your body, so it carries away the last remnants of distraction or stagnation.

Once you have finished these initial ablutions, lie back in the tub and relax. Turn your focus inward and contemplate what you are about to undertake. Consider that you are preparing yourself to face death. Do not take this lightly, but also do not be afraid. Simply think about your life, and what it means to you. Think about your experiences in coming to understand death. Approach the ceremony as if it were a real death. Reflect upon the things you leave unfinished, the words unwritten and unsaid. Think of the people in your life you would leave behind should you actually cross over this night. What would you say to them, if you only had one last goodbye? How do you think things would change without you in their lives? Try to be peaceful and serene as you prepare yourself for death. Let go of your regrets. Let the water cleanse your fear.

Before you get out of the tub, open the drain and let the water empty around you. Feel the tension and fear rinsing down the drain with the water. Allow anything else that is burdening you to drain away with the water. Sit in the empty tub for a few moments, breathing the lingering scent of the myrrh, feeling completely cleansed and clear.

When you are ready, stand and towel off with decisive movements. Imbue each little action with *gravitas* and intent. Dress standing in front of the mirror. Prepare yourself in your ritual garb in silence, trying not to think of what came before this moment or of what is soon to come. Lose yourself in your present actions. Focus on the task at hand and simply *be*. Place the medicine bag around your neck as a final gesture of preparedness. When you are finished dressing yourself for ritual, blow out any candles you have burning in the bathroom except one. Take this lone candle and use it to light your way as you proceed to the space of your altar. Make this a solemn procession as you approach the threshold space.

The Chöd Ceremony

Alexandra David-Neel was an adventurous woman who journeyed to Tibet in the early part of the twentieth century. She spent fourteen years touring that country, learning the language of its people and sometimes interacting among them in disguise. As a Westerner, she was fascinated by the magickal traditions of the people of Tibet, and she wrote about her investigations of their practices and beliefs in her landmark work, *Magic and Mystery in Tibet*.

The Chöd ceremony is one of the many extraordinary rituals that David-Neel describes in her book. A ritual that is intended to help an initiate overcome his or her fears, the Chöd ceremony was typically practiced in the most haunted location the initiate could find. Old cemeteries were a favorite spot, as were isolated woods that had a reputation for being haunted by demons and worse. As David-Neel recounts the rite, the initiates would pick a night to go out alone to the haunted locale. Often, they would bring rope, and they would tie themselves up to a tree or post so they had no hope to run. Then, bound and helpless, practitioners of this ceremony would call upon the ghosts, demons, and other denizens of the dark, inviting them to come and attack. Essentially, the initiates offered themselves up to be devoured, demanding that the monsters eat their flesh, just as the initiates themselves had eaten the flesh of other beings in their lives. They would invite the hungry ghosts to spill their blood, just as they had spilled the blood of other beings in their lives. They offered up everything that they had, inviting the most horrific and grisly end imaginable.

If the ceremony went well, visions of demonic beings would begin to pour out of the graves or the surrounding woods. These would descend upon the initiate, feasting on flesh and bone and blood. The initiate would experience this devouring as if it were truly being carried out. If practitioners of this ritual did not give in to fear or panic, they would eventually come to realize that they were not attached to their flesh or their bones or their blood. They would realize that the demons, however terrible, had no power over what was real in them. Nothing could touch the essence of what they really were.

David-Neel tells of masters who were known for performing this ceremony over and over again, each time gaining a greater insight into the impermanence of the flesh and the needlessness of fear. Students of shamanism will recognize certain elements in common with this practice and the process of shamanic initiation: in most cases, once the shaman enters the visionary state of death and rebirth, he or she is seized upon by spirits and demons. These horrific beings descend upon the shaman, tearing the body up. The shaman is often cut into pieces and devoured, and yet remains cognizant and aware of the process, observing from a perspective that is not limited to the flesh. A shaman's powers to heal are believed to arise from this sacrifice to the spirits. In many traditions, each devouring demon represent a different illness, and the shaman gains power over that illness if its demon tastes his or her flesh.

Our ritual of initiation is going to invoke aspects of the Chöd ceremony in addition to aspects of shamanic death and rebirth. Not only are you going to disperse the five winds and seek a taste of death, you are going to throw wide the gates of your threshold space and invite *anything* that answers to help bear you into the depths. This means that you will be destroying any of the safe barriers you set up around your threshold space. You will be shattering your own shields as well, laying yourself bare.

Before you make this ultimate sacrifice, be certain that you have all the ritual tools you will need. Here is a quick checklist:

- Silk-wrapped heart scarab
- Pomegranate juice, or red wine
- Offering bowl
- Ritual knife
- Pillow
- Blanket
- One candle (in addition to the candles of life and death)
- All the usual items on your altar (including a bowl of earth)
- Necromantic medicine bag

Death and Resurrection

With your single candle, approach the altar. Stare into the veiled mirror for the last few steps of your approach, gazing deeply into the shadowed reflection. In your mind, call to the shadows beyond the Veil and will them to take form and substance. Set the candle down as close to the center of the altar as possible, without it getting in the way. From your single candle, light first the candle of life and then the candle of death. This gesture formally begins the rite.

Close your eyes, bow your head, and wrap your hand around the medicine bag that ties you to your cemetery. You are going to invoke its energy now, merging the threshold space of your private altar with the archetypal threshold that is the city of the dead.

> RITUALIST: [Name of cemetery], I call to you. I stand at the swirling gates of shadow, and I call. May these gates become one Gate, and all the cities of the dead converge in this space, now.

Envision the cemetery in your mind as clearly as possible. See it shrouded in darkness, cradled in the arms of the night. Imagine all the familiar tombs and monuments spreading out around you. You stand at the heart, and the heart is centered here, right in front of your altar. When you feel the intersection of threshold space grow solid and more real, remove the medicine bag from around your neck. Open the bag and empty its contents into the bowl that holds the element of earth. Mingle the earth already in the bowl with the soil and other power items in the medicine bag.

> RITUALIST: Spirit to spirit, dust to dust, all spaces now converge.

Reach out and touch the token you keep on your altar to represent the grave of your Companion. As you touch the simple representation, close your eyes and remember what it felt like to touch the actual stone of the grave. Will yourself to experience both sensations at once, so you are simultaneously standing at your altar touching a token and standing at the grave itself, your hand upon the cold stone. Whisper the name of your Companion three times.

> RITUALIST: Companion, guide, and guardian! I call to you now as I stand on the threshold between the living and the dead. I call across space. I call across years. May my words resound through the darkness, drawing you now, drawing you here.

Hold out your hands and summon your power. Meet the eyes of your own reflection in the veiled mirror. Pull upon the connection you have forged with your Companion until you can feel the energy of the Companion near.

> RITUALIST: Come to my side and take my hand. Reach across the Veil and guide me to the other side. This night, I descend from the world of the living. This night, I join you to taste the mysteries of the dead.

Hold your hand out to the mirror in an inviting gesture. Do not be shocked if you feel ghostly fingers close around your own. Accept this gift and make contact in return, allowing a gift of energy to flow through your fingers to your Companion's spectral hand.

> RITUALIST: I thank you for attending. I ask that you guide me back to the world of the living once my journey comes to an end.

Bow your head to the shadowed image in the mirror. Then release your Companion.

> RITUALIST: And now, I summon all my other witnesses.

Take the power you have gathered internally and direct this into both hands. With a sweeping gesture, expel this gathered power outward to all the wards and barriers that exist around your altar space. Shatter every shield and every wall that has been constructed to keep spirits out.

RITUALIST: I shatter now the walls that stand to keep the spirits out. Good spirits, bad spirits, enemies, and friends—I invite you all! All you mortal and immortal beings, gather here, and gather now!

Envision the walls of your spirit temple crumbling around you. The wind of power still rising from you sweeps all the shards away. The space where you stand, a juncture of gateways, is open and clear. There is a roiling darkness at the edge of your perception, and it creeps closer and closer, no longer kept at bay. Turn, and address all the beings you feel gathering in your space. Make your next statement both a taunt and a challenge:

RITUALIST: Come and feast on me, spirits! In bits and pieces, I have offered up my vital force. Now I pour it out for you to consume.

Turn back to face the altar. Take the open bottle and pour some of its contents into the offering bowl. Take the offering bowl and lift it up, presenting it to your veiled reflection.

RITUALIST: The red of blood, the red of life, I offer up this sacrifice.

Lower the bowl slowly and set it back down on the altar. Now take the ritual dagger. Wrap your hand around the hilt of this tool and feel the energy woven into it. As you focus on the blade in your hand, make it exist not merely as a dagger of metal, but a dagger of spirit as well. Hold your opposite arm out over the bowl and use the dagger to slice the air just above your wrist. *Do not make contact with your physical flesh*, but draw the energy of the dagger through your own energy, at least an inch above your skin. Cut into your energy body instead of your flesh, so you can feel some of your vital energy flowing out. Hold your wrist over the offering bowl, allowing your energy to spill into the bowl. Mix the fluid in the bowl with the tip of the knife, saying:

RITUALIST: Blood to blood and life to life, I fill the bowl of sacrifice.

Clench your free hand and cease the flow of energy. Imagine that there is a gaping wound on your energy body and, as you watch, the lips of the wound slide closed. You may feel a little weak in the knees after allowing this energy to flow forth. Do not fight the sensation, but accept it. It is just the beginning of your sacrifice. Meet your eyes in the veiled mirror and steel yourself for what is to come.

> RITUALIST: I give myself to you, spirits! Piece by piece I cut myself free of this fragile flesh.

Set down the dagger and reach down with both hands to your root chakra. Feel this energy center, wrapping your fingers around it. Imagine that the energy center is a knot binding your spirit to your flesh. Your goal is to loosen the knot and unwind a small thread of it, but you should not untie the knot entirely. This is likely to feel very strange, but concentrate through the sensation. When you have a portion of the energy firmly in hand, hold this out toward the bowl and address the spirits.

> RITUALIST: This is my root chakra. It is the first step, called the Way of All Flesh. I unlock this gate so my life spills forth. Spirits! Attend this sacrifice of flesh.

Wrap one hand around the energy and take up the knife with your other hand. Imagine that there is a cord of energy trailing from your closed hand to your root chakra. Taking care not to actually cut yourself, use the dagger to sever this cord of energy. Hold the hand that grips a small portion of this severed energy over the bowl. Unclench your fingers and let the energy spill forth. Stir the mixture of fluid and energy with the tip of the dagger, saying:

> RITUALIST: Blood to blood and life to life, I fill the bowl of sacrifice.

Meet the eyes of your reflection once more. Set down the dagger and reach with both hands to the energy center two inches beneath your navel. Feel this center and reach into yourself, wrapping your fingers around the energy. As you did with the root, loosen and unwind this center and draw some of its energy forth.

> RITUALIST: This is my navel chakra. It is the second step, called the Well of Vital Force. I unlock this gate so my life spills forth. Spirits! Attend this sacrifice of vital energy.

Pull it carefully from yourself. Then take up the dagger and sever the tie. You will feel weaker, and you may begin to feel cold, but stand firm and continue the rite. Place the energy into the bowl and stir the fluid with the dagger.

> RITUALIST: Blood to blood and life to life, I fill the bowl of sacrifice.

Now you are ready for the next gate. This is the center that is tied to your solar plexus, just beneath the base of your ribs. Set the dagger down and reach into yourself as you have done with the other centers. Feel the glowing ball of energy; loosen and unwind it. Hold a portion of it forth and say:

> RITUALIST: This is my solar plexus chakra. It is the third step, called the Rampart of Will and Desire. I unlock this gate so my life spills forth. Spirits! Attend and partake of this sacrifice of will.

Take up the dagger and cut it loose. You may feel a fluttering or pressure just under your rib cage. Stand firm and continue with the rite. Let the severed energy spill into the bowl of sacrifice. Stir the fluid with the dagger, and say:

> RITUALIST: Blood to blood and life to life, I fill the bowl of sacrifice.

Lay down the dagger and reach for the energy center at your heart. Loosen this knot as you have for all the rest.

> RITUALIST: This is my heart chakra. It is the fourth step, called the Juncture of Sorrow and Joy. I unlock this gate so

my life spills forth. Spirits! Attend and partake this sacrifice of emotion.

Pick up the dagger again and cut the thread. You may feel a clench-ing in your chest and this may briefly affect the rhythm of your heart. Stand firm and continue with the rite. Deposit the energy into the bowl and stir everything with the dagger.

> RITUALIST: Blood to blood and life to life, I fill the bowl of sacrifice.

Put down the dagger and move now to your throat chakra, at the base of your throat. Wrap your hands around this energy and feel it glowing like a jewel.

> RITUALIST: This is my throat chakra. It is the fifth step, called the Utterance of Names. I unlock this gate so my life spills forth. Spirits! Attend and partake this sacrifice of voice.

You may find that your voice weakens after this point. Despite this, continue as best you can. With the dagger, sever a portion of this energy, then let it slip into the bowl. Stir the contents again with your dagger.

> RITUALIST: Blood to blood and life to life, I fill the bowl of sacrifice.

You have one more step to go before you are finished with the sac-rifice. Work past any unpleasant sensations and do not be afraid of how your body reacts to cutting away so much vitality. Set the dagger aside and reach up to the energy center located at the very center of your forehead. Cup your hands around this and draw energy forth.

> RITUALIST: This is my third eye. It is the sixth step, called the Path of the Blind Seer. I unlock this gate so my life spills forth. Spirits! Attend and partake of this sacrifice of vision.

Pull this last spark of vital energy away, and cut its tie to your flesh with the consecrated dagger, being careful not to actually cut your body. Let the last offering of energy fall into the bowl. Stir the fluid with the dagger.

> RITUALIST: Blood to blood and life to life, I fill the bowl of sacrifice. Six parts of my precious life have I cut away and offered up. Six gates have I journeyed, and the seventh is always what lies beyond. My flesh is undone.

Set the dagger down. Then snuff the candle of life.

> RITUALIST: I pass from life to death.

Snuff the candle of death.

> RITUALIST: From death, I pass beyond.

Snuff the final candle so there is no more light. Be certain you know where your heart scarab is. As darkness descends around you, gaze deeply into the mirror and place your hand on the heart scarab.

> RITUALIST: [Name of Companion], guide my steps as I descend.

Heart scarab in hand, turn away from the altar. Stare into the darkness surrounding you. If you see things in that darkness, do not be afraid. Lower yourself to your knees, then stretch out at the foot of your altar. Drape the blanket over yourself, rest your head upon the pillow, and lie as one dead. Fold your hands over your midsection, and clutch the charm to your heart. As you lay there, feel the effect of the sacrifice upon your body. Feel weakness spreading through your limbs. Your breathing may feel shallow. Do not fight this, but instead, give in. Focus on the way your body feels sluggish and detached from you. Let your limbs grown heavy and sink into that inner space. Call to mind your practice with the Dispersion of the Five Winds. Go through these steps again as you feel your body growing cold and heavy around you. Speak the stages out loud, in a whisper, or simply think them clearly to yourself.

> RITUALIST: My body is earth.

You feel how weak you are from the sacrifice. You turn your focus inward so you can better perceive your energy centers. They seem to be dim, and growing dimmer. Your body grows heavy around you, and it becomes difficult to move.

RITUALIST: Earth dissolving into water.

And the knot remaining at your root chakra loosens and slips free. Your limbs feel watery, as if all strength has flowed out of them. Then you begin to feel cold.

RITUALIST: Water dissolving into fire.

The energy remaining in your navel chakra unravels completely, flowing away. You are less aware of the cold and now instead you feel brittle and dry, like an autumn leaf threatening to blow away in the wind.

RITUALIST: Fire dissolving into wind.

The energy in your center and at your heart loosens, then disperses upward, as if carried on a breeze. That light, dry feeling heightens momentarily, and you feel some essential part of you carried away. You perceive a scattering of pin-prick lights, like sparks, on the insides of your eyelids.

RITUALIST: Wind dissolving into void.

The center at your throat unravels, its pale-blue light fading into the darkness. All the sparks fade. All sensation, hot or cold, pleasure or pain, begins to fade. You feel nothing from your body. Nothing at all.

RITUALIST: Void expanding into dark-light.

The last threads of energy at your third eye dissolve, and you let go completely, surrendering to the visionary state that is the core of death and rebirth. Darkness descends, and it is a darkness that is somehow luminous. You are floating in that darkness, perceiving everything and nothing at once.

As you hang, suspended, free of your body, a hand closes around your hand and draws you up, farther and farther away. Your Companion guides you through the swirling visions of the realm beyond. There is no way to script this part of your journey. It may take moments, or it may take hours. You are seeking a vision, an internal revelation. You will know it when you experience it. Once you experience it, you will be ready to return. If you find it difficult to return, focus on the feel of your hand clasped around the heart scarab. Use this as an anchor to your body. It may take a great effort to return to your flesh, but stay focused on the heart scarab. Allow its meaning and significance to guide you home.

Do not move immediately as you allow feeling to creep back into your limbs. As you reintegrate, go back down the steps of the Five Winds. Hold the heart scarab as a focus and whisper to yourself:

RITUALIST: Light descends back into void, and I tie myself back to my body.

Feel yourself reconnect at your third eye, the knot of energy tightening once more.

RITUALIST: Void descends back into wind, and I tie myself back to my body.

You reconnect with the center at your throat, and the knot of energy there tightens spirit to flesh.

RITUALIST: Wind descends back into fire, and I tie myself back to my body.

Feel the centers at your heart and solar plexus reconnecting. Feel the strengthening of the tie between your spirit and your flesh.

RITUALIST: Fire descends back into water, and I tie myself back to my body.

The center at your navel reintegrates, and you are almost completely tied back to your flesh.

RITUALIST: Water descends back into earth, and I am tied once more to my flesh.

The knot at your genitals reintegrates, and you are tied securely to your body. Allow yourself to adjust, stretching your legs and flexing your hands. Proceed slowly and with care, as your first attempts to get up may be shaky. Feel for the matches you left on the edge of the altar. Raise yourself up so you are looking once more into the veiled mirror, then strike a match. Use this flame to light the single candle between the candles of life and death. Focus for a little while simply on this single flame. Feel your own vital force sputtering like this weak little flame. Take the offering bowl that sits before you. Holding it in both hands, turn to face the shadowed room. Address the spirits that still are gathered there.

> RITUALIST: Six times I sacrificed a part of what I am. Six times I offered myself up to you. Severed from my vital force, I descended to the depths. I crossed into the realm of shadows, yet I have returned. Now I drink from the bowl of sacrifice, so I may be renewed.

Drink from the mingled fluid and energy from the offering bowl. You do not have to drain it dry, but drink enough to slake your thirst. It is more important to concentrate on taking back as much of the energy you placed here as possible. As you swallow the physical liquid, concentrate on also imbibing the mingled energies in the bowl. Feel this energy coursing through you, leaving you stronger wherever it flows. Replace the bowl on the altar. Then turn back to face the room.

> RITUALIST: I thank you, gathered spirits. And I release you to the night.

Hold open your arms and release the energy of the sacred space. Do not shatter the space as you shattered the barriers. Instead, allow the energy of the space to dissipate like a final, contented sigh. Turn back to your altar and pick up the paper token that represents the grave of your Companion. Touch this, and once again envision yourself simultaneously touching the actual stone of the grave.

RITUALIST: [Name of Companion], my guide, my friend, and guardian. I release you from your duties. You may go or stay as you please.

From the single candle, light the candle of life and the candle of death. Unwrap the heart scarab from its silk cover and contemplate its form. Think about how well this item represents you. Think of how it fails to represent you at all. Pass this item through the flame of the single candle until its edges singe. Before it is dangerously consumed in flames, drop the token into the liquid that remains in the bottom of the offering bowl. Though most wines aren't flammable, take caution when dousing a flame in any liquid. Watch as the embers sputter and die.

RITUALIST: This is who I used to be, but it is not who I am now. I have cut away everything and seen the truth in myself. I stand now, reconstructed, stronger and more alive for having tasted death.

Sit or kneel on the pillow in front of your altar and reflect upon your experiences in this rite. When you feel that you are ready, snuff the candles and relinquish the last vestiges of the sacred space. Eat a simple meal in silence, leaving a portion for your Companion and for all the spirits who witnessed your rite. (If you are having trouble feeling fully integrated with your body, go through the Dispersion of the Five Winds meditation as it appears on page 156.) Later, when you have the opportunity, bury the remains of the offering bowl.

Aftercare

Death and rebirth is a demanding ritual, and it can take a lot out of a person, mentally, emotionally, and energetically. As such, it is not a rite you can perform and expect to recover from in just one night. The experience of death and rebirth often drags up profound emotional issues and unresolved conflicts in one's personality, demanding a complete reassessment of one's relationship with self, community, and society. It can take an entire lifetime to fully process and integrate all of this material, but the first few weeks immediately following the initiation are especially difficult. The initiate is left in a delicate and vulnerable state, and in other cultures that observed death and rebirth rites, the initiate was often removed from regular society for a recovery period.

As already observed, our modern society moves at far too fast a pace for any of us to take weeks off from work to devote to this ceremony. We can no longer spend a fortnight exclusively preparing for this transition, nor can we devote weeks to a period of recovery. No matter how badly we may need time to ourselves, our jobs and our schooling and our worldly responsibilities do not just go away. In some respects, this is even a good thing, because it encourages us to achieve balance in our lives. The rent will not pay itself, so we are driven to find the middle ground between material existence and spiritual practice.

It will not be easy to perform this rite and then hit the ground running. Going to work or school a day or two after this rite will seem jarring, at best. All your senses will be heightened, and the mundane concerns of material existence may even seem a little unreal. Your body will be exhausted, and your mind will have too many concepts whirling around in it to properly focus. After such an eye-opening experience, the demands of the daily grind may not even seem worth the effort. When you truly grasp the wisdom of impermanence, doesn't the act of amassing wealth seem ridiculous? At times it may seem as though you get up to work at a job you don't like in order to make less money than your time is worth so you can buy lots of junk you don't need.

Seeing the world with eyes that have looked beyond can be difficult. But remember that the entire point of this path is to walk with a foot in both worlds. To be a true walker-between, you have to achieve a sense of perspective, and an ability to appreciate the beauty in both worlds at once. Here are a few tips to help with your reintegration.

Rest

If at all possible, allow yourself to sleep in until you wake up on your own the day immediately following the ritual. Don't set your alarm.

Don't promise to be anywhere. Just sleep in and enjoy the luxury of having no responsibilities to anyone but yourself for just one day. If this is absolutely not possible, then at least make certain that you get a full night's sleep each night for the next several nights. Eight hours is the average amount of sleep that most people need in order to feel rested, but some people need more and others need less. You will know what's right for your body. When you sleep, pay attention to your dreams. After such an intense experience, it is highly likely that new insights and new information will manifest in dream images. The ancient Greeks believed that the dreamspace verged upon the realm of spirits as well as the realm of the gods, and so you should not be surprised if your Companion or perhaps a patron deity appears to you with a message while you sleep.

Diet

Feed yourself well over the next few days, but use some wisdom in your choice of nourishment. Following such an intense spiritual experience, you may find that your digestion is affected. Some people truly are gifted with iron stomachs, and they can eat whatever they wish no matter what they have just survived. But the rest of us should be aware of the quality of our food during these times. Stay away from heavy, greasy foods. Eat simple but wholesome meals, preferably cooked at home. Stay away from foods with a lot of chemicals and preservatives, as you may find yourself suddenly sensitive to these things. Drink stimulants, such as coffee or tea, in moderation. Don't overdo it with your sugars. If you tend to maintain a rather unhealthy diet, you may want to take this opportunity to make serious changes in how you eat. You have just undergone a death and rebirth—use this to make a break with unhealthy eating habits, and treat your physical body with as much care as you have devoted to your spirit.

Emotions

The death and rebirth rite can drag a lot of unresolved emotions to the surface. Burning your heart scarab at the end of the rite demands that you take a hard look at how you perceive yourself, and what those perceptions mean. Some of the emotional issues that are brought to the forefront of your mind may be so complex that you cannot even truly wrap your head around them at first. All you can do is feel. This means that you may be prone to mood swings in the days and weeks following the ritual. Simple, everyday activities may inexplicably call to mind experiences you thought were buried. In addition to emotions that linger from your past, your current emotional state will also be vulnerable and raw. Situations that once were simple may inspire a much stronger emotional reaction than you are accustomed to. This could make dealing with friends and co-workers difficult.

Your first step in dealing with this emotional sensitivity is to be aware of it. Then, when your emotions surge unexpectedly, you should make every effort to maintain enough control to disengage from the people around you so you don't say or do anything you may regret later. Walk away from whatever seems to be inspiring the intense reaction, and do something to help yourself calm down. This can be as simple as counting to ten, or it may be more involved, like asking yourself why you are reacting this particular way. Often, once we understand the reason behind the emotion, we can get a handle on the emotion itself. Sometimes, however, emotions don't seem to have any rational explanation. In these cases, you should recognize how you feel and embrace the emotion internally, but make a conscious choice about how you are going to react to that emotion openly. Taking a moment to think before you just react to a particular emotion is always a good idea.

Energy

In addition to being more emotionally sensitive, you are likely to also find yourself more energetically sensitive immediately following this ritual. One of the main goals of the death and rebirth rite is to open yourself up more fully to your experience of the spiritual side of the world. This means throwing wide the door to your psychic sensitivities. Many of you may find that you are much more tuned in to the emotions of other people, and this might lead to problems when you are in large crowds. The emotions and energies of other people may suddenly seem very loud and you can become easily overwhelmed. You may also find yourself so tuned in to the world of spirits that you have a hard time differentiating between the living and the dead—a fact that can prove embarrassing when you start talking with the old guy on the street corner that no one else can see.

Just as with your emotions, your first step is to simply be aware of this heightened sensitivity. You will have to judge for yourself when this new level of awareness is distracting or overwhelming. If you feel that you need to shut some of your sensitivity down, make a conscious effort to shield yourself. Imagine a bubble of energy forming around you that keeps out everything you don't want. If a bubble seems a little too restrictive, try the image of covering yourself from head to toe with a semi-transparent veil—something that dampens some of what you're picking up but does not cut you off from energy entirely.

JOURNAL EXERCISE: STARTING A NEW LIFE

1. What were your expectations going into this rite? How do you think those expectations influenced your overall experience with the ritual?

2. How easy or how difficult was it to stick to the twenty-four-hour fast? How did you feel during your fast? How did you feel by the end?

3. When you invited the spirits to attend your rite, how keenly did you feel their response? Were you able to tell how many spirits joined you for the rite? Were there any new faces in the crowd?

4. When you sundered the barriers of protection, how did your experience of the ritual space change? Did you feel the spirits differently? Did they themselves respond to the sundering? Record any noteworthy sensations or experiences you had during this part of the ritual.

5. How strong was your connection to your Companion throughout this rite? Was your Companion helpful to you? Did you have any special experiences with this spirit?

6. What did it feel like to offer up each successive sacrifice of self? How did the loss of each energy impact your mind, your body, and your spirit? When you drank from the bowl of sacrifice after returning, how did this feel? How did these lingering sensations affect you once you were finished with the rite?

7. Describe your experience with the Dissolution of the Five Winds in this ritual. Were you able to feel yourself untying each successive knot? Were there any sensations with any of these stages that really stood out to you?

8. Describe your experience of crafting the heart scarab. When you burned it at the end of the ritual, how did this feel? If you were to craft a heart scarab right now, how would it be different from the one prepared for this ritual? Take some time to record your impressions of what has changed in you.

Back to Life

In this chapter, you have symbolically given yourself a new start. You have sacrificed your old self and crossed over, however briefly, into the realm of the dead. Seeking the help of the spirits and energies you've attempted to draw into your life, you have sought out a taste of death. And, as the heart scarab burned, you severed the final ties to your old life, emerging fresh and new.

But what does this mean for you? Who are you, now that you have stripped so much away? What are you to become? The death and rebirth ritual is an initiation, which implies that it is a beginning, not an end. You have returned to life, but what do you want out of that life now that you embraced the potentiality of death?

When you have recovered from the death and rebirth rite, set some time aside to deeply consider these questions. You may wish to think "out loud" in your journal, jotting down your hopes for the future and any life goals. What do you want to become, now that change is a part of your life and you have freed yourself from fear? You know that you can become anything, but the very lack of barriers may make it hard to decide on a path.

Construct another heart scarab. You may make it out of paper, or you may consider shaping a scarab from crafting clay that can be baked and hardened in the oven. Flatten the bottom as with traditional scarabs and use a pin or knife to scribe words and symbols on this underside. This scarab will be a more permanent item that can sit on your altar to remind you of what you shall become. Use it not only as an anchor to your ideal self, but as an anchor to the future that lies ahead.

Each time you approach your altar, take a moment to read the scarab and reflect upon your goals for the perfect you. Finally, don't be afraid to embrace change even with this item. If your goals change, or if your ideals of who you should become change, don't be afraid to alter the scarab. If you undergo such a radical change in your life that nearly everything concerning your future ideal changes, consider undergoing the death and rebirth ceremony again to destroy this heart scarab, then construct a new, more relevant one.

17.

WALKING THE
TWILIGHT PATH

You have come a long way on your journey. Since you began your work with the Twilight Path, you have contemplated the inevitability of your own mortality. You have looked upon death in all its gruesome reality, and you have studied the various responses that cultures from around the world have had to the reality of death. Throughout it all, you have worked hard to appreciate death, not as something ugly or terrifying, but as an elegant and imminent part of nature.

You have learned to let go of your fear, and through your fearlessness, you have become acquainted with spirits. You have let them speak to you, guide you, teach you about their experiences with transition. And, as a crowning act, you have embraced that transition for yourself, crossing briefly into the realm of the dead in order to better comprehend its mysteries. Having undergone this ritual death and rebirth, you now stand, renewed and ready, as a twice-born soul.

All of this work and preparation for death and rebirth begs the question: what do you do now? You have achieved a balanced perspective of both worlds at once, and you can interact equally with the living and the dead. But what is the ultimate purpose? What can you do with wisdom so hard-won?

The simple answer is: *apply it*. Thanks to your studies in the Twilight Path, you have achieved a unique perspective on life and death. While this perspective will certainly enrich your own experience of the world, it will become even more profound if you share it with others. The following sections offer some ideas for how you can put your experience with the Twilight Path to practical use, sharing its wisdom with others and using your abilities to benefit both the living and the dead.

Machemeister mausoleum compound in Woodlawn Cemetery, the Bronx, New York.

Servant of the Stones

For a good portion of this book, you have cultivated a relationship with a particular cemetery. There is no reason that this relationship should end. Continue working with your personal cemetery, and continue interacting with the spirits that inhabit your favorite graves. As part of your role as a initiated follower of the Twilight Path, make yourself a servant of the stones. Make regular visits to your personal cemetery. Clean off the graves. Weed the flower beds. Consider making contact with the cemetery association and volunteering your time at this cemetery. See if they will allow you to plant trees or flowers of your own.

There are many ways you can devote yourself to honoring your cemetery. Are you looking for a summer job? See what it takes to become a caretaker of the cemetery. If you don't do well out of doors, go down to your local library and do some research on the cemetery. Learn about your city of the dead's history, as well as the history of some of the people buried there. Look up the names of the artists who crafted some of the most breathtaking tombs. You may be able to do some of this research online, and you may even find that there is a group of taphophiles (cemetery lovers) in your area. Subscribe to their newsletter. See if they go on outings to other cemeteries. Learn about the relationship your city or town has had with the cemetery over the years. If your cemetery has a particularly interesting history, you may even consider writing an article about the cemetery to encourage others to appreciate the place. You may also consider giving tours to those who are interested, leading them to the most interesting graves or the most attractive monuments. Share your love of this place so others will take an interest in caring for it, too.

Palliative Care

Palliative care is given to people who are dying. It is the kind of doctoring that cannot cure or halt a disease. It is simply meant to make a person as comfortable as possible during their wait for the end. Your work with this path does not qualify you to counsel the dying, but it does give you a unique perspective on both life and death. To this end, you may consider volunteering some of your time at a nursing home or hospice, where you can help another living being face death without fear.

This does not mean that you need to spend your afternoons cleaning bedpans. Residents who are undergoing palliative care often appreciate someone who is willing to be a companion. Sadly, many close family members have trouble visiting their relatives once they begin the slow decline into death. And yet these people are still alive, and they have very real emotional needs. Consider offering yourself as a companion to someone who is facing death alone. Bring a book each day and read to them. If you are musically inclined, they may enjoy hearing you sing or play songs. Or you can simply hang out and converse. Talk about their life with them. Learn about their most important memories, so the lessons of their life can live on in you. Just being there as they face the end of a lifetime can be very helpful. No one should ever have to die alone, unless solitude is what they themselves seek.

Haunting Resolution

When someone is dying, he or she needs emotional support from friends and loved ones to help make the transition easier. Once someone has died, those emotional needs do not just go away. Many ghosts linger due to unfinished business. This business often takes the form of emotional attachments that remain unresolved. Perhaps the dead person experienced a violent death. Perhaps he or she simply died very young. Parents who are taken from their children before they are confident that those children are able to care for themselves can also linger, remaining behind to act as a kind of guardian angel for their loved ones. The emotions that tie ghosts to the lives they led before are not always negative ones, but sometimes those emotional ties prevent the ghosts from evolving beyond their most recent lives.

A few rare spirits are very self-aware and they have chosen to linger on the Otherside for reasons of their own. Other ghosts are often lost and confused, consumed with loneliness and unable to let go. As someone who is sensitive to spirits and unafraid of the dead, you are in a unique position to offer help to these lost souls. By reaching out and communicating, you can determine whether or not a spirit lingers in a place by choice, or if the dead person would be happier moving on. Consider offering your services to people who feel troubled by ghosts. Interview the people who have had disturbing experiences, and assess the situation. Examine the place where the haunting has occurred and determine the source of the trouble. Some supposed hauntings aren't even tied to the spirits of the dead. Some houses simply have unusual energy or are thick with emotional residues. The residents then pick up on these things, mistaking them for sentient spirits. Once you have determined the true nature of the haunting, if there is a ghost, reach out to it. Do not make the mistake of assuming that it has no right at all to be there. Too many spirit mediums are quick to send a spirit "into the light" without taking into account the rights of the spirit. You must remember that these are sentient beings with a right to free will. But if you reach out, and make contact, and discuss why the spirit is restless, you may be able to help that spirit solve his or her emotional ills.

Resolving emotional attachments still may not mean that the spirit is ready to move on. Be certain to let the spirit decide, then act as a mediator between the ghost(s) and the people who reported the haunting. As someone who walks in both worlds at once, help the living understand and accept their dead houseguest, and help the ghost understand the living who share this space. If the ghost has no intention of moving on, encourage the family to set ground rules of what is and is not acceptable behavior for the ghost. Communicate these requests to the spirit, and try to work something out so both the living and the dead can share their space without coming into conflict with one another. Only if the spirit shows no intention of getting along with the living should harsher methods be used. For ideas about driving spirits from a home or business, refer to Chapter 5.

Speaker for the Dead

Wicca and, to a certain extent, all of neo-Paganism, is focused on light, life, and love. Because there tends to be such a focus on the positive aspects of life, when the reality of death intrudes through the passing of a friend, coven member, or even an animal companion, it can leave a group emotionally devastated. Not all priests and priestesses feel comfortable working with death, even in the context of a funerary rite. But life is never certain, as you have learned, and death is something we face in little doses every single day.

If you belong to a group or coven, volunteer to be the Speaker for the Dead. Take up the responsibility of running any of the rites connected with the death and dying. Become involved with the planning for Samhain, and see about running the ritual for that potent holiday. Construct an altar to the Ancestors, and create a rite to honor those Ancestors that everyone can participate in. If the others around you have a hard time perceiving spirits, or if they are afraid to connect with beings from the Otherside, offer to intercede for them. Like a traditional shaman, you can mediate between the living and the dead, passing on communications and helping the living to adjust to the presence of any beneficial spirits that have chosen to look after them.

Prepare a funerary rite for your coven and circle for the eventuality that someone connected to your group may pass. Set up a memorial for key figures who have influenced the members of your group. The people thus honored do not always have to be friends and relatives. Honor the names of writers, artists, and great thinkers who have changed the world and then passed on.

Encourage the members of your group to be in touch with the transitions of their lives, helping them to create rituals that acknowledge the death of an old identity, or the end of a certain phase of their lives. Honor the passing of animal companions, for they profoundly touch our lives as well. Every life that has touched us and moved on is a death that should be honored, both out of respect for the spirit and for our own peace of mind.

The End of the Beginning

Death is change, and the fundamental purpose of the Twilight Path is to create change and to become changed. By inviting these changes into your life through your immersion in death, you bring about other achievements as well. The work in this book should leave you more at peace with your life, and filled with a deeper understanding and appreciation for the things and people in your world right now. By facing the reality of death and learning not to shrink away, you have gained power over your fear of death and are also less likely to fear the little deaths in your life represented by changes in your living situation, personal life, or career. And, by inviting the energies of death intimately into your personal space, you have opened yourself up to the world of spirits, learning to reach out and communicate with friends and companions on the Otherside.

There are myriad benefits and applications of these achievements, and we have touched upon only a few in this closing chapter. I hope these various examples help you to see that your work with the Twilight Path is hardly at an end. The death and rebirth rite is intended to open a doorway to new experiences, but it is not a door that you walk through once, never to experience again. Try performing the rite at least once a year, renewing yourself in body and mind annually on some special date, like your birthday.

At this point in your progress, you should have an intimate acquaintance with death in all of its aspects. Death as the end of mortal life. Death as the root of non-attachment. Death as a transition to another realm of being. Death as an initiatory experience. Death as the very embodiment of change. All of these various lessons combine to make you more aware and capable in your life right now, and the wisdom you have gained here is something that should be used to enrich your experience of the living world. Do not think that this path is at an end, for all of the exercises here have really only been preparation for a life lived in balance—walking in peaceful empowerment between the realities of life and death, mortality and immortality, the realm of the living and that of the shadows.

Every exercise and ritual in this book is something that you can and should perform over and over again. Each time you revisit a section, you will see things in a different light and uncover something more profound. The more familiar you become with certain rituals and visualizations, the easier it is to perform them without thought or hesitation. If you can lose yourself in the experience instead of worrying about whether or not you are doing it "right," you may uncover inner doorways you never thought to find.

Every step along this path, you have been reminded: death is a beginning and not an end. Our modern culture has such a negative view on death and dying that we need to be reminded of this fact. By continuing your work with the Twilight Path and embracing these energies every day in your life, you can serve as an example of death's empowering and transformational side. If we live by example, we can encourage others to overcome their own fears, until fearlessness touches everyone we meet in our lives. A world that is free of its fear of death is a world that is free from its fear of change. Be an avatar of that change in the world around you, embracing the beauty of both life and death and teaching by example so others learn to do the same. This is the heart of the Twilight Path: change yourself and you will change the world.

A pensive cherub sits in watch over a grave. Woodlawn Cemetery, the Bronx.

APPENDIX 1

TWILIGHT PATH INCENSE AND OILS

Holy and consecrated oils have been used for thousands of years in ritual. The strong, pungent scent of the oil helps you to focus on your intent, and many of the ingredients have a sympathetic effect toward the magick you are working as well. There are many magickal oils for spells devoted to light and life, but precious few commercially available for deathwork. Accordingly, I have decided to share a number of my own recipes for Twilight Path blends.

All the oils listed below are best created with pure essential oils. Mix the essentials in a neutral base of vegetable oil (almond oil or grapeseed oil, of cosmetic quality, often keep the best, but safflower or even canola oil will work just as well). Be careful to mix only a few drops of essential oil to every cup of vegetable oil; essential oils are very powerful and highly concentrated. Some may cause skin irritation in their undiluted forms if you get them on your hands, especially if you have allergies. You should take special care that you do not get essential oils directly on your skin if you are pregnant or nursing; a number of essential oils contain chemicals that, if absorbed through the skin, could be harmful to your child.

As long as you take the proper precautions to handle essential oils safely, creating your own perfumes and ritual oils can be a very rewarding process. While you can certainly just go down to your local occult supply store and pick up some oils that are already prepared, taking the time to create the oils yourself imbues them with a special potency. While it is not strictly necessary to make a ritual out of the creation of your oils and other ritual supplies, it can also help add extra kick to the mixtures if you prepare them formally in sacred space at an appropriate time. Unless noted otherwise, all of the blends that appear below are best prepared at night or during the twilight times of dusk or dawn. If you pay attention to moon phases and work this into your magick, then you will want to prepare these oils during the dark of the moon, from last quarter to the start of the New Moon.

Selecting a special bottle or jar to store each oil can also be part of the ritual. Pick out something that really appeals to you, an item that has a shape, color, or design that reminds you of the type of work this oil is intended for. Alternately, you can buy a plain bottle and decorate it with charms, ribbons, or precious stones. Clear bottles are acceptable, but you will notice that most essential oils come in bottles made of thick, amber glass. This is because light, especially direct sunlight, can break down the delicate chemicals that are the active constituents in the essential oil. If you choose to use a clear glass bottle to store your final blends, be certain to store this in a cool, dark place when you are not using it.

Not everyone is going to want to get this involved in the creation of their ritual items, but many of us do enjoy the act of consciously crafting our ritual tools. Don't think that you *must* have a special bottle or that you *must* create the oil at a special time in order for it to work correctly. However, it can still be fun to go all out. You may even want to incorporate the action of creating these items into a formal ritual, writing a short spell or prayer to say over the oil as you mix it, or asking certain deities or tutelary spirits to lend their power to your work.

For the oil recipes, I offer the ratio of essential oils in drops. Most bottles of essential oils will come already equipped with built-in droppers. Otherwise, you will want a glass eyedropper, and you should clean this thoroughly before you use it with each oil to avoid contamination of the scents. It should be noted that I have a rather keen nose, so if you find that the scent of a particular oil is not strong enough for you, slowly increase the quantity of essential oils in the mix. Just be certain to stick to the same ratios for all of the essential oils in the recipe.

To turn Twilight Path oil blends into body sprays or perfumes, use a 25/75 rule. That is, your perfume should contain about twenty-five percent (or slightly less) essential oil and seventy-five percent (or slightly more) dilutant. The dilutant is alcohol. Vodka can be used for this, or grain alcohol (aka Everclear), since these have no real scent, but there are laws against reselling perfume blends that use drinking alcohol as a base. Although more expensive, a better choice both scent-wise and law-wise is to use perfumer's alcohol for your base. There are sites online that sell perfumer's alcohol, such as www.snowdriftfarm.com. When everything's all blended, a drop or two of glycerin can be added as a fixative for the scent.

Cleansing Oil

- 4 drops Sage
- 1 drop Camphor
- 3 drops Rosemary
- ⅓ cup vegetable oil base

This is a general cleansing oil for use on yourself as well as your ritual tools. This is the one oil that should be crafted during the day and preferably during a waxing moon. You want this oil to contain solar power and the power of fire for burning away impurities and clearing unwanted energy. The oil itself has a strong astringent scent. As you prepare yourself for a ritual bath, dab a portion of this oil on the inside of either wrist and on either side of your throat, just beneath your jaw. Before you get into the bath, take a few moments to just inhale the scent of this oil and feel your pulse carrying its energy throughout your body. The oil will help clear your energy, zeroing it out so that you can start from a fresh state as you prepare for the rest of your ritual.

When you acquire a new tool for use on your altar, anoint the tool with this oil before you do anything else with it. This will clear the energy of the item so you have a clean, blank slate to start with. If you ever work with a tool and find that you are unhappy with the feel of its energy, you can use this oil to zero it out, clearing the energy so you can start anew. The act of cleansing your ritual tools will work best if you accompany the anointing with a wiping and rubbing motion of your hands. Call energy into your hands as you do this, and imagine that you are wiping and clearing away all the previous energy attached to the object. Use the clean scent of the oil as a reminder to help focus your intent. If the scent of the oil is not strong enough for you, it is safe to double the quantities of essential oils added to the vegetable oil base, keeping the same ratios between the essential oils.

Corpse Candle

- 4 drops Amber
- 4 drops Sandalwood (preferably Red Sandalwood)
- 2 drops Benzoin
- 1 drop Myrrh
- ⅓ cup vegetable oil base

This oil is to be prepared at night, preferably in the dark of the moon. Keep it on your altar to use prior to any spirit evocation. Before you attempt to communicate with or perceive spirits, rub a dab of this oil on your temples, throat, and the insides of your wrists. As you do this, clear yourself of any distracting thoughts or energies, gather your power into your center, and focus on your intent. Breathe deeply the scent of the oil as you focus. This is a fiery oil, and it will help to open you, clearing any blockages that dull your perceptions. Myrrh helps to tune this otherwise solar oil to your death-related workings.

Vision Quest

- 4 drops Sage
- 2 drops Lavender
- 2 drops Sweet Grass (optional)
- ⅓ cup vegetable oil base

This oil has the same basic application as Corpse Candle, but it is attuned more to the shamanic side of spirit work. If you take a more shamanic approach to your practices with the Twilight Path, this is a good oil to use to help open you and attune you to the spirits. Anoint the temples, throat, and wrists with this oil prior to vision questing or dreamwalking.

Jaguar Dreams

- 2 drops Cedar
- 3 drops Sage
- 2 drops Copal
- 1 drop Juniper
- ⅓ cup vegetable oil base

This is another spiritual vision oil with ingredients that are more attuned to shamanic work. Use as Vision Quest, above.

Crossroads

- 4 drops Cypress
- 3 drops Horehound
- 3 drops Myrrh
- ⅓ cup vegetable oil base

This oil helps to evoke the energies of the crossroads. Blend at night, in the dark of the moon. For added potency, take your work outside, and blend this oil either at the intersection of three paths or just outside of a cemetery (standing at the cemetery gate works best). This oil has strong associations with the goddess Hecate. Anoint yourself with this oil to enhance any threshold work.

Wake the Dead

- 3 drops Horehound
- 2 drops Musk
- 1 drop Saffron
- 3 drops Benzoin (listed as "Red Storax")
- ⅓ cup vegetable oil base

In his seminal work, *The Magic of Incense, Oils & Brews*, Scott Cunningham gives a recipe for loose incense which he calls "Raise the Dead." Cunningham instructs his reader to "compound and fumigate [this incense] about tombs and graves of the dead. This will cause spirits and ghosts to gather, according to ancient lore" (58). The first ingredient in Cunningham's original recipe, pepperwort, is rather hard to come by in essential oil form. It seems that these days, *Lepidium latifolium* is more likely to be used in cooking than in aromatherapy. I have found that pepperwort can be adequately replaced by horehound, a bitter herb that has ties to both Anubis and Hecate. Saffron, another one of Cunningham's ingredients, is a pricey oil that should be used with caution: the IFRA (International Fragrance Association) restricts its use to 0.005 percent in commercial perfumes. With a stretch, you can replace this with dark vanilla, but this significantly changes the tone of the scent.

Prepared as a ritual oil, this scent should be used on you and your tools as part of your preparation for calling up spirits. The blend can be used to create a loose incense as well, and in this case, you may be able to stick with Cunningham's original recipe. To do this, merely replace the horehound with pepperwort and dispense with the vegetable oil base. Fumigate your ritual chamber with this incense to assist in calling spirits. You may also go straight to the heart of things and burn the incense at the cemetery to assist in your work there.

Loose Incense

Loose incense is made up of pure resins and dried herbs, coarsely crumbled or ground and shaken together in a loose mixture. Such incense is typically burned in a brazier over a very low fire or on a hot charcoal. As the incense smolders, the smoke releases its scent. Self-lighting charcoals for use with loose incense are available at occult supply shops. These are the safest ways to burn this type of incense when you are working indoors. If you are working out of doors, a small fire that has been allowed to die down so that it is only red, glowing coals can also be used. Throwing this type of incense on an active fire burns the ingredients up too quickly and you will waste most of the effect of the incense.

Loose incense creates a lot of smoke, and so it is not always recommended for close indoor work, even when you're burning it safely. There are active ingredients in many of these herbs that are released in their smoke, and you can ingest those chemicals simply by inhaling the smoke. In several cases, this is precisely why certain herbs have been traditionally burned to induce visions or summon the dead. Even though none of the herbs used below are restricted or illegal, you still want to use moderation when working with them. Just remember: when working with loose incense, a little pinch goes a very long way. Another caution to keep in mind is this: many of the green herbs used in loose incense have a distinctive underscent reminiscent of marijuana. Some of your neighbors or family members may mistake the incense for something illegal, and then you will have some uncomfortable explaining to do, especially if the authorities get involved. Anything with sage, mugwort, or wormwood is especially prone to this kind of confusion, so keep that in mind when choosing which blends you want to use in your own work.

Like the blend I call Wake the Dead, most of the oil recipes listed in the previous section can be translated for use as loose incense. Rather than drops of essential oils, use the quantities listed as a reference for the proportions for each ingredient. Whenever the recipe calls for one drop of an essential oil, try using one tablespoon of the same herb, dried. I have found this substitution works best for making small, personalized batches of each blend.

Obviously, you no longer need a neutral base to dilute and carry the essential oils, so you can dispense with the vegetable oil when creating loose incenses of the previous blends. Rather than using essential oils, purchase the herb or resin in its natural form. Flowers, leaves, and woods should be dried prior to use in loose incense. Resins should be broken up into pieces that are no larger than a small pea. This is best done with a mortar and pestle, an item you can typically purchase at the same stores that sell incense ingredients.

Because essential oils can be costly or rare, loose incense blends are often easier to put together. In the following section, I've included a variety of recipes that I have used to good effect. As with your incense oils, these combinations are best blended at night or at twilight, during the dark of the moon. Store your blends in an air-tight container and keep them out of direct sunlight so they retain maximum potency.

Spectral Visions

- 1 part Dittany of Crete
- 1 part Wormwood
- 1 part Mugwort

This blend of loose incense combines three powerful herbs that have traditionally been burned to induce visions, especially visions of spirits. Wormwood is the active ingredient in the liquor known as absinthe, a potent alcohol with reputed hallucinatory properties. Traditional absinthe has long been outlawed in the United States because it was believed that continued ingestion of the chemicals found in wormwood led to madness and death. Absinthe has gained renewed popularity in recent years and many distilleries produce new varieties that are sold overseas. Not everyone agrees on the dangers of wormwood, but it is an herb that should be used with caution and only in moderate quantities. Rather than directly inhaling the smoke of this incense, burn it on a brazier so you can peer into the resulting smoke. The thick, white swirls are reputed to help facilitate spirit manifestations.

Beyond the Veil

- 2 parts Cypress
- 1 part Myrrh
- 2 parts White Willow
- 1 part White Chrysanthemum

This is another variation on the blend intended to help summon spirits of the dead. This version includes cypress and willow, two trees that have traditionally been associated with graveyards here in the West. Chrysanthemums also have strong associations with death. In Japanese folk belief, this is especially true of the white chrysanthemum. Blend this incense at night during a new moon and burn it to rouse the spirits and call them into your sacred space.

Mummy's Dust

- 2 parts Myrrh
- 1 part Cinnamon
- 1 part Benzoin
- 1 part Gum Arabic
- Sea Salt or Natron

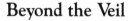

The ancient Egyptians used a number of exotic gums and spices in the process of mummification. Many of these were considered to be powerful apotropaics, warding off evil for the dead in the Afterlife. Mummies were preserved to last for eternity, and many of them have survived the millennia intact to our age. Because of the care and work invested in their funerary practices, the Egyptian cult of the dead has earned a kind of mystical awe from many modern Pagans. The following mix of resins and spices is inspired by the Egyptian funerary arts and it is intended to evoke the mystery and antiquity associated with the Egyptian dead.

Note: Natron is a type of salt that the ancient Egyptians would use to leech all the fluid out of a mummy. True natron is harvested in the salt marshes to the north of Egypt. You can make your own approximation of natron by taking equal amounts of sea salt and baking soda and blending them with a little bit of distilled water to make a paste. Spread the paste out on a cookie sheet and cook this in the oven at 150 degrees, until it has dried out completely. Crumble the dry sheet of natron and store in an air tight container until ready to use.

Phoenix Blend

- 3 parts Red Sandalwood
- 2 parts Cinnamon
- 1 part Gum Benzoin
- 1 pinch of Gum Arabic

In ancient Greece, it was believed that the mythical phoenix bird lived for five hundred years. At the end of that time, the bird returned to the place of its birth and began to gather cinnamon branches and the branches of other rare woods. This apparent nest actually was intended as a funeral pyre, and once the nest was completed, the phoenix burned itself to ashes. From the ashes of this pyre, a new egg emerged, and this would hatch even as the ashes of its predecessor cooled around it. The phoenix, rejuvenated and renewed, would be reborn, to live another five hundred years and repeat the process all over again.

I use the Phoenix blend incense for any rite or ritual involving death and rebirth. It is a heady, cloying scent that for some easily brings an altered state of consciousness. I personally find it deeply relaxing, and it puts me in a frame of mind that is ideally suited for ritual work. Prepare this blend at dusk or dawn in order to best capture the transitional energies of the phoenix.

Phantom Tears

- 2 parts Willow
- 1 part Sandalwood

White willow contains the active ingredient of aspirin, one of our most widely used painkillers. Long before aspirin was made commercially in the laboratory, villagers knew to chew the bark of the white willow as an analgesic. Willow is also a plant that has long been planted near graves, and this is especially true of the variety known as weeping willow. In addition to its healing properties, willow can be very effective for attracting spirits when mingled with sandalwood. Several varieties of sandalwood are available on the modern market. Yellow and white sandalwood are most prevalent and least expensive. For this mixture, I recommend red sandalwood. Red sandalwood comes from the heart of the plant, and it has the richest, most lasting aroma. It is a little more expensive than the more common forms of sandalwood, but the difference in scent is worth the extra dollar or two you will pay per ounce.

Kiss of Morpheus

- 3 parts Dittany of Crete
- 1 part Myrrh
- 1 pinch of Poppy Seed
- 2 parts Sandalwood

This is another blend that is useful for summoning spirits.

Eyes of the Dead

- 2 parts Mugwort
- 1 part Gum Mastic
- 1 part Wormwood
- 1 pinch of Powdered Orris Root

It is believed that burning the herb mugwort allows spirits to manifest themselves. Several of the witches I met in college suggested that mugwort actually provides some crucial energy that makes it easier for the spirits to appear. I have also heard that mugwort has a visionary effect on the summoner, which makes the senses more receptive to the subtle appearance of spirits. Wormwood, another main ingredient in this mixture, is mildly poisonous and was used a century ago in an alcohol known as absinthe. Absinthe had hallucinogenic properties, and those who drank a lot of it often had very vivid, mind-altering dreams. Because of these two ingredients, this incense should be used with caution. Try not to overdo it and try not to directly inhale too much of the smoke. Also be advised that when you burn this, it is going to smell very much like a less-than-legal herbal blend!

Elemental Blends

When you are performing the rites of the elemental mysteries, you are asked to burn incense as an offering to the element you are working with. Because the rites are primarily geared toward deathwork, any of the incense blends described above will suffice. However, some practitioners may feel that it is more appropriate to burn an incense that is attuned to the particular element. There are many excellent resources on the market that can provide a variety of recipes for elemental incense blends, including Scott Cunningham's *The Magic of Incense, Oils & Brews*, so you will not be at a loss for ideas. For those who are interested in making their own blends, I have included my favorite recipes for elemental incense below.

Embrace of the Earth

- 2 parts Patchouli
- 1 part Mugwort
- 1 part Vetivert

For the most ideal results, procure essential oil of vetivert and, rather than adding one part of the dry herb, sprinkle three or four drops of the oil into the mix of patchouli and mugwort. Toss the herbs together until evenly coated with the oil and spread them out to dry.

Tears of the Ocean

- 3 parts Lotus
- 2 parts Jasmine
- 1 part Spikenard

Kiss of the Flames

- 2 parts Amber
- 2 parts Dragon's Blood
- 1 part Cinnamon

For best results, use whole pieces of cinnamon wood rather than cinnamon powder. Powdered cinnamon is often cut with cassia powder (or substituted entirely). The taste is similar, but cassia is a completely different plant.

Breath of Twilight

- 3 parts Benzoin
- 1 part Lavender
- 1 part Lemongrass

As with Embrace of the Earth, the best results for this blend are obtained when you combine a dry ingredient with essential oils. In this case, make certain that you use granules of benzoin, not powdered benzoin. Put the granules in a glass jar sizable enough so that the benzoin only fills the jar halfway. Sprinkle three drops of lavender oil over the benzoin granules and quickly sprinkle two drops of lemongrass oil. Put the lid on the jar, then shake thoroughly, so the essential oils are spread evenly throughout the grains. Empty onto a cookie sheet or other surface and spread them out to dry. Wash and dry the jar before putting the coated granules back in for storage.

Incense Alternatives

For smoke-free households, there are alternatives to burning incense. One is the use of an essential oil atomizer, such as the models for sale at www.diffuserworld.com. Although delicate and moderately expensive, these gadgets very efficiently diffuse essential oils into the air, spreading the scent. Because they very quickly get a large quantity of essential oil into the air, they should be used for only a few minutes at a time. Twilight Path ritual oil or incense blend recipes can be adapted for use with a diffuser. For oil blends, simply blend the proper amounts of pure essential oils into a small glass container and omit the use of the vegetable oil base. For the incense blends, find essential oils of the required ingredients (in a few cases this may not be possible) and blend them together in the same proportion, again, simply blending straight essential oils without the use of a base. Store the blends in a cool, dark place between ritual to help them last longer.

A down-and-dirty option that I've used has involved a small pump-action spray bottle, two to three ounces of distilled water, and a blend of essential oils mixed in the same proportions as called for by the recipe. Put the water in the spray bottle, then add the essential oil, and seal the spray bottle. Shake vigorously, then spritz the scent throughout your ritual chamber. The bottle will need to be shaken thoroughly before each use, and the water will go stale after about a week. Still, it works in a pinch to give you the scent of the incense blend without actually burning anything. This will pretty much ruin the spray bottle for any other use, so be sure you pick up something small and inexpensive.

APPENDIX II

LEYDEN PAPYRUS RECIPES

The Leyden Papyrus is a manuscript of magickal spells and recipes from Hellenic Egypt. Written around the third century of the Common Era, this manuscript bears much in common with the Greek magickal papyri and gives a great deal of insight into the magickal beliefs and practices at work in the Hellenic world forged by Alexander the Great. The manuscript, torn in two pieces, is concerned primarily with three main types of magick: healing, love spells, and methods of spirit conjuration. The spells for spirit summoning include lamp and bowl divination, among other techniques. Those familiar with the methods of spirit evocation recorded in grimoires from the Middle Ages onward will immediately recognize influences from this much earlier work. In fact, a great deal of what is typically considered Goetic magick owes much of its language and structure to the magick recorded in this and similar papyri.

Many of the spells and recipes from this manuscript are supremely impractical for modern-day usage. In some cases, the ingredients are rare or impossible to obtain. Other spells call directly for animal sacrifice. One spell requires the magician to drown a falcon in a jar of wine. Another calls for the magician to burn alive two specific varieties of fish. The vast majority of modern practitioners would find such activities repugnant. Even so, some of the spells and recipes can be suitably adapted for modern use. Below are four recipes adapted from the Leyden Papyrus that deal directly with summoning spirits.

To Appease Spirits

During one of the spells for spirit evocation, the magician is told to place several grains of myrrh upon a willow leaf. This is then cast into the brazier as an offering to the spirits. If you have myrrh powder, you can use the willow leaf almost like a small spoon, scooping up a small amount of the powdered incense with the leaf and then throwing both leaf and powder into the fire. It is unclear whether a live or dried leaf is required for this operation; either should work satisfactorily.

To Make Spirits Appear

Gather the woody stalks of the anise plant together with copper sulfate (or alternately, crushed eggshell) and place these on the hot coals of the brazier. This incense is said to lend aid to the spirits you are summoning so they appear more clearly to you. Due to some scribal errors, the plant called for here may actually be horehound, not anise. Horehound may be what the ancients called "the Anubis plant," and so its use as a summoning incense would only be appropriate.

Another for Summoning Spirits

Grind together frankincense, beeswax, benzoin, pine resin, and a date stone with a little wine to make a paste. Roll the paste into a little ball and place on the burning coals.

This recipe has been adapted somewhat. The original recipe calls for styrax rather than benzoin. However, as styrax is the source of benzoin, the use of benzoin in the recipe is probably implied. I have taken a similar liberty in the substitution of pine resin. The initial translation calls for turpentine, which would yield a rather dangerous incense. Turpentine is highly flammable as well as being a poisonous lung irritant. Although I cannot be certain without seeing the original manuscript itself, I suspect that what was actually called for was terebinthus—a tree commonly used to produce turpentine. As turpentine is processed from pine resin, a safe alternative is to use the unprocessed resin itself. The recipe also calls for the use of something called "the Anubis plant." The translators of the 1904 edition of the Leyden Papyrus suggest that this plant is either stachys, known modernly as woundwort; or marrubium, better known as horehound. Several stalks of the whole plant are added to the coals along with the ball of mixed resins.

To See Spirits

Take several seeds from the white lupin, which the papyrus names as "the Greek bean." Put a portion of oil in a jar. Drop the beans in the oil and store this in a dark place for about a month. When the seeds are finished steeping in the oil, strain them out and use the oil to anoint your eyes prior to doing spirit work. While the manuscript seems to imply that you should do this by putting the oil directly in your eyes, I strongly recommend that you simply dab the tip of your finger in the oil and wipe a small amount across each eyelid.

From the description given in the manuscript, you probably want only a small amount of oil to soak the beans in. The original recipe requires that you check on the seeds after twenty days, at which time it says you will see a phallus and testicles—which is to say, the seeds will have germinated, the two halves of the bean splitting and a single shoot rising up between them (the Egyptians were often rather earthy in their descriptions). When you see this, you are supposed to seal the jar back up and leave it for another forty days, at which point the oil should take on a reddish tint (this might vary depending on the species and color of lupin being used). Once the oil has taken on this different color, it is considered ready to use.

APPENDIX III

OFFERINGS FOR THE DEAD

For many of the exercises in this book, you are asked to make an offering to the dead. Although a small portion of your own vital energy, gathered into your cupped hands and offered to the spirits, will suffice, many people find it helpful to offer some physical token along with the energy. Below is a collection of traditional offerings made to the dead. These offerings have been gathered from many eras and many cultures, in order to give you a wide variety of items to choose from. Read over the information gathered here and see if any of these offerings really speak to you. You may find that some of the spirits you work with appreciate one type of offering, while others have different tastes entirely. Do not be afraid to experiment, and if nothing here seems appropriate, let your intuition guide you to something that is.

Gifts of the Greeks

In Book IX of Homer's *Odyssey*, the hero Odysseus makes an offering to the dead as part of his preparation for calling the dead up from Hades. The offering described in the text is a classic offering made by the ancient Greeks, both to the spirits of their blessed dead as well as to their deities. If you wish to re-create Odysseus' famous offering to the dead, you should dig a trench or a small hole somewhere out of doors (a cemetery would be ideal, but be certain that you are not damaging public property). You should have separate vessels containing honey, milk, wine, water, and white barley meal. Once the trench is prepared, call out the names of the dead for whom you are making this sacrifice. Then pour a portion from each vessel into the hole. In the *Odyssey*, this offering precedes a rite of necromancy, where Odysseus summons spirits in order to seek wisdom from a deceased seer. A further offering of blood is made to the spirits, to give them the power to communicate with the living. You may forego the blood, but if you seek to communicate with the dead, an offering of your own vital energy can help provide the same kind of power.

Bread of the Underworld

According to the ancient Greeks, there is a portion of Hades called the Asphodel Meadows. This field, overgrown with asphodel flowers, was where ordinary souls went in the afterlife. To the ancient Greeks, asphodel was considered the favorite food of the dead. The ancients themselves ate the plant, roasting or boiling the bulbs. It was a widespread practice to plant asphodels around the tombs of the dead, in part as a food offering to those buried there.

Asphodel bread is still prepared in some countries. This bread is made by boiling asphodel bulbs in water, then mixing a portion of the bulbs in with flour as the bread is prepared. I have adapted the recipe for my own use, making offering loaves to leave at the cemetery or to put out on nights of high spirit activity, such as Samhain.

The bread is edible to humans as well as spirits—just be very certain of the species of bulb you are using (*Asphodelus ramosus*) before making this bread to eat!

- 3 cups flour
- 1 tablespoon sugar
- 1 tablespoon salt
- 1 ounce yeast
- 2 small asphodel bulbs, boiled, then mashed
- 1 ¼ cups hot water
- 2 tablespoons olive oil
- 2 teaspoons chopped rosemary
- 1 teaspoon chopped basil

Mix two cups of the flour together with the sugar, salt, and yeast in a large bowl. In a separate bowl, mix the herbs with the remaining cup of flour. Add hot water to the first mixture, then mix in the oil and mashed asphodel bulbs. Beat slowly, adding the remaining cup of flour with the herbs in gradual portions. When the dough is evenly mixed, set it aside for about thirty to forty minutes. You may lay a damp cloth over the bowl and set it someplace warm (such as your stovetop) for better results. After the dough has risen, punch it down and knead it a few times. Shape the loaf and place it in a greased loaf pan. Cover and let it stand for another thirty minutes. The loaf should double in size again due to the action of the yeast. As the loaf is rising, preheat your oven to 375 degrees. After the thirty minutes is up, place the loaf in the oven for forty to forty-five minutes. You may brush the top with butter.

For a much simpler, down-and-dirty version of this bread, get a package of pizza dough mix. Follow the directions on the package, but when you are kneading the dough, add one mashed asphodel bulb and half a teaspoon each of rosemary and basil. Shape the dough into a thin, flat round, brush with olive oil and any additional herbs, and cook thoroughly.

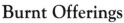

Burnt Offerings

Taking a cue from the Chinese festival of hungry ghosts, you can also burn items that you wish to give to the dead. During the festival of Ullamban, which occurs on the fourteenth night of the seventh lunar month, the living give the dead paper items that are copies of real-world items. There is ghost money, sometimes also called hell money, which is often printed up to look like real cash. Many companies also produce paper cars, paper houses, and other facsimiles of real-world articles that are believed to help the dead live comfortably in their world. The items are burned, and it is believed that destruction in the flames then transfers these items from the world of the living to that of the dead.

Libations to the Dead

A libation is an offering of some manner of drink, such as milk, water, or wine. A cup or bottle of fluid is offered up to the dead, then spilled out upon the ground. In some cases, the fluid is poured over the gravestone; in others, it is poured either directly onto the earth of the grave or into a little hole dug specifically for this purpose. Libations are not made strictly to the dead, and they do not necessarily have to be made at the graveside itself. Of course, libations are best made out of doors; otherwise, they leave quite a mess to clean up.

Liturgy of Funerary Offerings

The ancient Egyptians had a long and involved shopping list for their traditional offerings to the dead. In the "Liturgy of Funerary Offerings," more than a dozen types of bread and meat are proscribed as offerings to the dead, along with fresh fruit, vegetables, incense, oils, beer, and wine.

Spirits for the Spirits

Congolese people give offerings of palm wine or beer to the dead. For example, at a wedding, if the bride's father is deceased, he is offered libations of wine and beer, just as his living brothers are given these to drink.

Copper Bells

The Hohokam Indians of the American Southwest would include many tiny copper bells as funeral offerings when they cremated their dead. The intended purpose of the bells, beyond that of simple offerings, is unknown. Other traditional Native American offerings include cornmeal and tobacco.

Living Folk Traditions

According to Orion Foxwood, in the Appalachian tradition, one brings whiskey or another potent liquor to the crossroads as an offering to the spirits there. Similarly, in New Orleans Voodoo, the Loa who looks after the dead, best known as Baron Samedi, is appeased with offerings of rum steeped in hot peppers. In my workings with him, he's also expressed a fondness for rum-soaked cigars.

Other Offerings to the Dead

In funerary traditions the world over, three things are repeatedly left as offerings to the dead: fresh fruit, fresh flowers, and a lit candle or candles. In Western funerary practices, flowers have become such a part of the presentation of a coffin during the wake that many florists make more money off of the dead than they do selling roses for somebody's sweetheart. Candles, also, are a significant enough part of the Western funerary tradition that many cemeteries provide small enclosures near graves where a candle can be lit and protected from the wind.

But, aside from tradition, why do we leave such offerings to our dead? Do we really think the deceased is going to eat the offerings of food? Can a corpse appreciate the beauty and scent of cut flowers? Is there any need to leave a candle burning in the dark at the side of a grave? Probably not, but all of these items contain some form of vital energy, as Dion Fortune points out in her slim volume, *The Book of the Dead*. In this respect, the dead are not expected to eat the physical oranges left out for them, but the living energy that is still in the freshly plucked fruits may provide some nourishment to the spirits. The same process is at work with a candle, whose living flame gives off energy in the form of both heat and light. According to Fortune, some of this energy transfers to the spirit-world in a form that the deceased can harness.

APPENDIX IV

SOME DEITIES ASSOCIATED WITH DEATH

Anubis (Egyptian)

Depicted as a man with the head of a jackal, Anubis presides over several aspects of death and the afterlife but is most notably a god in charge of the process of mummification. In essence, Anubis is the mortician of the gods, safeguarding the knowledge of preparing the body and presiding over funerary rites. Anubis is also one of the deities who appears in the Egyptian Book of the Dead in the Hall of Judgment, presiding over the weighing of the heart of the deceased.

Atropos (Greek)

According to Greek myth, a human's lifespan is in the hands of three women. They are the Fates, and it is their duty to shape the thread of life, to measure each life's span of days, and finally, to cut the thread when that life has reached its proper conclusion. Atropos is the name of the elderly woman who cuts the thread at life's end. She is a somber crone figure, and she is unyielding in her duties. She is such a fearsome figure that atropine, a deadly poison found in the belladonna plant, was named in her honor.

Azrael (Hebrew)

Also Azriel; another variant may be Uriel. Azrael is the Hebrew angel of death. In Exodus, when Moses visits plagues upon Pharaoh in an attempt to coerce him into letting the Israelite people go free, one of the plagues is the death of all the firstborn in Egypt. Azrael is the angel who goes from house to house, taking the firstborn, and thus is the angel that the Passover preparations guard against. In Leilah Wendell's necromantic tradition, Azrael is the very personification of death, and he appears as a skeletal angel clad in sweeping black robes.

Baron Samedi (Voodoo)

Baron Samedi (Baron Saturday) is a jolly, foul-mouthed loa in Voodoo specific to the New World. He has no African counterpart, although that does not stop him from being both a popular and a powerful spirit. He is often depicted as a skeleton wearing a top hat and tails. He smokes cigars and wears sunglasses, frequently with one of the lenses knocked out. His preferred colors are black or purple —funeral colors appropriate for a god of the dead. Because Voodoo is a syncretic religion, combining African traditions with Catholic beliefs, each loa is associated with a particular saint. In the Baron's case, his Catholic counterpart is St. Gerard, the patron saint of expectant mothers. This may seem an odd coupling, since Baron Samedi is the loa of death and cemeteries, but like so many death gods and goddesses throughout the world, the Baron is also a god of fertility, since life and death are just two sides of the same coin. His wife is Maman Brigitte, a protectress of gravestones. He is also known as Baron Cemetière (of Cemeteries) and Baron La Croix (of the Cross).

Cernunnos (Celtic)

Literally "the horned one." Cernunnos is a Celtic god of fertility and of the hunt. He is traditionally depicted as an ithyphallic deity with horns. As a fertility god, Cernunnos may not seem at first involved with death, but he plays an integral part in the energies involved with renewal and regeneration. He presides over culling and taking in addition to growth and fertility, making way for rebirth and preventing decay and stagnation by destroying the old, the weak, and the infirm. Cernunnos is the god most often adopted by modern Wiccans as the consort of the Mother Goddess. In this capacity, he also becomes a dying and rising god. Through the cycle of the year, he appears as the consort of the Lady. He mates with her and then dies so that he may be reborn through her.

Charon (Greek)

The ferryman who carries souls across the River Styx. A son of Nox, goddess of the night, Charon plays a relatively minor role in Greek mythology, but he is a compelling figure nonetheless. Depicted as a gaunt and pale man with burning eyes, Charon has appeared again and again in literature about Hell and the afterlife. His most noteworthy appearance, and perhaps the one that has fixed him irrevocably in the modern imagination, is in Dante's *Inferno,* where he fulfills his age-old role of ferrying the dead across the underworld's first great river.

Dakinis (Tibetan Buddhist)

Not goddesses per se, Dakinis are divine beings who appear in visions. Depicted as many-armed women, Dakinis are often naked save for a garland of skulls. Dakinis are vampire-like, and they are often shown with fangs and red, pointed tongues, much like the Hindu goddess Kali. They drink blood, typically from a special chalice fashioned from the top of a human skull. The Dakinis carry a ritual dagger, and this little curved blade has the power to cut through worldly attachments. For all their terrible appearance, Dakinis are closer to the Western idea of angels than they are to demons. Their purpose is to demonstrate the insignificance of the flesh. They appear to people who are dying, urging them to overcome their illusions about physical life so that they may move beyond the Wheel of Death and Rebirth and be free from incarnation.

Dionysus (Greek)

Dionysus was the god of wine and merriment, as well as the god of drama and a god of the wilderness. A mystery religion grew up around Dionysus and he became another incarnation of the dying and rising god. His death and rebirth were celebrated in the Eleusian Mysteries with wild orgies of drunkenness and dramatic portrayals. A cult of wild women, known as the Maenads, were associated with him. They were said to drink themselves into a frenzy in worship of him and then run naked through the forests and wild places. They would hunt down any hapless travelers they happened to encounter in this state, killing them with their bare hands and then feasting upon their flesh and blood.

Duma (Hebrew)

According to Gustav Davidson's *Dictionary of Angels*, Duma is the angel of the silence of death. He is an attendant of the official angel of death, Azrael. Duma was actually adopted by the Israelites from Babylonian myth. In the tale of Ishtar's descent into the underworld, Duma is the guardian of the fourteenth gate of the realm of the dead.

Ereshkigal (Sumerian/Babylonian)

Ereshkigal is the sister of Ishtar and goddess of the Underworld. Her name means "Lady of the Great Earth" or "Lady of the Great Below." She is a goddess of death, and she presides over the Sumerian underworld, a place of shadows and dust where the spirits of the dead huddle in darkness.

Although she is not necessarily evil, Ereshkigal can be grasping and cruel. She's featured as the antagonist in the myth of Inanna's descent into the underworld. Inanna, or Ishtar, goes to visit her sister in her shadowy kingdom, proceeding to the first gate of the underworld. Ereshkigal, seeking to rob her sister of all her power and dignity, has sent word to each of the gatekeepers to demand a gift from Ishtar at each gate she passes. Along the way, she surrenders her crown, her girdle, her earrings, and sundry other pieces of jewelry until she arrives, naked, to stand before her sister's throne. Ereshkigal refuses to let Ishtar return to the land of the living, hanging the goddess's naked body on a post for all to see. In the end, a cry for Ishtar is taken up by the remaining gods and she is rescued, but not before her corpse has been debased and abused by Ereshkigal in her shadowy realm of the dead.

Hades (Greek)

Hades is the brooding brother of Zeus who was given command over the land of the dead. He is a dark and taciturn god who speaks little and laughs less. The one high point in Hades' existence was his love affair with Persephone, goddess of the spring and daughter of the harvest goddess Demeter. He was hardly subtle in revealing his amorous intentions: one day, when Persephone was out gathering flowers with her mother in the fields, Hades erupted from beneath the earth in his dark chariot, scooped Persephone up, and carried her down to the underworld with him. Persephone objected loudly to this treatment and begged to be returned to the sunlit world with her mother. Hades, taciturn as ever, refused to let her go. Meanwhile, Demeter searched the world over for her daughter, and in her grief, she caused the grain to wither and winter to fall upon the land.

Lest all humanity starve under these conditions, the gods of Olympus importuned Hades to return Persephone to her mother. But Hades stood firm to his claim over her as his wife. Had Persephone simply refused his hospitality during her stay in the underworld, all would have been well, but at one point she grew hungry and ate six seeds from a pomegranate offered her. As in many traditions, eating the food of the dead taints you with death, and so for this reason Persephone was tied to Hades and his shadowy underworld. A compromise was struck between mother and husband, and Persephone was allowed to spend half the year in the sunlit lands with her mother, and this was the time of the year when spring broke forth in the land and all was renewed. The other half of the year she was forced to spend in the

underworld with Hades—one month for each seed she had eaten—
and during her absence, winter raged across the land, bringing death
with its chilling grip. Hades' Roman counterpart is Pluto.

Hecate (Greek)

Hecate is the goddess of the crossroads or tri-via (a place where three
roads comes together). She is also a goddess of night and a goddess
of conjurations. As such, she is traditionally a goddess of magick and
witchcraft. She is depicted as a triple-faced goddess, a typical moon
goddess characteristic that demonstrates a link to the moon's mutable
faces. Several invocations to Hecate depict her as a blood-thirsty goddess who revels in the howling of dogs and the shedding of blood. This
violent, destructive nature is part of her identity as a dark goddess.

The dark goddess owns all those things that are threateningly,
subversively feminine: darkness, blood, the hidden and occult, and
of course, destruction, that terrifying other half of woman's more nurturing generative powers. Where the goddess is the womb that creates, the dark goddess is the *vagina dentata*, the womb that devours
her own creation. Attended by howling dogs, associated with tombs
and lonely places, darkness, night, destruction, and blood, Hecate,
Queen of the Night, is a very formidable representative of the dark
goddess tradition.

Hel (Norse)

Also known as Holle or Holde. The Norse goddess of the underworld,
Hel is a fearsome giantess of striking appearance. Half of her face is
that of a beautiful, if severe, maiden, and the other half is a mis-
shapen mass, devoid of features and unformed. This stark duality in
her appearance is a striking example of the association of death with
thresholds. Hel is at once formed and unformed, a grown woman and
a creature still waiting to be born. She is a much-feared and much-
misunderstood goddess in the Norse pantheon, and her reputation is
made perhaps worse by her identity as daughter of Loki, that inveter-
ate trickster.

Hermes (Greek)

Hermes is the quintessential psychopomp, the guide of the dead. Both a messenger and a trickster god, he is the ultimate go-between, walking the thresholds of matter and spirit, living and dead. In his aspect of Hermaphrodite, he even walks between the polarities of gender. In the myth of Orpheus and Eurydice, it is Hermes who is called upon to lead Orpheus' young bride out of Hades and back into the mortal world, and it is Hermes who leads her back to the shadowy depths once Orpheus fails to hold to the stricture that he not look behind him until emerging from the world of the dead.

Kali (Hindu)

The "black lady" of India, Kali is both consort and feminine counterpart of Shiva the destroyer. Kali is depicted as naked to the waist with garlands of skulls and severed heads hanging from her neck and waist. She is often also depicted with fangs and with a long, protruding, pointed tongue. These features represent her blood-thirstiness as well as her lustiness. She is a terrible warrior-goddess who viciously strikes down all who oppose her.

In one of the stories concerning Kali, she became so overwhelmed with bloodlust that no one, neither god nor man, could stand before her without being slain. Finally, as she laid waste to thousands before her, the gods went to her consort Shiva and begged him to put an end to her rampage. He went before her, but in her rage she hardly even recognized him. She struck him down before she could stop herself, but then, as she realized what she was doing, she stopped herself from killing him. Instead, she danced out the remainder of her fury on his body as he lay stretched out beneath her. Like Sekhmet, Kali also shares strong associations with blood, especially with menstrual blood. In addition to her role as goddess of death she is also a goddess of lust and fecundity.

Khonsu (Egyptian)

Depicted as a child or as a falcon-headed god whose headdress combines both the full and the crescent moon, the Egyptian god Khonsu is known as "the traveler." Khonsu is a deity associated with fate and with judgment, and he is among the many gods attributed with the creation of the world by the Egyptians. Khonsu's child form is grimly misleading, for he is an inimical deity known for eating the hearts of the dead. As one of the many creator-gods, he seems to reserve the right to judge his creations, retiring to the chthonic realms where he metes out his punishment of obliteration to those who are unworthy of life in the immortal realms.

Libitina (Roman)

Libitina was the Roman goddess of death, corpses, and funerals. Her consort was Orcus, a god who was very likely a holdover from the pantheon of the Etruscans, a mysterious ancient people who inhabited the Italian peninsula before the Romans. Libitina's very name was synonymous with death, and her temples contained the registers of the dead. In time, her temples housed all equipment and personnel connected with funerals, including gravediggers. Although Libitina was rarely remembered in sacrifices and her name has become obscure, her image will seem hauntingly familiar. She was traditionally depicted as a winged figure swathed in black robes. She would hover like a spectral bird of prey over her intended victim, face hidden in shadow and dark wings outspread. Her name may have been forgotten over the millennia, but her image lingers still in the guise of both the Grim Reaper and the Angel of Death.

Lilith (Hebrew, Sumerian, Babylonian)

In rabbinical lore, Lilith is said to be the first wife of Adam, made to be his equal in all things. Adam, something of a chauvinist at heart, finds he doesn't much like a bride who will not lie beneath him during sex, and so he has God cast Lilith from the Garden. Adam is given Eve as consolation who, by her creation from a part of Adam, is necessarily subordinate to him. Lilith, however, is left to range out in the wide world and consort with demons. She becomes a mother of demons and an adversary of the children of Adam. In one capacity, she is a killer of infants, sneaking into their cradles and sucking their blood. In her other capacity, she is a seductress of men, whom she also subsequently devours and destroys. She is associated with owls and with beasts of prey and is commonly depicted as a beautiful woman with wings and the talons of a bird of prey. She is also a minor spirit in Babylonian and Sumerian lore. Her consort is Gelal, and she leads a band of similarly blood-thirsty spirits known as the *lilu* or *lilitu*.

The Morrigan (Celtic)

Known as the Battle Crow, the Morrigan is a warrior-goddess associated with death on the battlefield. One of the many Celtic deities who has a triple aspect, the Morrigan also appears as Baebh and Macha. She is most often depicted suited up for war, complete with armor and spear. Ravens are her sacred birds and their presence upon the battlefield indicate that she is nearby. She can be a cruel and bitter goddess and is a terrible foe. It was she, in her aspect of Macha, who finally engineered the downfall of the great hero Cuchulainn.

Odin (Norse)

The Norse god Odin is All-Father and wisdom-keeper, but in many respects he is also a chthonic deity. In order to gain the wisdom of the runes, Odin sacrifices his eye and hangs for nine days on the World Tree. As the Hanged Man, Odin has strong connections to the archetype of the dying and rising god, and his death-like trance aimed at gleaning otherworldly wisdom echoes the initiatory trance-states of traditional shamans. Odin is well known for riding Sleipnir, the eight-legged horse birthed by Loki. Eight-legged horses are not uncommon in myth, and they have especially strong associations with shamans. Some mythologists suggest that the eight-legged horse represents the funeral bier, carried as it is by pall-bearers at each corner, providing a steed with eight legs. Odin is also a psychopomp, as we see in his capacity as instructor of the valkyries or "choosers of the slain." The valkyries may be the battle-maids who take the heroic dead from the battlefield, but it is Odin All-Father who is the true force behind their decisions. In addition to all of this, Odin's sacrifice of vision gives him one eye that looks into ordinary reality while the other sees into non-ordinary reality. Thus he is a threshold god, transcending the realms of spirit and matter, the living and the dead.

Osiris (Egyptian)

One of the many dying and rising gods associated with the harvest, Osiris became the god of the Egyptian underworld through a series of misadventures. It seems that Osiris' brother Set was jealous of the place Osiris held among the gods, and so he plotted to kill him. Set got hold of his brother's measurements and, knowing that Osiris couldn't refuse a gift that was skillfully and ornately crafted, had a wooden box fashioned to fit Osiris snugly as a coffin. Then Set threw a feast in his brother's honor and, dragging out the exquisitely carven trunk, Set tricked Osiris into testing its fit by laying down inside of it. Of course, once Osiris lay within the trunk, Set clapped the lid shut and secured the thing tightly so poor Osiris had no hope of getting out. Then he tossed the trunk, Osiris and all, into the Nile. When Osiris turned up missing, his wife, Isis, began a search for him that ranged all over Egypt. Finally, when she had located the trunk and was about to claim the body of her husband, Set came by and, in a rage, tore the body of Osiris into thirteen pieces and scattered them across Egypt. So Isis laboriously started her search anew and, piece by piece, gathered the body of Osiris. She located twelve of the pieces, but the thirteenth, his phallus, had been swallowed by a fish in the Nile, and so she had to fashion one from clay. Finally, with all the pieces of her murdered husband, Isis set herself to the task of preparing his body for burial. She had Anubis, the jackal-headed god to help her. With Anubis' help (as he was a god in charge of the process of mummification), she put the body back together and went through the long process of mummifying him. Once he was properly interred, his spirit returned and he was able to take his place as god of the underworld. Thus he became an enduring symbol of death and resurrection and there was little his jealous brother Set could do about it.

Sekhmet (Egyptian)

Sekhmet is the dark aspect of the Egyptian mother goddess Hathor. Ordinarily, Hathor is a nurturing goddess of plenty, depicted either as a heifer or as a woman bearing a headdress made up of the horns of a cow with the disk of the sun between them. Sekhmet is her dark-of-the-moon counterpart, linked to the menstrual cycle of the goddess. She is most often depicted as a statuesque woman with the head of a lioness. It is said that one day Hathor was transformed into Sekhmet and, thirsting for blood, she went out upon the land and began hunting for victims to slake her thirst. She ranged far and wide, killing all she encountered and drinking their blood. Like a ravaging lioness, her jaws and mouth were covered with blood. Finally the gods became afraid and sent some of their number to put an end to Sekhmet's blood-thirsty ravages. In time she was subdued and she returned to her gentler aspect as Hathor. Sekhmet embodies the forces of death and destruction that necessarily serve as the counterbalance to the generative, nurturing aspect of Hathor. She is woman empowered by her blood, and her priestesses wore wigs dyed heavily with henna in honor of this strong link to the vital fluid. In addition to her ties to power and blood, Sekhmet is also a goddess of drunkenness, for in one aspect of her mythic cycle, she was tricked by the gods into drinking beer dyed red to keep her from destroying any more of humanity.

Shiva (Hindu)

Part of the Hindu trinity of gods, Shiva embodies the forces of destruction that pave the way for new creation. In his aspect of Shiva Nataraja, he is depicted as an androgynous dancer, in a balance between the masculine and feminine, who keeps chaos at bay with his eternal dance. In one hand, he beats the drum of time, which sets the rhythm to his dance. In another hand, he holds a flame, symbol of the destruction that renews. With a third hand, he makes a hand signal, known as a *mudra*, which indicates "Be not afraid." This cautions those who are witness to the dance not to fear even their own destruction as it is ultimately regenerative and positive. Another hand gestures to his feet, one of which is raised off the ground in motion, the other of which is stationary and stands firmly upon the back of the dwarf of chaos. Thus it is through his eternal dance of creation and destruction that Shiva keeps chaos at bay. Both the moon and the Ganges are caught in his wild hair. His locks fly out in wild disarray and around his waist there coils the Kundalini serpent, a symbol of both sexual and transformative energies. Shiva's consort and feminine counterpart is the goddess Parvati who appears in a dark goddess aspect as Kali, the black lady.

Valkyries (Norse)

The name of these demi-divine beings literally means "choosers of the slain." These fierce Norse battle-maidens hover above every heated battle, seeking out those heroes who are to die and carrying them off to Valhalla, the home of the gloriously slain. They are the handmaidens of Odin, the All-Father, and it is he who instructs them who to claim and who to spare among the heroes of the battlefield. One valkyrie of note, Brunhilde, was Odin's favorite. She was a proud girl who disobeyed her father and refused to claim the life of the hero Sigurd. For this she was punished by Odin and placed in an enchanted slumber. She was guarded by an impenetrable ring of fire until the day that a great warrior, her destined husband, would come along and free her. Once the warrior Siegfried released her from the spell, she would live out her days as a mortal woman, never to soar the clouds above the battlefield with her sisters again.

Yama (Hindu, Buddhist)

A god whose origin lies in early Vedic myth, Yama is the god of death in both Hindu and Buddhist traditions. In most myths, Yama is the first mortal who died and was able to navigate the afterlife to the celestial realms. This primacy allowed him to become the Lord of the Dead. In other traditions, Yama is already the god of death even before the first mortal succumbs to his inevitable call. *Yama* can be translated as "twin," and in some traditions he is paired with a female counterpart, Yami, who is seen as his sister. A child of the sun, Yama appears with green or red skin, riding a water buffalo. He carries a loop of rope or a noose, which he uses to lasso the souls of the dying in order to carry them off to his realm.

BIBLIOGRAPHY

Aima. *Perfume Oils, Candles, Seals & Incense*. USA: Foibles Publications, 1981.

Auerbach, Loyd. *Hauntings and Poltergeists: A Ghost-Hunter's Guide*. Oakland, CA: Ronin Publishing, 2004.

Baumgartner, Anne. *Ye Gods!: A Comprehensive Dictionary of the Gods*. Syracuse, NY: Lyle Stuart, Inc., 1984.

Belanger, Jeff. *Communicating With the Dead: Reach Beyond the Grave*. Franklin Lakes, NJ: New Page Books, 2005.

Bellows, Alan. "The Remains of Doctor Bass." *Damn Interesting*, October 29, 2007. DamnInteresting.com. Sourced December 1, 2007.

Brennan, J. H. *Occult Tibet*. St. Paul, MN: Llewellyn Publications, 2002.

Budge, E. A. Wallis. *The Liturgy of Funerary Offerings*. New York: Dover Publications, 1994.

Coughlin, John. *Out of the Shadows: An Exploration of Dark Paganism and Magick*. Bloomington, IN: 1st Books Library, 2001.

Chang, Garma. *Teachings of Tibetan Yoga*. New Hyde Park, NY: University Books, 1963.

Choron, Jacques. *Death and Western Thought*. New York: Collier Books, 1963.

Christian, Paul. *The History and Practice of Magic*. New York: Citadel Press, 1969.

Cunningham, Scott. *Cunningham's Encyclopedia of Magical Herbs*. St. Paul, MN: Llewellyn Publications, 1985.

———. *The Magic of Incense, Oils & Brews*. St. Paul, MN: Llewellyn Publications, 1986.

Curtis, Vesta Sarkhosh. *Persian Myths*. Austin, TX: University of Texas Press, 1993.

David-Neel, Alexandra. *Magic and Mystery in Tibet*. New York: Penguin Books Inc., 1929 (1975 reprint).

Davidson, Gustav. *A Dictionary of Angels, Including the Fallen Angels*. New York: Free Press, 1994.

Davidson, H. R. Ellis. *Gods and Myths of Northern Europe*. New York: Penguin Books Inc., 1964.

———. *Myths and Symbols in Pagan Europe*. Syracuse, NY: Syracuse University Press, 1988.

El Mahdy, Christine. *Mummies, Myth, and Magic*. New York: Thames and Hudson, 1989.

Eliade, Mircea. *Death, Afterlife, and Eschatology*. New York: Harper & Row, 1967.

Evans-Wentz, W. Y. *The Tibetan Book of the Dead*. Oxford, England: Oxford University Press, 1960.

Forman, Werner and Stephen Quirke. *Hieroglyphs and the Afterlife in Ancient Egypt*. Norman, OK: University of Oklahoma Press, 1996.

Fortune, Dion. *Dion Fortune's Book of the Dead*. York Beach, ME: Weiser Books, 2005.

Gonzáles-Wippler, Migene. *Santeria: The Religion*. New York: Crown Publishers, 1989.

Griffith, F. and Herbert Thompson. *The Leyden Papyrus: An Egyptian Magical Book*. New York: Dover Publications, 1974.

Grof, Stanislav. *Books of the Dead: Manuals for Living and Dying*. New York: Thames and Hudson, 1994.

Grof, Stanislav and Christina. *Beyond Death: The Gates of Consciousness*. New York: Thames and Hudson, 1995.

Guiley, Rosemary Ellen. *Harper's Encyclopedia of Mystical & Paranormal Experience*. New York: HarperCollins, 1991.

Hamilton, Edith. *Mythology*. Boston, MA: Little, Brown & Co., 1942.

Harner, Michael. *The Way of the Shaman*. San Francisco, CA: HarperSanFrancisco, 1990.

Harrison, Ann Tukey. *The Danse Macabre of Women*. Kent, OH: Kent State University Press, 1994.

Henderson, Joseph L. *The Wisdom of the Serpent: The Myths of Death, Rebirth, and Resurrection*. Princeton, NJ: Princeton University Press, 1990.

Hornung, Erik. *The Ancient Egyptian Books of the Afterlife*. Trans. David Lorton. Ithaca, NY: Cornell University Press, 1999.

Huntington, Richard. *Celebrations of Death: The Anthropology of Mortuary Ritual*. Cambridge, England: Cambridge University Press, 1979.

Kalweit, Holger. *Dreamtime and Inner Space: The World of the Shaman*. Boston, MA: Shambhala Publications, 1988.

Bibliography

Knappert, Jan. *African Mythology*. London, England: Diamond Books, 1995.

Kübler-Ross, Elisabeth. *Death: The Final Stage of Growth*. New York: Simon & Schuster, 1975.

———. *On Death and Dying*. New York: Simon & Schuster, 1969.

Lewis, James. *The Death and Afterlife Book*. Canton, MI: Visible Ink Press, 2001.

Madden, Kristin. *Shamanic Guide to Death and Dying*. St. Paul, MN: Llewellyn Publications, 1999.

Métraux, Alfred. *Voodoo in Haiti*. New York: Schocken Books, 1972.

Nairn, Rob. *Living, Dreaming, Dying*. Boston, MA: Shambhala Publications, 2004.

Newberry, Percy. *Egyptian Scarabs*. Toronto, Ontario: General Publishing Co., 2002.

Obayashi, Hiroshi. *Death and Afterlife: Perspectives of World Religions*. Westport, CT: Praeger Publishers, 1992.

O'Flaherty, Wendy. *Hindu Myths*. New York: Penguin Books Inc., 1975.

Ogden, Daniel. *Magic, Witchcraft, and Ghosts in the Greek and Roman Worlds*. Oxford, England: Oxford University Press, 2002.

Osho. *And Now, And Here: On Death, Dying and Past Lives*. Essex, England: The C. W. Daniel Company, 1995.

Parkinson, R. B. *Voices from Ancient Egypt: An Anthology of Middle Kingdom Writings*. Norman, OK: University of Oklahoma Press, 1991.

Penczak, Christopher. *The Witch's Shield: Protection Magick & Psychic Self-Defense*. Woodbury, MN: Llewellyn Publications, 2007.

Pinch, Geraldine. *Egyptian Mythology*. Oxford, England: Oxford University Press, 2002.

Rangdrol, Tsele Natsok. *The Mirror of Mindfulness*. Kathmandu, Nepal: Rangjung Yeshe Publications, 1987.

Rinpoche, Chökyi Nyima. *The Bardo Guidebook*. Kathmandu, Nepal: Rangjung Yeshe Publications, 1991.

Rodman, Selden and Carole Cleaver. *Spirits of the Night: The Vaudun Gods of Haiti*. Dallas, TX: Spring Publications, Inc., 1992.

Southall, Richard. *How to Be a Ghost Hunter*. St. Paul, MN: Llewellyn Publications, 2003.

Starhawk. *The Pagan Book of Living and Dying*. San Francisco, CA: HarperSanFrancisco, 1997.

Sullivan, Lawrence E. *Death, Afterlife, and the Soul*. New York: Mac-Millan Publishing Company, 1989.

Thurman, Robert. *The Tibetan Book of the Dead*. New York: Bantam Books, 1998.

Toynbee, J. M. C. *Death and Burial in the Roman World*. Baltimore, MD: John Hopkins University Press, 1971.

Trelawny, Edward. *Recollections of the Last Days of Shelley & Byron*. New York: Carroll & Graf Publishers, 2000.

Wendell, Leilah. *Encounters With Death: A Compendium of Anthropomorphic Personifications of Death from Historical to Present Day Phenomenon*. New Orleans, LA: Westgate Press, 1996.

———. *The Necromantic Ritual Book*. New Orleans, LA: Westgate Press, 1995.

———. *Our Name is Melancholy*. New Orleans, LA: Westgate Press, 2002.

Yon, Michael. "American Aghori: An Introduction to Kapal Nath." *Vice Magazine Online*. Viceland.com. Sourced December 1, 2007.

INDEX

A

absinthe, 43, 267, 270

afterlife, 24, 30–31, 105–106, 109–114, 129, 203, 268, 278, 283, 285, 294, 296–299

Aghori, 78–79, 93–94, 299

Akh, 108

Akhu, 108

Alexander the Great, 6, 273

Altar, vii, 21–28, 32–35, 37–39, 49–55, 58, 60–63, 67, 77, 94–96, 98, 100, 113, 115, 130–131, 133–140, 142–145, 159, 167, 171, 173–174, 180, 184, 186, 188, 190, 192–193, 196–197, 201, 207–208, 212–213, 227–231, 233–236, 240, 243–244, 250, 256, 262–263

Ammit, 111

Amulet, 29, 107, 111, 114

Anatomy Warehouse, 33

Ancestors, 32, 35, 45, 121, 169, 256

Angel Gabriel, 125, 195, 221

animal companion, 256

Anubis, 32, 44, 107, 111, 113, 128, 264, 274–275, 283, 292
Ars Moriendi, 82
asafetida, 71
Asphodelus ramosus, 279
Atropos, 283–284
Auerbach, Loyd, 174, 295
Azrael, xviii, 284, 286
Azrael Project Newsletter, xviii
Aztecs, 6

B

Ba, 108–109
Bardo Thodol (see Tibetan Book of the Dead)
Bardo state, xvi, 50, 131, 150, 153, 223, 299
Baron Samedi, 59, 281, 284
Bass, Dr. Bill, 84, 295
Benu bird, 108
bindu, 152
Body Farm, 84
Bone Room, The, 33
Botox, 5
Buddhist, xviii, 34, 149, 285, 294
Byron, Lord, xxii, 126, 199, 299

C

cairn, 121
canopic jars, 110
Çatal Huyuk, 128
Catholic, xviii, 8, 22, 42, 67, 125, 284
Celtic, 129, 285, 291
cemetery, viii, xviii, xxii, xxv–xxvi, 4, 16, 19, 25, 43, 70, 73, 87–88, 91, 121–123, 132, 163, 167–171, 173–178, 180–181, 184–185, 187–188, 190–193, 195–198, 200–203, 207–210, 212–214, 216, 221–222, 232, 234, 252–253, 258, 264–265, 278, 281, 284
Cernunnos, 285
Chakra, 50, 150–151, 156, 159, 161, 237–239, 241
Charon, 91, 172, 188, 285
Chatterton, Thomas, 78
Chöd ceremony, 232–233
Christian, Paul, 28, 296
Christmas carol, 10, 120
Chrysanthemums, 42, 44, 267
coffin, 24, 29–30, 107, 114, 119–120, 122, 125, 135, 189, 206, 216–217, 281, 292
Columbine (artist), 33–34
corpse, xviii, 11, 42, 45, 78–80, 84–87, 101–102, 105, 107–111, 114, 119–121, 127–129, 138, 141, 144, 187, 189, 203, 206, 215, 262–263, 281, 287, 290
coven, 256
covered urn, 30
cremation, 78, 123, 125–126
crow, 30, 129, 134, 247–248, 251, 287, 291, 297
Cuchulainn, 291
Cuhulain, Kerr, 64
cypress, 29, 43, 132–133, 189, 264, 267

D

dakini, 69, 285
Danse Macabre, 80–83, 297–303
David-Neel, Alexandra, 232–233, 296
DaVinci, Leonardo, 84
death mask, 45, 102

death process, v, xvi, xxvii, 4, 50, 77, 85, 101, 150–151, 153, 156, 160, 183, 188, 224–303

death's head moth, 31

deathwork, xviii, xxv, xxvii, 6, 21, 23, 27, 37, 60, 193, 196, 259, 270

Demeter, 227, 287

Der Totentanz (see Danse Macabre)

Dickens, Charles, 120

Dionysus, 42, 286

Dis, 59

Dispersion of the Five Winds, 154, 156, 159, 161, 225, 233, 240, 244

dorje, 68

dreamcatcher, 69

dreamstate, 158

dreamwalking, 154, 263

Duma, 286

dying and rising god, 59, 285–286, 291

E

Easter, 8

ecstatic dance, 41

Edison, Thomas, 173

Egyptian, 24, 32, 44, 59, 82, 106–107, 109–111, 113, 122, 128, 168, 188, 268, 283, 289, 292–293, 297–298

Egyptian Book of the Dead, 82, 106–107, 283

Eleusian Mysteries, 286

embalming, 10, 79, 120–121, 135, 166

energies of death, xi, xviii, xx, xxii, xxv, xxvii, 8, 14, 17, 21, 23–26, 32–34, 37, 45, 49, 52, 54–55, 58, 61, 77, 80, 150, 154, 185–188, 209, 225, 257, 285

entities, 58, 60, 67–69

epitaph, 124, 129, 208

Ereshkigal, 286–287

Etruscan, 59

Eurydice, 289

EVP, 173

excarnation, 128, 143

F

faeries, 9, 67

fey (see faeries)

Field of Asphodels, 31, 44, 278–279–303

Flatliners, 3

Fortune, Dion, 64, 281, 297

Foxwood, Orion, 281

Fumigation, 70–71, 264–265

funeral, viii, 9, 19, 42, 79, 91, 93, 114, 118, 120, 129–130, 132–145, 213, 222, 224, 268, 281, 284, 291

G

Ganges River, 125, 294

gargoyle, 66

Ghost Hunters, 173

goddess, 22–23, 29, 32, 35, 45, 59, 69, 107, 109–110, 114, 127–128, 227, 264, 284–291, 293–294

goês, 224

Gothic, ii–iv, xviii, xxi–xxii, 14

Grandmother Spider, 69

graveyard poets, 199

Great Pyramids, 106

green fairy, 43

Grim Reaper, xiii, 9, 19, 29, 81, 84, 290

H

Hades, 227–228, 278, 287–289
haunting, 203, 254–255
heart scarab, 111, 188, 226–227, 229, 233, 240, 242, 244, 246, 249–250
Hecate, 29, 32, 43–44, 264, 288
Heket, 29, 107
Hel, 45, 288
hell money, 280
Hermes, 289
Highgate Cemetery, 122
Hindu, 93–94, 125, 189, 285, 289, 293–294, 298
Hohokam Indians, 281
Hopkins, Rev. John Henry, 10, 299
Horace, 29
Houses of Eternity, 112
hungry ghost, 232, 280

I

impermanence, viii, 77–78, 94, 100, 103–104, 146–147, 211, 233, 245
incense, ix, 6, 8, 11–12, 25–27, 37, 50, 52–53, 71, 94, 100, 113, 134, 137, 140–141, 143, 190–191, 213, 229, 259, 264–267, 269–270, 272, 274–275, 280, 295–296
inhumation, 120–121, 123, 129
Ireland, 9, 66, 124
Ishtar, 286–287
Isis, 107, 292
Itonde, 59
Izanami, 59

J

jackal, 109, 283
jack-o'-lantern, 66

K

Ka, 108–109, 112
Kali, 93, 216, 285, 289, 294
Kalma, 59
Keats, John, 124, 166
Khepra, 188
Khonsu, 289–290
Kostinice Ossuary, 87

L

Leyden Papyrus, ix, 273–275, 297
libation, 280
Libitina, 290
Lilith, 290
Liturgy of Funerary Offerings, 112, 280, 296
Loki, 45, 288, 291
Longfellow, Henry Wadsworth, 38

M

Maenads, 286
Maerin, 59
magick, 40–41, 43, 47, 71, 196, 259–260, 273–274, 288, 296, 298
Mary Queen of Scots, 29
mausoleum, 36, 117, 122, 176, 252
medicine bag, viii, 185–186, 188–189, 192–193, 196, 212, 230–231, 233–234
medieval church, 67
meditation, vii–ix, xviii, xxii, xxv–xxvi, 33, 41, 54–55, 113, 117, 147, 153, 160, 163, 170, 174, 184, 192, 201, 208, 227, 244
memento mori, 28–29, 32
Memorial Day, 168
Middle Ages, 28, 80–81, 84, 273
Middle Kingdom, 106, 298
mirror, 7, 28, 47, 50–52, 54, 94–96, 98–102, 104, 113, 134, 136–137, 139–140, 142–144, 146,

174, 180, 190–192, 230–231, 234–235, 237, 240, 243, 298
Moksha, 94
Monroe, Robert, 154, 225
Moody, Raymond, 28
Morrigan, 291
mortician, 32, 80, 107, 283
Mother Earth, 121, 136
mummification, 106–107, 109, 111, 268, 283, 292
mummy, 107, 109–112, 188, 226, 267–268

N

nadi-wheel, 50
Native American, xvii, 69, 128–129, 185–186, 224, 281
natron, 109, 114, 120, 267–268
near-death experience, xii–xiv, xvi–xx, 153–155
necromancy, 223–224, 278
necropolis, 167
need-fire, 71
Neith, 109
neo-Paganism, 8, 255
Nephthys, 59, 109
Nergal, 59
New England, 123
New Orleans, 121, 281, 299
Nile, 112, 292
non-attachment, xiv, xx, 79, 103–104, 257
non-ordinary reality, 40–41, 45, 292
Norse, 45, 288, 291, 294
Nuit, 24

O

obelisk, 195
Odin, 291, 294
Odysseus, 278
Odyssey, The, 278

Old Kingdom, 106
Opening of the Mouth Ceremony, 112, 114
orbs, 173
Orcus, 290
Orpheus, 199, 289
Osiris, 109, 292
Otherside, ix, xiii–xvi, xx, xxiii, 28, 58, 70, 117, 121, 169, 175, 180, 193, 205–206, 208–209, 226, 254, 256–257
Otherworld, 9, 106, 109, 111, 224
Our Name is Melancholy, xviii, 299
out-of-body experience, 154–156, 161, 225
Oya, 59

P

palliative care, 253–254
Papa Ghede (see Baron Samedi)
Penczak, Christopher, v, 64, 298
Persephone, 227–228, 287
Pharaoh, 106–107, 113, 284
phoenix, 10–11, 108, 268–269
phurba, 68–69
piercing, 7
plague, xiv, 71, 82, 84, 183
Pluto, 288
pomegranate, 227–228, 233, 287
prana, 150
Pre-Raphaelite, 78
psychic attack, 65
psychomanteum, 28
psychopomp, 221, 224, 289, 291
Puritans, 123
putrefaction, 79–80, 85
Pyramid Texts, 106

Q

Qingming Festival, 197

R

Reincarnation, 125
Remembrance Day, 168
Rice, Anne, 43, 229
rigor mortis, 85
Rimbaud, Arthur, 43
Rite of Seven Gates, xix
ritual bath, 8, 50, 94, 133, 137, 140, 143, 213, 230, 262
ritual garb, 41, 231
ritual mask, 45
rlung, 150
Roman, 30, 203, 223, 288, 290, 298–299
Romantic, xxii, 14, 78, 80, 127
rosary, 189

S

sacred space, 21–23, 40, 49, 57–58, 115, 133, 137, 143, 169, 176, 178, 184, 190, 192–193, 243–244, 260, 267
sacrifice, 5–8, 12–14, 17, 21, 95, 233, 236–241, 243, 249, 274, 278, 291
Samhain, 256, 278
saponification, 86
sarcophagus, 113–115
scars, xii, xx, 95–96
sea change, 127
Sedna, 59
Sekhmet, 289, 293
self-initiation, xix–xx, xxvii, 212, 225
Serket, 109
Seth, 109
Shakespeare, William, 127
shaman, ii, xiii, xvii–xxi, xxvii, 68, 121, 128, 211, 223–225, 233, 256, 263, 291, 297–298

Shelley, Mary, 126
Shelley, Percy Bysshe, xxii, 126, 199
shielding, 60–61, 64, 221, 233, 235, 248, 298
Shiva, 93, 289, 293–294
shrine, 110
Skulls Unlimited, 33
sky burial (see excarnation)
Sleipnir, 291
soap mummies (see saponification)
Southall, Richard, 173, 299
spirit-chaser, 66, 68
spirits of the dead, xii–xiv, xvi–xxi, xxiii, xxv, 7, 9, 12–14, 22–23, 28, 32–35, 40, 42–45, 49–55, 57–58, 60–64, 66–71, 77–78, 84, 89, 91, 95–96, 100, 102, 107, 109, 114–115, 125, 129, 133–134, 136–137, 139–141, 143–146, 149, 154–155, 158–161, 169, 171–173, 175–181, 184–185, 187, 190–193, 197, 200–211, 217–219, 224–226, 228, 233–239, 242–244, 246, 248–249, 251, 253–257, 261, 263–265, 267, 269–270, 273–275, 277–281, 284, 286, 289, 291–292, 299
spirit-temple, 61–63
stela, 112–113, 123
Stoker, Bram, 29
Stone Age, 120–121
Swinburne, Algernon Charles, 76, 199

T

Talmud, 31
taphophile, 171, 253
Tarot, xi, 4
tattoo, 6–7

Tempest, The, 127
Thoth, 111
threshold state, xx, xxiii, xxvii, 45, 49, 54–55, 58, 64, 134, 154, 184, 213, 225
Tibetan Book of the Dead, xvi, 82, 150, 153, 223, 296, 299
Tibetan Buddhist, 34, 285
Tomb Sweeping Day, 197–198, 200
towers of silence, 128, 145
Trelawny, Edward, 126, 299
Tutankhamen, 111

U

Ullamban, 280
underworld, 44–45, 59, 109, 176, 191, 225–228, 278, 285–288, 292
ushabti, 106, 114

V

valkyries, 291, 294
vampire, 31, 86–87
Victorian, 9, 31, 44, 122
Virgil, 2
Voodoo, 59, 281, 284, 298
vulture, 128

W

Wallis, Henry, 78, 296
wards, 31, 64, 67, 106, 166, 235, 268
Watchtowers, 25, 60
Wendell, Leilah, v, xviii, 284, 299
Wheel of Death and Rebirth, 125, 286
Wicca, 8, 255
Wilde, Oscar, 43
willow, 29, 43–44, 132, 137, 189, 198, 267, 269, 274
witches, 49, 57, 60, 64, 270, 288, 298
Woodlawn Cemetery, xxvi, 4, 16, 25, 70, 88, 122, 168, 200, 207, 222, 252, 258

Y

Yama, 294
Yarilo, 59
yew, 43–44, 132, 189
Yngona, 59

Z

Zitui, Jie, 198
Zoroastrian, 128